Józef Piłsudski, 1867–1935

Józef Piłsudski, 1867–1935

ANDRZEJ GARLICKI

Edited and translated by
John Coutouvidis

SCOLAR PRESS

Abridged, edited and translated from the Polish *Piłsudski* by Andrzej Garlicki

Published by
SCOLAR PRESS
Gower House
Croft Road
Aldershot
Hants GU11 3HR
England

Ashgate Publishing Company
Old Post Road
Brookfield
Vermont 05036
USA

British Library Cataloguing-in-Publication data

Garlicki, Andrzej
    Jósef Piłsudski, 1867–1935. – Abridged ed
    I. Title II. Coutouvidis, John
    943.8033092

    ISBN 1–85928–018–8

Library of Congress Cataloging-in-Publication Data

Garlicki, Andrzej.
    Józef Piłsudski : 1867–1935 / by Andrzej Garlicki : edited and translated by
John Coutouvidis. – New abridged ed.
        p. cm.
        Includes bibliographical references.
    ISBN 1–85928–018–8
    1. Piłsudski, Józef, 1867–1935. 2. Heads of State–Poland–Biography. 3.
Poland–History–20th century. I. Coutouvidis,
John. II. Title.
    DK4420.P5G35 1995
    943.8'04'092–dc20   94-23977
    [B]   CIP

Typeset in Sabon by Photoprint, Torquay
and printed in Great Britain by Biddles Ltd, Guildford

Contents

Hints on Pronunciation and Terminology

The following hints on pronunciation of frequently recurring Polish names and terms used in the text are given once only and relate solely to sounds foreign to an Anglophone:

Józef Piłsudski (sound j as y in yell, o as oo, e as e in get, i as ee in eel, ł as w in pew, u as oo in wood: Yoozef Pewsudski): the subject of this biography.

Andrzej Garlicki (sound rz as j in jardiniere, c as ts in ants: Andjey Garlitskee: author and Professor of Modern Polish History at Warsaw University.

Zułów (u and ö as oo in look: Zoowoof: the place of Piłsudski's birth, some 60 km north of **Wilno** (Veelno) in Lithuania. Wilno and its district were incorporated into Poland in October 1920 by General Lucjan Żeligowski on orders from Piłsudski.

'Ziuk' is pronounced Zeeook: Piłsudski's nickname as a youth.

'Wiktor' is pronounced Veektor. Piłsudski's pseudonym as an activist in the PPS: **Polska Partia Socjalistyczna** (sound y as i in ink, cz as ch in chunk). The Polish Socialist Party.

Endecja is pronounced Endetsya. The term is made up using N.D. the initials of the National Democratic (**Narodowa Demokracja**, pronounced Narodova Demokratsya) Party, the main political rivals to the followers of Piłsudski.

Roman Dmowski (Roman Dmovskee): leader of the Endecja or leading **Endek**.

Wincenty Witos (Veetos): leader of the largest peasant party, the **Piast** – named after the medieval Polish ruling dynasty. Piast was much less sympathetic to the socialists than the Liberation (**Wyzwolenie**: sound ie as y in yes) Peasant Party, the second largest of the peasant political groups of the Second Polish Republic which was constituted in 1921.

Sejm, The lower house of Parliament, is pronounced Seym.

Sulejówek is pronounced Sooleyoovek: Piłsudski's place of residence on the outskirts of Warsaw during his self-imposed seclusion, 1923–1926.

Ignacy Mościcki (sound ś, and si, as sh in sheet): Piłsudski's candidate as President of Poland, elected President by the Sejm following the coup d'etat of May, 1926.

Sanacja (sound a as a in art: Sanatsya: clean up – the term used by the regime which ruled Poland from 1926 to 1939.

List of Illustrations

Between pages 78 and 79

Editor's and Translator's Preface

Andrzej Garlicki's *Józef Piłsudski, 1867–1935* was published in 1988, at a moment of great change in Poland. It was the year which saw the beginning of the end of rule by the Communist Party which had been in control of the Polish state since 1947. In 1989 the first free and fair elections in the country since the Second World War gave Poland the lead in Eastern Europe's sudden rush towards democracy and away from Soviet hegemony. Lech Wałęsa, the leader of Solidarity, became President in 1990 in a campaign which witnessed the juxtaposition, on election posters, of his image with that of Piłsudski's.

Judging by reports out of Poland during this period of revolutionary change, the memory of Piłsudski remained strong and his name often associated with contemporary events in that country. Writing in the *New Statesman and Society*, 22 June 1990, Marek Kohn had this to say of developments in Warsaw:

> That the distant past has a more authentic claim to life here is rapidly being recognised in matters of symbolism. The crown has been restored to the head of the eagle on the national shield. Paris Commune Place has reverted to its pre-war name of Wilson Place. The custodians of the past are often youthful. A teenage boy runs a stall . . . , selling books about Soviet atrocities. He is a member of the Shooters' Association, the youth section of a right-wing nationalist party. The name recalls the riflemen's units around which Polish forces were built during the First World War. The heavy-whiskered image of their organiser, who later became the authoritarian national leader, Marshal Piłsudski, can be seen among the banners at the gates of the university . . . . The students have renamed the place after him; a patriotic gesture, but a somewhat ominous way to greet democracy . . .

Similar concern was expressed by Tony Paterson writing in *The European*, 30 July–2 August 1992:

> Poland may have been the first eastern bloc satellite to shed its communist shackles, but . . . the country shows worrying signs of reverting to the political and economic mire it languished in before the Second World War. . . . When it was last an independent democratic state, before the war, governments managed to remain in power for an average of only ten months, and the autocratic leader Marshal Piłsudski eventually assumed dictatorial powers. The parallels with today's Poland are striking. . . . Lech Wałęsa, has shown an understandable irritation at successive govern-

ments' failure to govern effectively. His response has been to
demand fundamental changes to the Polish political system
. . . (even threatening) to assume the office of prime minister
himself as the only means of ending protracted political
chaos. Piłsudski must be smiling in his grave.

Why the repeated reference to Piłsudski? He was the foremost Polish
statesman of the Second Polish Republic, 1918–1939. As one of the
founders of the independent Polish State, Piłsudski's policy involved the
use of armed force; in his opinion the only measure of a nation's
strength. He regarded Russia as Poland's worst enemy. His Legions
became the Polish army which defeated the Red Army in the War of
1919–1920.

Foreign domination of Poland had left a lasting impression on
political outlooks and the conduct of national policy since the mid 18th
century when Poland was little more than a client state of Russia; the
termination of her statehood, which came with the partitioning of
Poland between Russia, Prussia and Austria, followed by increased
Russian control of an even greater portion of her territory in the
settlements following the defeat of Napoleon in 1815, left many Polish
people with a hatred of their oppressors. Their fear of occupation,
together with a pride in the glories of historic Poland, were factors
contributing to the extreme nationalism which characterized Polish
political life, uniting Poles of widely differing political persuasions in a
yearning for freedom. This was regained at the end of the First World
War when Piłsudski became independent Poland's first head of state.

The political system over which Piłsudski held sway, directly or
indirectly, was fragmented. No party or grouping was strong enough to
provide a firm basis for stable government. The constitution of the
Second Polish Republic which was finally adopted on 17 March 1921
was modelled closely on the French system: real power lay with the
legislature made up of a *Sejm* (lower house) and a Senate. Of the two
houses of parliament, the Sejm was vastly more powerful. The president,
as titular head of state, had the right to appoint the government but not
to dissolve parliament. In this way Roman Dmowski's National
Democrats (*Endecja*), Piłsudski's greatest political rivals, hoped to
insure themselves against him if he became president after the
forthcoming elections, in 1922. The *Endecja* dominated the right in the
spectrum of Polish politics. Theirs was basically a middle-class party,
supported by white-collar workers and much of the intelligentsia – the
dominant urban class. In the elections of 1921 and 1922 the party
formed joint lists with the Christian National Party of Labour. This
Catholic party gradually freed itself from dependence on the Endecja
and in 1925 changed its name to the Christian Democratic Party,

(*Chadecja*). In the centre was the *Piast* party (PSL-*Piast*) led by Wincenty Witos and supported in the main, by well-to-do peasants. (This was the largest of five peasant parties that contested the 1922 elections.) On the left was the Liberation Peasant Party (PSL-*Wyzwolenie*) and the Polish Socialist Party (*Polska Partia Socjalistyczna*), PPS. On the extreme left was the politically insignificant Communist Party of Poland, KPP.

In the period from 1918–1926, when Piłsudski overthrew the parliamentary regime, no fewer than 14 governments held office. After the May coup of 1926, the key positions in the state administration had been filled by military personnel who had a disdain for the democratic process and a worshipful regard for Piłsudski's dictates. Therefore by 1930, when Piłsudski was losing his vigour others were hesitant to take a lead. The government styled itself 'Sanacja' which denoted the 'reform' it had in mind for parliament. It tried, at first, to exercise power constitutionally but by the elections of 1928 Piłsudski was losing the support he had had, from the parties in the centre and on the left, because of his outspoken criticism of the Sejm. He ignored opinion contrary to his own; democratic procedures were foreign to his nature. In this he had the support of the government who muzzled any effective opposition. The neglect of informed opinion, in matters of domestic and foreign policy, was symptomatic of a deep malaise in the governance of Poland and a characteristic of Polish affairs of state beyond Piłsudski's death in 1935.

Józef Piłsudski has personified independent Poland. Successively convicted terrorist, socialist agitator, cavalry officer, commander-in-chief and vanquisher of Trotsky's Red Army, democratic president and dictator, he became the embodiment of Polish statehood.

What then of Andrzej Garlicki's biography of this extraordinary Pole? His *magnum opus* (over 300,000 words in length it has, to date, sold over 150,000 copies in three editions) was the culmination of 30 years' work. In 1961, he completed research for his doctorate, begun in 1958, on the origins and formation of the Polish Legions. He developed his thesis over the next ten years and, in 1972, after approval by the Historical Council of the University of Warsaw, submitted this work for publication. Yet, despite a contract with his publisher, the text was withheld from the printing press.

As Professor Andrzej Garlicki recalls in the preface to the complete (1988) edition of his *Józef Piłsudski, 1867–1935*:

> One of the most valued documents in my private archives is the letter from the publisher's director informing me that he had renounced the contract because there was 'little interest in the

subject'. This was patently untrue, yet all efforts to obtain information as to what actually were the objections concerning the typescript ended in vain. In Kafkaesque fashion, the typescript circulated around various offices, leading a life on its own quite independent of that of its author. Now and again news arrived that this or that reader had expressed a positive opinion about the manuscript, but all to no avail.

Yet, time worked to the text's advantage. An awkward situation had developed. Either a condemnation of the typescript must be formulated or agreement given for its publication. A decision was taken. As can often happen in such cases permission was obtained to publish *part* of the typescript in an official academic publication on two conditions. Firstly, that its title would make no mention of Piłsudski. Secondly, that a few pages at the beginning would be added in order to set the text in a wider social context, and thus ensure that the book would not begin with the birth of Józef Piłsudski.

I accepted these conditions without hesitation. I wrote a few pages about the situation in Poland under Russian occupation after the January Rising of 1863 and I invented the title 'Back to the sources of the "Belvedere Camp" '. (The name given to the governing group within the Belvedere Palace, Piłsudski's official residence in Warsaw as head of state.) This made no sense in terms of a title of what was to be the first volume of a biography of Piłsudski and under normal circumstances I would never have contemplated such a departure. The book eventually appeared in 1978 in a print run of 5000. The breakthrough had been achieved. There were to be no more problems in renewing permission to publish the volume nor indeed with subsequent volumes of the biography which followed in quick succession.

During his visit to Staffordshire University in October 1992, I asked Professor Garlicki to elaborate further on his experiences with the censor. He replied:

Although the first volume of the biography was ready in 1971 and I wanted to publish it, this was impossible. So why did it become possible, in part at least, in 1978? I suppose, that was as a result of a new generation in the ruling elite of the Party. Although Gierek, in power between 1970–1980, was in charge of the party when my volume was complete, both party and state apparatus still reflected the Gomułka period: 1944–1948, 1956–1970. In other words, this was the generation who were politically active in the Second Republic, and to them Piłsudski was not an historical figure but political enemy. In each of his speeches Gomułka pointed out the superiority of the Polish People's Republic over pre-war Poland. He addressed his speeches to people, who, like himself, lived and worked in pre-war Poland.

By contrast, the group of people who came to power with Gierek had spent their childhood and early youth in post-war Poland; pre-war Poland did not play any role in their political biography. Piłsudski was simply an historic figure. It was not advisable to aggravate Moscow by propagandising him, but it was no longer a political problem; hence the consent to publish the first part of the biography under a changed title and in a limited edition. It appeared in 1978 and was sold out in a matter of a few weeks.

How could more copies be printed? The rules on censorship contained a loophole. A text which had once been censored and published could be printed in a new edition provided it did not contain any changes. In such circumstances second censorship was not required. My publisher and I took advantage of these rules and in the next year, a second edition of 20,000 was in circulation and soon after a further 30,000. The political bodies put on a brave face; in such circumstances they could do little else.

However, there was no chance of publishing the complete Piłsudski biography. This possibility did not occur until 1988, a year before the final collapse of the communist system. Censorship still was active but no longer concerned with pre-war history. For Jaruzelski (1981–1989) and his acolytes in the party, pre-war Poland was ancient and remote history. Moreover, Gorbachev (1984–1991) was in Moscow with his *perestroika* and *glasnost*! A biography of Józef Piłsudski could appear in Poland at such a time and thus the eventful political history of Eastern Europe had a direct bearing on its publication.

Was Professor Garlicki's experience of censorship an experience common to other Polish academics? An article, published on 11 August 1989 in *The Times Higher Education Supplement* suggests not. Describing academic life in communist Poland, Zdisław Krasnodębski, a sociologist at the University of Warsaw, stated:

> Most people are inclined to think about our ... society in quasi-Orwellian terms. That is, in terms of total state control over the public and private life of citizens, the repression of every manifestation of independence and the omnipresence of Big Brother watching the individual's every step. ... The Orwellian model may perhaps describe well enough the system as the Communist Party intended it to be, but not how that system actually functions after so many years in power.
>
> What then is the reality of the situation? Let me explain this by reference to the example I know best – the example of the university. When I talk to Western colleagues who have never visited Poland and tell them that at the university, my colleagues and I are not as deprived of academic freedom as Westerners seem to imagine, I am always treated as though I were some sort of communist sympathiser or agitator, at any rate as someone to be treated with considerable suspicion.
>
> Of course it is true that in principle everything is tightly regulated by the Ministry of Education. There are, on paper, strictly outlined programmes for university life. But, in reality, during the 15 years of my university career, nobody has ever shown any political concern with what I taught or indeed with anything I have published.

Clearly, Andrzej Garlicki's experience was somewhat different. His subject could give offence to the Kremlin and therefore it had to be censored. He would however agree with Krasnodębski's description of academic life in communist Poland: 'In general, the system did not work in the economy let alone in academia'.

Which brings us to another set of questions: to what extent has the book been affected by censorship? Has Andrzej Garlicki different and more independent views? Did he insert or omit certain passages only to make the whole palatable to the government of the day? How far did he manage to satisfy the requirements of censorship by party, publisher and academic peers without compromising his work?

Briefly reviewing the first volume of Garlicki's biography, Professor Wacław Jędrzejewicz notes in his *Piłsudski: A Life for Poland* (New York, 1982, p. 375): 'A biographical sketch covering the years to 1922, written very unevenly – certain parts in great detail, others (the Legions, war with Russia 1919–1920) practically omitted. Lacks a bibliography; written with an eye to censorship in Poland and Marxist ideology'.

Questions relating to Professor Garlicki's and other sources are addressed in the bibliographical essay which is appended to this edition.

With regard to evenness of coverage, it is the case that Professor Garlicki writes relatively little of the Legions and of the Russo-Polish war. This is not surprising. As noted above, Piłsudski's legions became the Polish Army which defeated the Red Army in the war of 1919–1920; in the context of Soviet–Polish relations during the 1970s, it would have been impossible for him to have dealt fully with this episode without giving offence to the Kremlin. Here was one more concession that had to be made to the censor.

I believe that Andrzej Garlicki has adequately explained and justified the textual adjustments he has had to make. But what of Marxist ideology? Was he a member of the party? Were passages of Marxist analysis also a genuflection to the political correctness of the day?

I confronted Professor Garlicki directly over these questions. His answers were equally direct: 'Where I employ a Marxist approach I do so out of the conviction of its appropriateness. There are passages which could be rewritten as new material surfaces. My own opinions have altered over time. It could not be otherwise. But I would retract nothing from the book.'

Andrzej Garlicki's *Piłsudski* is the first biography of the man to have come out of Poland for two generations and one which could not be published in Poland until the Soviet grip had been loosened. His book is much more than merely a product of its time; it is not only a gripping story of a great man's life, but also an important work of new European scholarship; and, in contrast to many studies of Piłsudski, of which

Professor Wacław Jędrzejewicz's biography cited above is an example, Garlicki is not offering us a portrait to be worshipped as an icon.

This new edition of *Józef Piłsudski, 1867–1935* attempts to convey faithfully in English the machinegun-like style of Andrzej Garlicki's Polish: pointed statements rapidly released in short bursts; each paragraph presenting a close pattern on his chosen target. As translator and editor I am entirely responsible for any errors made in this new edition; I can only hope that what the original has lost in this abridged version of Professor Andrzej Garlicki's *Józef Piłsudski, 1867–1935* can, in some way, be compensated for by introducing him to a wider readership.

This new English edition owes a great deal to the help I received from my darling wife Merrilyn. I am extremely grateful to her for advice and assistance at every stage of its production in manuscript form. It owes as much to the late and sadly missed Wacław Wacewicz. I also wish to thank Molly Kempton who typed the text, Owen Tucker who drew the map and Alexandra Garlicka who supplied the photographs, for enhancing this edition with their work; Alec McAulay for his enthusiastic support and expertise as our publisher; Andrzej Garlicki for his wisdom and the pleasure of his company at The Boat House, Barlaston, Staffordshire.

J.C.
10 February 1995

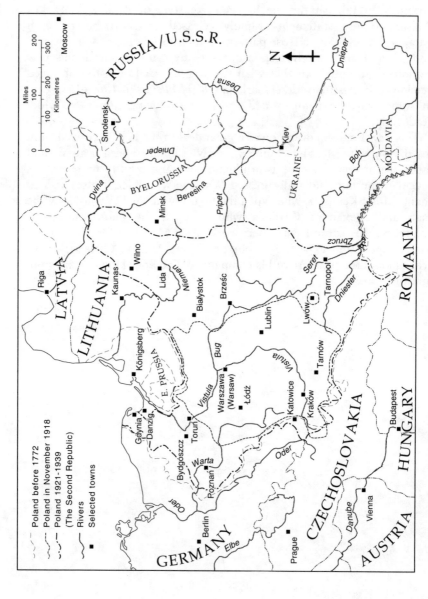

Pre-partition Poland and the frontiers of the Second Republic with adjacent countries.

CHAPTER ONE

Youth and Exile

Józef Klemens Piłsudski was born on 5 December 1867 into a family of landed Polish gentry living at Zułów, some 60 km from Wilno in Lithuania. (See map. The link between Poland and Lithuania dates from 1389 when Prince Jagiełło of Lithuania married the Polish Queen, Jadwiga. The Jagellonian empire included territory in the east stretching from the Baltic to the Black sea. At first Poland and the eastern borderlands or *Kresy* merely shared a monarch but by the end of the 16th century they had fused politically into a single Commonwealth or *Rzeczpospolita*. Its social, economic and cultural life, until the middle of the 18th century, was dominated by the Polish gentry or *slachta* into which the local aristocracy was absorbed, by a rapid process of Polonization. The Commonwealth went into decline in the 17th and 18th centuries by which time it came under Russian dominance. Poland was then partitioned between Russia and Prussia in 1772. The second partition, which also involved Austria, occurred in 1793. The third partition, by all three powers again, took place in 1795. This was followed by the incursions of the Napoleonic wars, resulting in increased Russian control of an even greater portion of Polish territory in the settlements after the defeat of Napoleon in 1815. Ed.)

The Piłsudski estates were sufficiently large to support an opulent lifestyle but not large enough to sustain and survive the financial blunders of its owner, Piłsudski's father. By July 1874 debt forced the family to move to Wilno and led to eventual bankruptcy. The move to Wilno came as a great shock to the young Piłsudski, known to family and friends as 'Ziuk', for whom Zułów symbolized prosperity and happiness.

The fourth of 12 children, Ziuk was closest to his elder siblings, Helena, Zofia and Bronisław. His upbringing owed much to Polish traditions and patriotism, inculcated through forbidden literature of the great Polish writers and through observance of national custom and religion. The sense of duty to uphold Polish consciousness was very high, as was its price. Repressive measures, begun after the insurrection of 1863 (the January Rising), were brutal and intense. Tsarism terrorized the Polish population, an ethnic minority in Lithuania, but did not break its patriotic spirit.

Piłsudski's sense of identity was severely tested when he began his formal education at the Russian high school in Wilno. The educational aims of the authorities ran counter to everything he held dear. The school had to bring up citizens loyal and obedient to the Tsarist Empire. It had to Russify. The clash between the ideals inculcated at home and those of the school curriculum led inevitably to conflict. Yet, although these circumstances generated feelings of rebellion in Piłsudski they also prevented manifestation of them. Restraint was urged by his family, who knew that public display of a rebellious attitude would have severe consequences.

Very few verifiable facts exist with which to build a picture of Piłsudski's school years. There are sources which reveal that he was punished three times with detention; once for using the Polish language in school and twice for 'not honouring his principals' outside the school. As regards his academic ability, a confidential school report stated: 'Józef Piłsudski does not always do his homework conscientiously; written work is satisfactory, in class he tries to be attentive, and shows special interest in science'. A former teacher adds: 'Piłsudski was clever at mathematics, but his attitude to other subjects was somewhat reckless; his school attendance was rather poor, and his frequent absence was excused because of sickness or family circumstances; his attention in the classroom left much to be desired'.

In private Piłsudski always preferred Polish to Russian literature which explains his inadequate knowledge of the Russian language, written and spoken. To the school he seemed a problem pupil; he was disobedient as well as high-spirited.

Piłsudski's liveliness and good humour were encouraged at home. According to Bronisław, his elder and more placid brother, Ziuk was pampered as the family favourite who enjoyed drawing attention to himself at any gathering. Sadly, his self-centredness very often developed into selfishness, which could be unpleasant for people around him; Bronisław often complained of Ziuk's selfish behaviour.

Piłsudski's strong personality found early expression in a conspiratorial youth circle called 'Spójnia' (Union). Founded in 1882 it soon had a membership of 16 young students attracted to it by a liking for secret organizations and for self-expression. They bought books and journals which formed the basis of a lively exchange of ideas and views. The discussions were sometimes naïve, sometimes worldly. The circle read Darwin, Comte, Huxley, Spencer, Draper, and Büchner. It is doubtful whether the young conspirators always understood what they read, but theirs was an ideological search typical of the new generation which was born soon after the collapse of the January Rising (1863) and which grew up in a period of utter disaster for the Polish population of the Russian Empire, a time of impetuous change which transformed the

Polish nation. For this generation it was imperative to define its attitudes and seek out a new code of behaviour and a new way of life.

The general response of youth is to rebel against adult conformity, which is often interpreted as passivity and opportunism. In this case their situation was atypical and much more complex. The older generation could not direct the young or show them the right way to act since they were themselves confused by the course of events. The far-reaching changes in social structure were as startling as they were incomprehensible. The adult world was as lost as the world of youth.

This generalization was true of the gentry and particularly true of the intelligentsia and it can, in varying degrees, be applied to different Polish regions. The fact remains, however, that the early 1880s witnessed the appearance of many young conspirators. Rebels against Russian authority, their actions were influenced by the romantic myths, legends and daring of the secret revolutionary organization, *Narodnaya Volya* (National Will). These culminated in the assassination of Tsar Alexander III in 1894, an event which eventually destroyed Bronisław Piłsudski. Ziuk, whose commitment to conspiratorial work was for the time being less than that of his elder brother, was also implicated.

On 2 September 1884 Piłsudski's mother, Maria, died. Although she had been in very poor health and bedridden for some time she continued, under very trying circumstances, to run the Piłsudski household. This extremely ill and exhausted woman displayed great courage and a cheerful disposition to the very end.

A year after his mother's death and against his father's wishes, Piłsudski enrolled to read medicine at Kharkov University, an institution set in a grim, provincial town which contrasted unfavourably with his beloved Wilno. At the university he was in contact with a students' circle but, at its first meeting, he was bitterly disappointed. He found himself amongst a majority of Russian students to whom he found he could not relate. He regarded them as oppressors of the Polish nation and withdrew from their company. At the end of the academic year in Kharkov, he visited his brother Bronisław in St Petersburg and returned to Wilno. In August he applied for admission to Dorpat. Unlike many in the Russian Empire, this university, at which lectures were delivered in German, enjoyed a relatively liberal ethos; it was far more European in character than Kharkov. However, his admission was delayed and he could not commence his studies in 1886 but instead remained in Wilno where he went through a deep emotional crisis. In the depths of his despair he sometimes became suicidal.

Whilst in Wilno he renewed contacts with school friends and together with a few others on vacation from St Petersburg organized a secret circle. Little is known of it, though Piłsudski later recalled some of the material he read as a member. There was Wilhelm Liebknecht's *In Defence of Truth* and he also attempted the first volume of the Russian edition of *Das Kapital*. Its abstract logic, which urged the dominance of materialism over individualism, did not appeal to Piłsudski. His position on this was typical of the majority of the young intelligentsia. They used socialism as a weapon in their struggle against the Tsar, accepting its democratic bid for equality, justice and freedom but rejecting the programme of class struggle which was a product of scientific socialism. In reality theirs was the ideology of a liberal-democratic middle class which could serve as the starting point for further evolution in the direction of either Marxism or nationalism; it could be transformed into something completely different.

Socialism was, at that time, the only ideology committed to action and struggle. Therefore anyone who rejected loyalty to the Tsar, opportunism and conformity in favour of action, gathered under the flag of socialism, even though sometimes barely understanding what it represented. The saying by Clemenceau: 'He who is not a Socialist in his youth, will be a rascal in his old age', is more than a well-phrased aphorism. Many of these young people would stand by socialism as conventionally understood, others would find themselves aligned with workers' revolutionary movements, and others still would soon cross to the other side of the barricades. But this was the course of events over decades. The Wilno secret circle, which Piłsudski joined after his return from Kharkov, was of a general, ill-defined nature but for one overriding aim: the defence of the Polish nation from a brutal policy of denationalization as practised by the Russians in Lithuania.

It is difficult to ascertain just how far Piłsudski was involved in the workers' movements in Wilno, because of the lack of sources other than his own article: 'How I became a Socialist'. However, it is well known that through its Petersburg connections, Wilno's circle took part in terrorist actions against prominent Russians. This activity included a plan, masterminded by Józef Łukaszewicz (from Wilno) and Aleksander Ulyanov (Lenin's brother) to assassinate Tsar Aleksander III.

The first assassination attempt took place on 10 March 1887. Three more abortive attempts followed before, finally, the conspirators were arrested by police. During the interrogation one of the conspirators, Michał Kanczer, betrayed the organization. This led to the arrest of Józef Piłsudski on 22 March 1887. On 2 April 1887 he was incarcerated in the Peter and Paul fortress in St Petersburg.

During the criminal proceedings brought by the authorities against the conspirators, Józef Piłsudski gave evidence as a witness. His brother Bronisław was sentenced to 15 years in penal servitude. Piłsudski was sentenced to five years exile in Siberia; a 19-year-old suddenly facing the most traumatic experience, a victim of political unawareness of the heart of the matter and the gravity of its consequences. Now he paid the price. Destined for Siberia bitter, disappointed and broken, devoid of any sense of purpose and of any certainty in the rightness of his actions or in the usefulness of his sacrifice.

On 25 May 1887 a group of sixty prisoners, including Piłsudski, left prison in Moscow and went via Nizhni Novgorod, to be put on a barge which took them along the Volga and Kama rivers to Perm. From Perm they went by rail to Tyumen and then again by barge to Tomsk prison. After two weeks in Tomsk prison they began the next stage of their journey on foot, 560 km to Krasnoyarsk, and another 1100 km to Irkutsk. This journey took four long, hard months.

Prisons in Wilno, St Petersburg and Moscow where Piłsudski had been held were luxurious in comparison with stopping-places between Tomsk and Irkutsk. In filthy, primitive cells, surrounded by criminals, Piłsudski was the only Pole and this made him feel very lonely and depressed. On the rivers the barges were overcrowded and stuffy, either very hot or intensely cold. To add to their discomfort the prisoners suffered the bites of small Siberian flies which caused very painful swellings. Relations with guards were extremely tense.

This prolonged journey left a distinct stigma on the psyche of the exiles. The immeasurable distances; the wild, awe-inspiring landscapes; the utter dependence on the mood of the guards and local authorities, would have broken the morale of any but the toughest characters. In a letter Piłsudski wrote of the total divorce from normal life, as like being 'thrown into an abyss where one cannot feel ground under one's feet'. This 'first political group' – such was its official name – arrived in Irkutsk on 4 October 1887 and it was for the local governor to decide the eventual place of exile.

Piłsudski was destined for Kirensk on the river Lena, 1000 km north of Irkutsk. He started his journey on 13 December, travelling by cart about 100 km each day and after ten days, the day before Christmas Eve, he reached a small town or village called Kirensk. There lived there quite a sizeable colony of exiles among whom Piłsudski met Stanisław Landy and his wife, resident in Kirensk since 1882.

Landy, 12 years older than Piłsudski, was a member of the first socialist circles in Warsaw. He was arrested in 1878 and sentenced to 12 years of penal servitude, later commuted to exile. He was a well-read person and very interested in science. The Landy family, who remained in Kirensk until November 1888 when they were permitted to move to Irkutsk, played a major role in Piłsudski's Siberian years. During his stay in Kirensk, Piłsudski was on very friendly terms with them and stayed with them for days on end like a member of the family.

Piłsudski's exile can be divided into two periods: the stay in Kirensk until July 1890 and the stay in Tunka from August that year. Very little is known about the first ten months in Kirensk, but deportees endured only limited supervision or restriction of their movements: escape was practically impossible because survival in the wilderness for long was so unlikely. During Piłsudski's stay in Tunka a ban on movement was introduced but not very rigorously enforced.

Exiles lived in rented quarters and received ten roubles a month for their keep, though some, including Piłsudski, had this allowance stopped. It seems that the authorities took little interest in how the deportees lived. Inevitably life in such surroundings and among so many people of such different backgrounds was very difficult and there was no help from the authorities. Many of the deportees worked for local merchants and many took to hunting, sometimes for fun, but more often as a way of income.

In the spring of 1889 Piłsudski met Landy's sister-in-law, Leonarda Lewandowska, who was a few years older than he. Thirty letters remain from Piłsudski to Leonarda, dated from 25 March 1890 until 11 December 1891 and one from the later days, undated but written in about 1893; Leonarda was Piłsudski's first real love, but little is known about her as she died very young, committing suicide in about 1900.

Ziuk's love letters to Leonarda sketch for us personal features of the young Piłsudski giving us an insight into the sincerity and the frankness of his loving and his being loved. This sincerity gave him real pleasure. Acquaintance was soon transformed into deeper feelings. Piłsudski became a daily guest of Leonarda's and he spent more and more time with her. In the difficult conditions of Siberian exile, Leonarda was more than the first woman he fell in love with. Their affection for one another embodied and substituted for everything that he was missing; home, security and thoughts of a future.

His time with the Landy family also compensated for his solitude and the separation from his family, especially since he could not organize his own life. The most mundane tasks daunted him: domestic work, like cooking, washing up and cleaning, filled him with dread. In two letters dated October 1890 he wrote to Leonarda about his phobia of all domestic work and about how he hated the untidy shambles of his quarters.

All these domestic problems had been solved by July 1889 when Piłsudski began to live a secret and intimate existence with Leonarda and towards the end of her stay in Kirensk they openly lived together as a couple. In exile circles and among revolutionaries this type of liaison happened frequently and was generally accepted. Of course there was the usual gossip but it was not malicious.

In March 1890 Leonarda left Kirensk for Irkutsk. Her separation from Piłsudski was expected to be very short as both hoped that Piłsudski would get permission to live in Tunka and that on the way there he could stop in Irkutsk and see her. However, in a letter dated May 1890 he wrote to her of his difficulties in obtaining the required permission and of how much he missed her.

While still in Kirensk he was depressed by the news that 22 April saw the end of Leonarda's exile which meant that she might not wait very long for his arrival in Irkutsk. Two months later he arrived there and they met again but their joy was short-lived because on 22 July Leonarda started the long trek home and their hope that Piłsudski could see her in Krasnoyarsk evaporated.

On 6 August 1890 Piłsudski arrived in Tunka, a village 200 km south-west of Irkutsk. In a letter he wrote to Leonarda from there, dated 13 August, he said: 'Tunka is not for me. It is a Godforsaken place, suited only to labourers; for them Tunka could be a paradise with no restriction on movement . . . for periods of up to 10 days. The people here generally seem to be satisfied, though their attitude towards the oppressor is beyond the nihilistic, suffice it to say that I will undoubtedly be seen as an aristocrat which I don't like. Anyway, life here is bearable, people are quite active, having discussions, playing games, and reading newspapers or journals – of which there are plenty.'

In a letter dated 10 December, 1890, Piłsudski declared his intention of being like the others, participating in their activities, as well as reading more books. However, he did not follow through his commitment. 'I cannot do it, . . .' he wrote in another letter dated 22 April 1891, in a period of lethargy.

Instead he resumed his hunting, playing cards and chess, and talking into the small hours. Quite often he could not even find the time to write to Leonarda and might manage only a few hasty words in the weekly post which then took six weeks to reach its destination. A reply from Leonarda took twice as long. Major worries about which he wrote to Leonarda from Kirensk were firstly a shortage of money and secondly the possibility that the authorities would prolong his exile in Siberia, as they had with others. He was still a young man with little experience of life and the prospect of additional years in exile horrified him.

He also shared with Leonarda his concern about what he could do when he returned to normal life. He had no profession except teaching, which he did not like, and ignorance of how to start a new life practically paralysed him. Letters from home were not optimistic, debts were high and rising every year and the prospect of having to auction off the remaining estates became even more likely.

Lamenting his lack of professional qualifications, he was also self-critical of his own laziness and lack of self-discipline. In reply to a question of Leonarda's about his morale, he wrote to her on 16 March 1891: 'I cannot say it is very good. There are moments when I am conscious of something hanging over me which makes me dissatisfied with myself, people around me, and the life I lead'.

He blamed his feelings of inadequacy on his upbringing. His parents had 'inculcated in me confidence in my ability and recognition of an unusual assignment or special destiny which went with this. Faith in it is very deep in me; but at the same time they did not teach me perseverance, which explains why many of my intentions remain intentions only . . . and that is why I feel so degraded in my own eyes and in the eyes of others'.

On 16 February 1891 Piłsudski informed Leonarda that he had made various literary attempts, none of which were finished. He expressed doubt over whether he could achieve anything. 'I must confess that you, my dear, are my only encouragement to any work. I dread taking my place with ordinary people and crave fame that I should be worthy of you, although I think that you could love me whatever I am, as you do now.'

Piłsudski's psychological state of mind was dominated by colossal frustration. His frantic ambition and craving for fame required a freedom of action he did not possess. As he imagined, his chances of a start after his return to normal life were still very slim. The possibility of making his way, rising in the world and putting his energies to good use was almost inconceivable. This was the reason for his frustration and time wasting. Piłsudski belonged to the category of people who could not come to terms with life in exile. He found it unbearable that he was there at the bidding of others and not through personal choice, though he was not yet a revolutionary.

For revolutionaries, the future could be visualized in one of two ways: survivors from prison and exile, who returned to normal life would again have revolutionary action as their aim. Those whose spirit was broken by repression dreamed of a quiet life, peace and stability. Nothing suggests that Piłsudski was involved in any conspiracy against the Tsar or even foresaw such a possibility. He certainly never mentioned the subject in his letters to Leonarda, but this might have been to allow for the fact that letters could fall into the wrong hands. The tone of that correspondence was very pessimistic about the future and full of gloom.

A case could be made that Piłsudski's companions in exile influenced him to recognize his potential as a revolutionary. Such a development is suggested in various biographies. At the same time it would be normal and psychologically understandable for a young man uprooted by fate from his own circles to dream of returning to his own environment. Although exile fostered his hatred of his oppressors, it did not negate his will to return to normal life.

One must examine Piłsudski's feelings towards Leonarda in the context of his psychological state. She was the constant stable factor and fixed point of reference in an uncertain future, the only being who made any sense of planning ahead. It was the thought of spending the ensuing years together which gave some meaning to his life. Leonarda, however, was ill-suited to this role. She was too pessimistic and too much of a worrier, which Piłsudski did not like; these aspects of her personality unnerved him.

She worried continuously about the state of his health, which is not surprising since he wrote to her about it most particularly. While in Kirensk he wondered if he had TB. In Tunka he suffered often from 'flu, toothache or catarrh though nothing more serious. More than anything else, however, the knowledge that letters took six weeks, and that anything could happen in the meantime, kept Leonarda in a permanent state of worry. She was more and more doubtful about the prospect of their marriage.

Other factors tended to foster this doubt: Piłsudski often neglected his correspondence with her, and when he found the time to write he mentioned two women exiled in Tunka: Gubarewa and Lidia Łojko. Of Gubarewa he wrote that she would easily fall in love with him with the least encouragement from him. He mentioned her illness and how everybody bustled around her. He described one night-time session when he comforted her with compliments, 'which worked better than morphine'.

That annoyed Leonarda and she wrote expressing the hope that such interest did not give him pleasure. A reply dated 4 March 1891 reassured her since: 'Conquest would be too easy; her nature is too straightforward ... to engage my mind, and ... I love my Olesia (Leonarda) too much to seduce other easier women. If I do seduce another, it gives me no particular pleasure'.

Leonarda remained unconvinced and she asked him whether his feelings towards her had changed. In a letter written on 22 April 1891 he denied this and promised that if such a thing should happen he would tell her honestly. However difficult and unpleasant this was he would not cheat her.

Such reassurances were devalued by an increasing number of references in his letters to Lidia Łojko. Leonarda's anxiety increased and their relationship approached a difficult juncture. Leonarda's earlier suspicions were proved correct about the end of July when she received a letter dated 24 June: 'Leosiu, I have not written to you for all this time because I hadn't the heart to tell you that our relationship cannot last. Forget me, Leosiu! I am not worthy of you. And forgive me if you can. . . . Be happy dear. Goodbye, perhaps for ever. Ziuk'.

Leonarda's worst fears confirmed, she wrote off immediately demanding an explanation. At the end of October she received his refusal to go into further detail to preserve, 'the confidentiality of the third person concerned'. He did confess, however, that he had entered another relationship while still in love with Leonarda and that this was not only dishonourable but also 'short-lived and painful for me and her because of my love for you'. The liaison ended 'with bitterness on her side and another stain on my character'.

Piłsudski sought Leonarda's forgiveness which she had, in fact, sent in a previous letter in which she had also explained that her love for him was of a motherly sort involving understanding and forgiveness. Devastated by what had happened she was determined to fight to regain his love.

In a following letter, and desperately wanting more news, Leonarda wished to 'penetrate your thoughts, your soul, to be able to see inside you and find out what is happening'. But no further letters came from Tunka. Unexpected changes permitted no further contact. Piłsudski and seven others were officially notified that, from then on, their correspondence would be censored. It is unlikely that this worried Piłsudski unduly in view of further comments he made in his last letter to Leonarda: 'I am close to tears when I think of the past and about how things have turned up since. I decided to re-assess our relationship on my return home when I can see you and talk to you face to face. How can one write about these things? The pen does not listen to the dictates of my love and my mind is unable to express in words what I feel. I want to talk to you about everything but I am unable and unwilling to write to you'.

On 20 April 1892 Piłsudski's exile came to an end. Against all the odds it was not extended and he was permitted to leave Siberia, but banned from living in the university cities of Tver and Nizhni Novgorod. Delay in the arrival of money from home for the return journey meant that he left Irkutsk on 24 May, somewhat later than planned, and, because of bad spring roads, he did not arrive in Wilno until 30 June.

Piłsudski returned a completely changed man. The five years of his exile saw his development from youth to maturity. Left completely to his own devices and the difficulties of Siberian life, he had finally developed an inner toughness. He saw another world, came into contact with men of action and freedom fighters. Living with such people and taking part in their discussions revealed a milieu quite unlike the one he had known until then. And was he fascinated by it all? To some extent he was, but far less than is suggested in some hagiographic biographies. The ideological disputes so typical in these circles, were for him incomprehensible and unfamiliar. He was simply not interested in them though he had undoubtedly broadened his knowledge of socialist ideology.

By the time Piłsudski returned home his family's financial situation was grim. While he was away his family had sold the Suginty estate and in 1892 sold Zułów by auction, so the only estate left was in Żmudzi-Tenenie. His assumption that he would have to seek employment on his return proved correct. Of course he could stay with his family for some time but this was not a long-term solution. Neither was one easily found elsewhere. Continuation of his studies required a lot of time and he had in any case lost interest in medicine. Office work was even less tempting and held out few prospects for the future. He lacked knowledge of agriculture so this was hardly a possibility. In a sense exile had left him marginalized, an odd man out. He had lost his foothold on the ladder to success and this was made worse because nothing suggested any prospect of change. This made him feel alienated and useless. Useless but free.

CHAPTER TWO

The Party Activist

Much had changed during the five years Piłsudski had spent in exile. During the period 1887–1888. Poland under Russian occupation witnessed a marked growth in working class activity. Strikes in Białystok, Łódź, Warsaw and in the Dąbrowa Basin provided clear evidence of this. These spontaneous strikes were economically motivated and were not widespread but they had great significance for the development of the consciousness of the working class. The strike on 1 May 1890 in Warsaw was supported by eight to ten thousand workers. Taking into consideration the weakness of the workers' movement in the face of Tsarist persecution this number is very impressive. The following year, despite mass arrests before the May holiday and despite the alertness of the authorities, 30,000 workers (according to workers' sources) were on strike. The first of May 1892 fell on a Sunday. In Warsaw a workers' demonstration took place. In Łódź the May festivities turned into a six-day general strike. It erupted spontaneously and spread beyond Łódź to Zgierz and Pabianice. An estimated 60,000 workers took part. The 'mutiny of Łódź' demonstrated the strength of the working class, its competence in organization and its ability to conduct and sustain the struggle.

These years witnessed other political developments. In 1886 the weekly *Głos* (Voice), founded by Jan-Ludwig Popławski and Józef Potocki (alias Marian Bohusz) began to appear in Warsaw. In the Russian nationalist tradition, *Głos* concerned itself with the interests of the masses, acting as their mouthpiece. It appealed to peasants as well as workers, to all who laboured for their livelihood. By the end of the 1880s several socialist groups had also formed. Broken up by previous arrests they soon revived to rekindle class consciousness amongst the workers.

In 1886 Zygmunt Balicki formed a secret Union of Polish Youth, known as 'Zet', in the Congress Kingdom of Poland. (*Kongresówka*: called into existence at the Congress of Vienna in 1815; in 1874 absorbed into Russian occupied Poland. Referred to in the text below as the Kingdom or Kingdom Poland. Ed.) Organized on the Masonic model and deeply conspiratorial, with secret initiation in three stages, it aimed to achieve independence for Poland on the basis of political, national and social justice. A year later, in 1887, Zygmunt Miłkowski (alias Teodor Tomasz Jeż), participant in the struggles of 1848 and

1863, and a popular writer residing as an émigré in Switzerland, published a pamphlet: 'Concerning active defence and a national fund'. In it he strongly condemned both supporters of conciliation and positivists for abandoning the goal of Polish independence. He advocated an all-Polish secret organization, which would prepare society to fight for independence, and the creation of a national fund to support the struggle.

In 1887 Miłkowski's initiative gave rise to the Polish League, based in Switzerland. It met with a surprisingly favourable response. To those circles within the intelligentsia and among the townspeople unwilling to accept socialist ideology the rebuttal of positivism enabled them to see what a policy vacuum they were in. In the event of the expected conflict between the occupying powers, the Polish League called for action to regain an independent Poland with pre-partition boundaries intact; this was very attractive to the erstwhile non-socialists.

As a clandestine organization the Polish League was active in the three partitioned parts of Poland: Prussian, Russian and Austro-Hungarian. It worked closely with Zet and attracted editorial sympathy from Lwów's *Przegląd Społeczny* (Social Review) and Warsaw's *Głos* (Voice). On social issues, the Polish League echoed vague democratic émigré programmes. It opposed the principles of international socialism and condemned 'socialist revolution'. Its patriotic platform was bourgeois-democratic in character and advocated the necessity for change while retaining the values of capitalism.

The slogans of the Polish League found a patriotic resonance among the youth, and in the older generation they were accepted as a means of countering socialist ideology. Until the Polish League was formed, socialism alone stood for action against the occupying powers. Now a revolutionary movement began to form which could be a very effective weapon against socialist influence and which also presented a programme of patriotic activity.

In 1893 activists of the Polish League, with Roman Dmowski at their head, effected a *coup d'état*, transforming the Polish League into the National League (*Liga Narodowa*) with its headquarters in Warsaw. This marked a distinct turn in the direction of nationalism and gradual renunciation of an armed struggle for independence.

What of these events reaching Wilno? Undoubtedly echoes of news about the existence of socialist conspiratorial organizations in Warsaw, certainly – though after some delay – news about the May Day demonstrations and the 'mutiny of Łódź'. Since *Głos* reached Wilno, information about new ideological movements, arguments and discussions were well known. News also reached Wilno by different routes from various countries of Europe about the strength of the socialist movement, about its widening parliamentary presence and about trade unions.

Wilno was something of a backwater, out of the main current of events. Devoid of industry and consequently of a working class, the town did not experience a violent period of development like Warsaw, Łódź or in the mining towns of the Dąbrowa Basin, but some changes did occur, all the same. During the five years of Piłsudski's exile its political atmosphere altered significantly.

A small group of socialists came together, though little was known about them and they had no programme or organization, nor led any active political work except for making a few speeches and holding discussions. Piłsudski met them socially after his return from exile.

This situation changed at the beginning of 1893 when on 16 January Stanisław Mendelson crossed the border at Wierzbołów. Still only 35 years old, he had behind him a rich political past. In the years 1875–1878 he was one of the organizers of the first socialist circles. Threatened by arrest, he fled to Lwów, and from there to Switzerland. He was the founder and first editor of the Polish socialist periodicals: *Równość* (Equality), *Przedświt* (Pre-Dawn), *Walka Klas* (Class War). He kept in contact with Frederich Engels and participated in the founding congress of the Second International. He was, moreover, an initiator of the Paris Assembly in November 1892.

The idea of unifying the Polish socialist movement emerged at the Brussels congress of the Second International in 1891 when a Polish delegation declared a union to be 'in the interest of socialist progress in Poland and in the interest of international socialist politics . . .'. The initial intention was to call an assembly from the three occupied parts of Poland, but so many difficulties arose that it was finally decided to assemble socialists from Tsarist Poland alone.

The meeting which took place in Paris, lasted from 17 to 23 November 1892. It was attended by 18 representatives of a number of socialist groups: 'Second Proletariat', 'Workers Union', 'Commune of National Socialists', 'Independents' and 'Union of Polish Workers'. After heated and at times very controversial discussions, they accepted resolutions to establish a 'Union of Polish Socialists Abroad' (*Związek Zagraniczny Socjalistów Polskich* – ZZSP.) The delegates' assignment at the end of the Paris conference was to report on its proceedings and resolutions and to unify socialist groups at home in creating the Polish Socialist Party (*Polska Partia Socjalistyczna* – PPS).

The introduction to the draft programme of the PPS was written by Mendelson and a much abridged version was published in the fifth issue of *Przedświt*. Mendelson gave a Marxist analysis of the situation and of the task facing the Polish working class, claiming that the Socialist

Party, under the banner of international revolution leading to universal liberation, alone represented the national interest. 'Only the Socialist Party can save the country from suicidal politics, which are trying to force upon us the rich and lower-middle class.' He emphasized that the Polish Socialist Party (PPS) demanded 'the complete removal of class governments, which found their expression in today's state system' and was committed to gain political power, 'for the proletariat and by the proletariat'. This was to be achieved 'only when the proletariat was able to exert adequate political strength'. For the present it was agreed that the PPS would fight for an 'independent democratic republic', bourgeois-democratic in character.

Mendelson crossed back into Russian occupied Poland on 16 January 1893. After his arrival in Warsaw he came into contact with activists of the Union of Polish Workers and of the Second Proletariat. In February–March these organizations came together in the PPS. The ZZSP also acceded to the PPS, but this was of no practical importance as contact between Russian occupied Poland and the émigrés was broken.

The resolutions of the Paris Assembly were accepted by the majority of socialist activists with distrust. Doubts were aroused by a proposed programme for independence which avoided international solidarity of the proletariat in a revolutionary fight for socialism. They were afraid that a patriotic programme would lead to the negation of the class character of the workers' movement.

This response resulted from a socialist perspective which, with certain simplifications, was based upon the following logic: the aim and mission of the proletariat is the struggle for the realization of socialism. It can be introduced only by way of a proletarian revolution, which would engulf all European countries. Victory of the proletarian revolution would mean solving all national problems, including Poland's. Such a premise meant that to embark on a programme for independence would deflect the attention of the Polish proletariat from more important aims and would direct its energy away from the revolutionary struggle towards activities contrary to its class interest.

Those who accepted the precision and logic of this sequence of thought made a mistake of paying insufficient attention to the enormous (especially in Polish circumstances) mobilizing role of independence slogans, as was pointed out later by Lenin. This is not to say that they were bereft of patriotic feelings and characterized rather by national nihilism or cosmopolitanism. Nothing could be more wrong. Having conducted a class analysis of the movement's aims, they recognized a general proletarian revolution as the only real way to solve national problems.

During his stay in Russian occupied Poland, Mendelson got in touch with the socialist group in Wilno. He also met Józef Piłsudski. There is no record of the discussion or discussions between Piłsudski and Mendelson. We know only of their consequences. In a March issue of *Przedświt* there appeared two letters from Piłsudski, dated 1 February and 17 February respectively. In the next issue of the paper other correspondence followed and in May more, under the title 'To Jewish comrade socialists in the annexed Polish provinces' together with a letter to the editors about the case of Bronisław Piłsudski. (See above.)

Piłsudski's dreams, while in exile, of working as a writer, found a chance of realization. However, the meeting with Mendelson had more important results. It opened for Piłsudski the possibility of action in the newly born PPS, and this gave him an aim in life and a way out from the *impasse* of hopelessness. The community to which Piłsudski returned from exile found no place for him and, in any case, there was nothing to match his ambitions. Activity in the PPS allowed him to find himself and to break free of the feeling of uselessness.

The PPS programme was for him clear and understandable. It was consistent with the independent tradition of his childhood and youth and with that which he had absorbed through contacts with socialist ideology – the proletariat, the mass of the people was the deciding power of the future and in the struggle for independence. There was also an additional factor. In joining a nascent party, he could play an important role and even decisive role while at the same time avoiding the strenuous hardships of climbing the political ladder and of dominating successive layers of a hierarchy. These did not yet exist because the party was only just launched.

It was much easier than for activists in the territories occupied by the Russians. He joined a PPS unimpeded by the stamp and dogma of any earlier group and his five years of exile gave him authority. The party having been created from people of different views, politically and ideologically, this was an exceptionally favourable position. Piłsudski had another advantage over many activists. With few wants in life and deriving a small but sufficient income from the remaining family estate, he was able to devote himself entirely to the party's cause.

The Wilno group renamed itself the 'Lithuanian Section' of the PPS, but this had no apparent effect on its numbers or level of activity. It is not known whether contacts were resumed with Warsaw or whether Piłsudski maintained contact only with London, where the leadership of the Union of Polish Socialists Abroad (ZZSP) had moved.

Relations between the PPS organization in Warsaw and the ZZSP became distinctly strained. PPS activists, who are usually referred to in the literature as the 'old' PPS, became increasingly uneasy with the ideological tendencies of the ZZSP. It was felt that *émigré* activists were abandoning class and revolutionary positions and ZZSP periodicals reaching the country confirmed these suspicions. The 'old' PPS also protested against insulting references to the people of Russia in these articles.

The pace of events was hastened by Stanisław Wojciechowski's arrival in Warsaw during the first days of June. As emissary of a ZZSP alarmed by the way things were developing, he believed that compromise was not possible; the 'old' PPS had rejected the programme of the Paris assembly. Only the Lithuanian Section of the PPS remained faithful to the ZZSP. That is why, after finding out what the situation was like in Warsaw, Wojciechowski left for Wilno, where he met Piłsudski. At the end of June or beginning of July 1893 a meeting was held in a forest near Wilno. Apart from Wojciechowski, it was attended by Józef Piłsudski, Stefan Bielak, Aleksander Sulkiewicz and Ludwig Zajkowski. The participants referred to the meeting as the first assembly of the Polish Socialist Party.

Given the fact that the assembly represented only itself, there is no need to draw from it any far reaching conclusions; the coming into being of a political movement, especially an illegal one, very often represents no one but its founders in its early stages. All that matters is how things develop in the course of time.

The participants of the self-styled 'first PPS assembly' entirely approved the programme of the Paris Assembly. This was not surprising since two (Sulkiewicz and Wojciechowski) of the five were participants of the Paris Assembly and the rest had already accepted the Paris programme. On Piłsudski's initiative, it was decided to define relations towards Russian revolutionists. It was also decided to set up in that part of Poland under Russian annexation an illegal paper and to represent the PPS on the Union of Polish Socialists Abroad (ZZSP) at the forthcoming congress of the Second International.

In fact, as a result of the split of the Warsaw organization and numerous arrests there was no national PPS actually in existence. However, the system of smuggling subversive literature was functioning well. During 1893 nearly 22,000 copies of different publications (including 6140 copies of *Przedświt*, 167 copies of Jewish and 203 copies of Russian pamphlets) crossed the frontier.

This was principally to Sulkiewicz's credit. Of the same age as Piłsudski (born on 8 December, 1867) he was a descendant of a Muslim Tatar family long settled in Poland. Brought up in an atmosphere of Polish patriotism, he was; as early as 1887, a member of the Second Proletariat, and subsequently participated in the Paris Assembly. Though a Mohammedan he could join the civil service and in 1890 he was appointed a clerk at the Town Hall in Suwalki. He then worked in customs, first at Władysławów, then, until the autumn of 1900, in Kirbarty in the region of Wierzbołów, adjacent to East Prussia. There he most effectively organized points of entry for illegal literature and for the illegal transport of people across the border. He was an excellent organizer and conspirator, having the ability of re-knitting the constantly torn network of party communication.

This illicit literature, known in party jargon as 'bibuły' (tissues), played a most important part. First of all it facilitated the awakening of class and national consciousness of the proletariat; in PPS literature greater emphasis was placed on developing a national consciousness though the socialist theme was also propagated. The literature was varied and targeted at different groups; it ranged from appeals and flysheets aimed at a popular audience to *Przedświt* and pamphlets and books relating to socialist theory destined mainly for the intelligentsia.

The delivery of 'bibuły' to particular groups was most often the first step in any attempt to form a party organization. In the initial period of PPS activity, as indeed later, party literature was randomly distributed to houses or factories and displayed on walls. This relatively safe method did not involve a lot of people. Its disadvantage was that material often fell into the wrong hands and was destroyed. Attempts were therefore made to organize the distribution better.

Circulation of as many illicit publications as possible was the main aim, since with their 'illegal' status the amount and territorial spread of 'bibuły' gave spectacular proof of the activity and strength of a political group. Other criteria for assessment were difficult to apply. Strikes and May Day demonstrations could not be credited to any one party, though as a rule they too were preceded by illegal appeals.

The strength of a revolutionary political movement in the wider social consciousness was, it seems, in proportion to the amount and spread of its illegal publications. This quality proved to be very important. Because of it, a small but well-organized group could create the impression of being much stronger and more numerous than it was in reality, and at the same time draw in potential supporters.

In the first half of February 1894 in Warsaw, the PPS convened its second assembly which was attended by nine people. They instituted the party's structure and decided that its highest authority would be the assembly called 'about once each year'. Taking part in it would be 'persons having the confidence of the party', which meant that members of the second assembly were almost automatically nominated. The assembly also selected the Central Workers' Committee (*Centralny Komitet Robotniczy* – CKR), which had the authority to appoint new members in whom there was confidence, after agreement with the 'highest possible number of existing trusted personnel amongst the organization's members'; it also had authority to appoint new trusted personnel to the next assembly. The assembly decided the membership of the CKR, which nevertheless could supplement its numbers, as necessary, for instance, in case of arrests or absence from the country. The CKR's brief was to direct the party's work in its entirety and especially in organizing and directing the work of Local Workers' Committees (*Miejscowych Komitetów Robotniczych* – MKR). The party's basic unit or cell was the 'circle of agitators.'

Relations between the PPS and ZZSP were also discussed. The CKR was instructed, in agreement with the ZZSP, to work on and publish 'an article about relations with the patriotic party'. The assembly again pointed out the need to publish various material in a workers' paper which was to inform and to agitate as well as to highlight the work and experiences of conspirators whether free or imprisoned.

The assembly appointed the following to the CKR: Jan Strozecki, until his arrest chief organizer of the work of the PPS, Juliusz Grabowski, Paulin Klimowicz and, as the representative of the Lithuanian Section, Józef Piłsudski. With the help of Wojciechowski and Sulkiewicz, the latter was to set up a printing press for the publication of *Robotnik* (The Worker).

This was a difficult commission. An appropriate printing press had first to be found and transported from abroad to a location where it could be reasonably safe to print the paper. Then there was the problem of newsprint; although paper was readily available, the purchase and transport of a sufficiently large amount could raise suspicions. It was also necessary to ensure the production of an adequate number of copies and to organize their distribution. Thus it was an undertaking fraught with obstacles.

Wojciechowski purchased a printing press in London and arranged for its shipment home. It arrived at Królewca on 13 May 1894 and was transported to Lipniszek, a small village near Wilno located 12 km from the railway station at Bastuny, where Kazimierz Parniewski, who had just finished his studies in Moscow, ran a pharmacy. Parniewski had met Piłsudski in Wilno through Dominik Rymkiewicz. Piłsudski persuaded him to open a pharmacy in a remote settlement as a cover for the printing operation. They decided on Lipniszek. It had its drawbacks because conspiratorial activity was difficult in such a small place; the frequent arrival of unfamiliar people would inevitably arouse suspicion. Władysław Gławacki, hired as compositor, took up residence in accommodation rented by Parniewski.

The first edition of *Robotnik* appeared on 12 July. It contained ten pages each 22 cm × 14 cm in a run of 1200. It was datelined June 1894, Warsaw. This information was clearly false. The editorial stated that the aim of the paper was the furtherance and defence of the interests of the working class, adding that 'if the paper is to survive it cannot be published in a foreign country, therefore we publish it in Poland'. The second edition appeared in August but was dated 3 July and the next edition was dated 27 October.

At the end of August 1894 a wave of arrests hit the PPS. Of the CKR committee only Piłsudski and Pietkiewicz remained free. These arrests were particularly harmful to the PPS because the main burden of conspiratorial work now depended largely on one man, Strozecki. Also as a consequence of these arrests, the third conference of the PPS, planned for September 1894, was called off. The decision did not however reach Wojciechowski, returning from London with Jodko-Narkiewicz, until they had reached the border and met with Sulkiewicz. Wojciechowski returned to London. Jodko-Narkiewicz decided to meet Piłsudski and other party activists.

Witold Jodko-Narkiewicz (Jodko), three and a half years older than Piłsudski, already had behind him a very rich political history. He came from a very wealthy family which made him financially independent. While still at grammar school he had learned about the ideology of socialism and as a student he joined the Second Proletariat. Threatened with arrest he moved to Prague where he qualified as a lawyer. Next he settled in Switzerland where he associated with the Mendelson group. He wrote articles for *Przedświt* and *Walka Klas*, and travelled illegally throughout occupied Poland. He was one of the organizers of the Paris Assembly in 1892, and after Mendelson's departure from the ZZSP he took over as editor of *Przedświt*.

Thus, in the autumn of 1894 Piłsudski met a fellow activist of great political and organizational experience. Nevertheless Piłsudski held an advantage over Jodko; after the spate of arrests, all the PPS activities were concentrated in his hands. He was now not only editor of *Robotnik* but also in charge of all PPS activities. Though the party was paralysed by arrests, *Robotnik* continued in publication, and the party network, despite some difficulties, was rebuilt.

In January 1893, Piłsudski had met Mendelson who drew him into the creation of the PPS and after less than two years Piłsudski had practically taken sole charge of the organization's activities. It was a career as instant as it was brilliant. Piłsudski worked in difficult conditions, in a nascent illegal organization threatened with destruction by arrests, and weakened as a result of the exodus of its most active members from Russian occupied Poland. Continuously for over seven years Piłsudski was to head the party's work in the Russian sector. Regardless of his organizing abilities, his influence on people at every passing year strengthened his position as a party leader.

In December Piłsudski took part in the Congress of the ZZSP in Zurich. It was his first foreign trip. Piłsudski wrote to Sulkiewicz to say that he had had a pleasant journey although he had had to borrow money and had been troubled by 'various nationalities who jabbered away in heaven knows what language, but not in Polish'. There is no record as to what impression the contact with the democratic countries of Western Europe had made on Piłsudski. Undoubtedly this journey widened his horizons. Yet its most important aspect was his meeting in Zurich for the first time in person the leaders of ZZSP. Piłsudski knew only Stanisław Wojciechowski and Witold Jodko-Narkiewicz. Now he made the acquaintance of Feliks Perl, Bolesław Jędrzejowski, Aleksander Dębski, Zygmunt Balicki, Stanisław Grabski, and Romuald Mielczarski. This meeting must have had quite a shaping influence on Piłsudski's political persona.

What was Piłsudski's outlook at the time? How did he see the programme of the PPS and in what direction was he leading the party? The third question is easiest to answer, but this answer would be incomplete without answering the first and second questions. The fundamental difficulty is that we have at our disposal, in Piłsudski's articles, only the official material. His letters to the ZZSP are of a similar nature. In correspondence to *Przedświt*, in articles in *Robotnik*, his personal points of view are influenced by his position as party activist. Nevertheless it does seem possible to outline the general features of his political profile using such sources.

One edition of *Robotnik*, contained a major article entitled 'Russia', written by Piłsudski. It begins with the statement that the greatest 'enemy of the Polish working class is Russian Tsarism'. This meant that in time it had to come to 'open war between the Polish working class and Tsarism, not for life but for death'. In preparation he advised seeking out those opponents of the Tsar who shared with them a common purpose. One of these was the International Workers' Movement, 'of which we are part' and 'whose most illustrious representatives' were Marx, Engels, Liebknecht, and Bebel.

Further, Piłsudski discussed the relationship of the Russian population and the Tsar. He began with the peasants whose interest lay in the toppling of Tsarism but considered that the 'lack of consciousness of this class, its ignorance and its slavish outlook – consequences of history and of the present Russian economic system', not only made a peasant rising against the Tsar impossible, but made peasants 'a tower of strength on which Tsarism is built'.

In his view the Russian working class was 'too weak and unaware of its task'. Capitalism in Russia was at a stage when it did not meet any

opposition from the working class which it brought to life. Piłsudski
emphasized the peasant character of the Russian proletariat, and stated:
'we can no longer delude ourselves and must recognize that the creation
of a strong working class party in the present economic and political
circumstances in Russia, is impossible and will long remain so'.

Next, he analysed the respective positions of the nobility and the
bourgeoisie in Russia. Of the former he said that 'it is a class sentenced
to disappear' and he considered that it had no 'weight on the scales of
fate'. As to the latter, their economic privileges led them to seek a
political role but 'liberal bourgeoisie opposition meant weakness and
timidity'.

This line of reasoning led its author to two conclusions. Firstly that
the revolutionary movement in Russia 'had never been a mass
movement, and always relied only on individuals'. Nothing was likely to
change in the near future as capitalism evolved very slowly. But,
secondly 'fortunately, within the Russian state, besides Russia there
were other countries, subjugated by force and linked to Tsarism by
prison chains, which had to be taken into account. The peoples of these
countries – Poles, Lithuanians, Latvians, Ruthenians – occupy territories
earlier belonging to the Polish Republic. These territories have a
different historic tradition and are at a different stage of economic
development with national and religious persecutions breeding hatred
towards an unfamiliar political structure'. Therefore, resumed Piłsudski,
'all these conditions suggest that precisely from them will emerge the
strength which will crush to dust the might of Tsarism. In this struggle
the Russian revolutionary movement can play only the supporting role
of a helper'.

The main problem the Polish workers' movement had, in assessing its
options, was its relationship to the Russian revolutionary movement.
Marx and Engels frequently pointed out that Tsarist Russia represented
the main force of counter-revolution in Europe and that movements
such as the Polish national insurrection, which might lead to the
overthrow or weakening of Tsarism, were revolutionary.

However, during the 1890s, especially in the second half of that
decade, the situation began to change. Capitalism in Russia, despite
setbacks in its development, became an ever stronger internal threat to
Tsarism, creating in Russia a force capable of overthrowing it. When
Piłsudski wrote his article about Russia, such potential seemed hardly
possible, though what signs there were had already been noticed by
Polish revolutionaries. At the time the Russian workers' movement was
at an embryonic stage, but before long fundamental change was
inevitable and as their activities gathered pace the Polish situation began
to lose the significance attributed to it by the founders of scientific

socialism. The only real way to effect the national and class aims of the Polish proletariat would be by co-operation with the Russian revolutionary movement.

Nevertheless, for Piłsudski the analysis of 1895 remained the unchanged credo; the logic of which was that the main aim of the movement was to prepare for a people's insurrection that would create an independent and democratic Poland. Only then would the working class be able to undertake the fight for the realization of the socialist system. It had far-reaching implications. First of all, it defined relations toward other social groups and classes. Almost automatically, it moved the problem of allies from a class to a national plane. To simplify, one can say that alliances and compromises were permitted with all those who for some reason declared themselves against Tsarism. In the struggle conducted in *Robotnik* and *Przedświt* against the Polish rich, the PPS focused their attention on the loyalty and treason, respectively for or against the national interest, of landowners and the bourgeoisie.

The concept of a people's anti-Russian uprising found echoes in the romantic tradition which moulded the youthful views of Piłsudski. The Messianic conviction of the special role of the Polish nation translated into a faith in the special role of the Polish working class in the overthrow of Tsarism.

The working class was to be the force which would regain the independence of Poland. Therefore, despite having to postpone full realization of class aims they must continue the struggle to diminish exploitation and improve working and living conditions and also seek to attain that which had already been achieved in the West without changing the basic system. It was primarily in this regard that the PPS differed from the National League (*Liga Narodowa*) in the 1890s. Their differences were not then great, though in later years a polarization would develop due both to an awakening in the consciousness of the working class and a growth in the feeling among the middle classes and the gentry of being under threat. This was to deepen through differences of orientation towards the prospect of war between the occupying powers.

It was time to define relations between the PPS and the National League. One of the resolutions of the second meeting of the PPS, compelled the CKR to reach an understanding with the ZZSP. The editorial to the fifth edition of *Robotnik*, dated 30 November 1894, focused on those who called themselves socialists but who did not support 'skirmishes against factory owners', and only participated in the distribution of patriotic literature, 'with a shade of socialism'. They could not, it declared, be termed socialists, 'because the PPS was first of all the party of labour, its aims and pursuits, expressions of the interests of the working class; it leads towards a class war against the capitalists, preparing for it and organizing the masses. It demands political independence as required by the class interests of Polish workers as well as the workers of other countries who through their representatives – Engels, Liebknecht, Plekhanov – wholeheartedly applauded our endeavours in this direction'.

The editorial article averred further, that a great many dream about independence, but 'all these patriots are not meeting proletarian requirements; they do not want to notice obvious class divisions which exist in class society. They call for national unity, but not for class struggle. Thus the difference between us and the patriots is clearcut'.

This distinction would, time and again, be reflected in party programmes. One of the resolutions of the Third PPS Congress recognized the necessity for a formal party statement concerning its attitude to the National League and also declared that no member of the PPS could join any other secret political organization.

Let us, however, return to the organizational activities undertaken by Piłsudski since the destruction of the CKR in the arrests of August 1894, just before Ludwik Kulczycki had been co-opted onto the CKR. Kulczycki was 28 years old and had eight years' experience in the workers' movement. He was also one of the founders of the Second Proletariat and was already well known as a propagandist in socialist circles. He was interested in sociology and in history and was a supporter of the struggle for a 'constitutional system' in Russia. He introduced this, as a slogan, to the PPS manifesto.

On 20 March 1895, Wojciechowski arrived in Wilno, not, this time, as an emissary but to resume activities in the Russian sector. While away from Poland he had learned the trade of a compositor and, amongst other things, assisted with the printing of *Robotnik*. Using the pseudonym Kazimierz Paszkiewicz, he rented a flat on the outskirts of Wilno near to Lipniszek where the printing press was located. To maintain the strictest secrecy the address of the printing shop was known only to Piłsudski and to Sulkiewicz.

Time and again in the correspondence of PPS activists, the problem of the party's lack of strength was mentioned, but numbers remain unknown. However, it does seem likely that in the middle of the 1890s the membership was rather small. And whilst the question of numbers is obscured by a lack of evidence, at best there were probably fewer than 50 members, though, of course many more found themselves in the orbit of influence of the PPS. For contemporaries operating in conditions of conspiracy, even much more than for historians, membership was unascertainable. A none too large but well-organized group could easily give the impression of a powerful party: all the more so if continuity of action were maintained as, for instance, with the printing of *Robotnik*. This publication, and its well-organized distribution at home and abroad, undoubtedly gave the PPS great political capital and spread a conviction about its strength which could not actually be verified.

The need to develop the PPS was urgent. A situation in which the party continued only to print and edit papers could not go on much longer, if only because workers, aroused by its publications, had to have the opportunity of joining a viable party organization. But this was much more difficult than just sustaining publication and distribution. These activities required only a few people (not counting *émigré* support) while to expand the network of the PPS organization required many more and adequately prepared ones at that.

At the third party rally the decision was taken to form more 'circles of agitators'. The aim was to gather together agitators directly involved with organizational work. Another resolution regarding party tactics required party members to equate 'the evolution of the power of the socialist movement in our country . . . with the growth of PPS strength' and to direct all their energy exclusively to this end.

It is also worth noting the resolutions of the rally in connection with relations to other nationalities within the Russian state. The task of the PPS was to awaken national separatism as a fundamental element in weakening Tsarism; the party's imperative lay in the overthrow of Tsarism and could be achieved in support of nations conquered by Tsarism. Organizationally, it was decided that the re-constituted CKR would have three members and that it would appoint deputies.

Shortly after the rally, in September, Kulczycki was arrested. An illegal publication was found in his possession, and, under examination he confessed to receiving it from Piłsudski. This incident would have its own particular meaning after Kulczycki's escape from exile, later, in 1899.

More immediately, Wojciechowski was co-opted to join the CKR. Its work was influenced by the close friendship which lasted between its three members and the more so now because it became politically monolithic. Sulkiewicz, as a civil servant, could not take part in running the activities of CKR. Wojciechowski had to sacrifice much of his time on printing *Robotnik*. Piłsudski thus became the most active member of the CKR.

In March 1896 Piłsudski left for London to arrange for the printing of a number of pamphlets. He prolonged his stay there because he took part in the London Congress of the Second International and on the way back he stopped in Kraków and Lwów returning on 16 September. During this half year Wojciechowski had, in effect, been the only working member of CKR at home, managing to publish just three editions of *Robotnik*, so it is little wonder that he proposed the transfer of the paper to London.

Before Piłsudski's departure there appeared in the thirteenth issue of *Robotnik*, dated 9 February 1896, the declaration of the Social-Democracy of the Kingdom of Poland (*Socialdemokracja Królestwa Polskiego*, SDKP) stating that 'after consultation with our entire organization in Poland, we have decided to join together with the Polish Socialist Party. Thus, as from today, we cease to operate as an independent organization . . . and we will continue to operate within the frame of one organization, the PPS, and in accordance with its programme'. This statement, signed in the name of the executive committee of SDKP, actually represented only one regional organization in the Dąbrowa Basin, the others having been crushed by arrests. In consequence, for over four years, the PPS remained the only workers' party in Russian occupied Poland.

The main thrust of party activity continued to be the publication and distribution of its literature. In May 1897, there appeared the first edition of the illegal paper *Górnik* (The Miner), edited by Tytus Filipowicz. Ten issues appeared by 1900. In April 1898 a popular science quarterly *Światło* (Light), edited by Bolesław Jędrzejowski was launched. Seven numbers of *Światło* were produced by 1900. They were printed in London, as was *Przedświt* which appeared every month. In 1899 the number of copies produced of various publications had reached 100,000. Of course it is difficult to establish the actual readership. Periodicals such as *Robotnik* and *Światło* were generally delivered to specific subscribers. Similarly with pamphlets. Flysheets or appeals had, as a rule, a wider range. Though some copies were destroyed by recipients, many more were passed from hand to hand. It would not be an exaggeration to say that in the course of one year 30–40,000 people came across PPS publications. Independent of the impact of their contents, the scale of activity in publishing and distribution strengthened belief in the effectiveness and mass popularity of the party. The myth of the PPS became an accepted social fact, functioning independently of the actual organizational possibilities of the party.

As detailed a history as possible of the PPS in its first years of existence is essential to explain the political career of 'Comrade Wiktor' (by which pseudonym Piłsudski was now known, remaining 'Ziuk' only to his closest friends). It was a career constantly under threat of arrest, prison and Siberia, but one with a clear aim and ever greater authority amongst the party's elite. This actually meant in the party as a whole, since the PPS continued to be an elitist party. It also meant authority in wider circles outside the party, mainly, but not exclusively, among the intelligentsia. For security reasons this authority had to be anonymous.

And, importantly for the future, Piłsudski was not dependent on the applause of the crowd. Such external trappings of authority were not for him. He identified real authority with organizational control and in the PPS he had an ever widening range of authority.

Only a few years had passed since his return from Siberian exile and the feelings of hopelessness. By contrast, Piłsudski's life now was full of action, with work to fill every day editing and printing *Robotnik*, writing appeals and articles, keeping up correspondence with the ZZSP, constant travel to raise funds and to make and maintain party contacts, all of which required a great deal of energy. The contrast with the picture, drawn in Piłsudski's Siberian letters, of the indolent youth lacking in self-discipline is striking.

Piłsudski was no orator. He lacked the ability to captivate an audience through clarity or dramatic quality of speech – he tended to use complex construction which clouded clarity and effective communication. He could write far more convincingly. Reading the correspondence from this period and comparing it to the letters from Siberia one is struck by the incomparably greater ease of the later communications. The Siberian letters are in a Polish full of Russian words and grammatical gremlins. The letters to the ZZSP are characterized by a good easy style and increasing use of literary metaphors. His letters, rather than his published articles, are evidence of this because of their spontaneity. It is clear that Piłsudski had been reading widely: in the letters of this period, there are dozens of well chosen literary allusions and quotations from various great works. He remembers schoolboy Latin and uses French and German quotations, as well as Russian.

Yet despite his abilities as a writer, he was not a theoretician or party ideologist. He was exclusively interested in the immediate, agitative value of the written word. There is not a hint of any attempt to contribute intellectually to accepted ideology. His attitude to sharp ideological controversy in the European workers' movement was one of complete indifference, and he rated political activists and parties exclusively in terms of their attitude to the question of an independent Poland or their possible use to this end.

Piłsudski did not believe in the possibility of revolution in Russia and did not consider it in his plans. For the realization of the aim which he put before the PPS – the rebuilding of an independent, democratic Poland *without social change* – revolution in Russia was not indispensable. He assumed that, in its appropriate international setting, a mass Polish uprising would achieve these aims. How realistic this was is another matter. Unlike Piłsudski, others recognized that changing the social structure was the primary aim and that the fate of this development was inextricably linked with the possibility of revolution in

Russia; one could, perhaps, imagine the rise of an independent Poland, but in determining general aims, everything related to the revolutionary movement in Russia.

In these first years of the existence of the PPS, Wilno was the centre of party activities. The printing works of *Robotnik* were located in Wilno and the CKR worked there. However, because of the small number of workers in Wilno, the influence of the party was weak or even non-existent. In a sense this gave conspirators an easier task, as the police were less alert, and the chances of discovery and denunciation by provocateurs and informers were small.

Quite a small circle of progressive intelligentsia lived in Wilno, often connected with the PPS, through political sympathy or simply on social grounds. Within this circle Piłsudski grew closer to Roman Dmowski who, since November 1893, lived close by in Mitawa. Prior to his escape over the border in February 1895, he very often visited Wilno. His frequent visits were attributable to the magnetic attraction of 'the beautiful lady', Maria Koplewska Juszkiewicz. Born in 1865 in Wilno, at the age of 16 she started higher education in St Petersburg. She was beautiful and highly intelligent, with a well-developed sense of humour. A year later she married a wealthy engineer, Juszkiewicz by name. Their marriage was not a happy one and despite the birth of a daughter, Wanda, they divorced. Maria was, partly for reasons of political conviction, in close contact with secret organizations and as a result was arrested several times. She eventually moved to Warsaw and joined the *Głos* (Voice) circle. She paid for this by being arrested and sent to Wilno.

The daughter of a well-known Wilno doctor, she had numerous friends and acquaintances. She soon became a leading light of the town's progressive intelligentsia. Her house became one of its meeting places; a focus of that circle's social life. Party matters involved her only slightly but she assisted when help was required.

Piłsudski became Maria's frequent guest. Their friendship turned to love but marriage was out of the question because Maria was a divorcee and a Catholic wedding would have been impossible. In such cases the solution was a change of religion. On 24 May 1899, in Łomża, pastor K. Mikulski authorized Piłsudski's change of religion from Roman Catholic to Protestant.

One month later, on 25 June, in the Evangelic-Augsburgian church in Paproc Duża in the district of Łomża, the first banns of marriage between Józef Klemens Piłsudski and Maria Kazimiera Juszkiewicz *née* Koplewska were published. The banns were repeated over the next two Sundays and on 15 July their wedding took place.

While on this subject, we may note that Piłsudski again changed religion during the First World War from Protestant to Roman Catholic. He was indifferent to religious matters, like many of the intelligentsia of his generation. He well understood that for the sake of his political career in Polish society, belonging to the Roman Catholic church was a necessity.

Domicile in Wilno was impossible for the Piłsudskis. Maria was too well known and he was wanted by the police. In Warsaw too they could easily have been found. They chose to live in Łódź. No one in the city knew them and there were good communications with Warsaw. Piłsudski's marriage coincided with the departure of Wojciechowski who was totally exhausted with conspiratorial activities.

At the fourth rally of the PPS which took place on 7 and 21 November 1897 an addition was made to the CKR; Aleksander Malinowski was elected to serve beside Stanisław Wojciechowski and Józef Piłsudski. The new member was a 27-year-old engineer whose strenuous party activities brought him to the attention of the authorities and who had had to escape across the border. In any event, he managed, for a time, to ease Wojciechowski's burden of work. Fatigue was not the only reason why Wojciechowski chose to emigrate. He also decided, at the end of 1898, to marry Maria Kiersnowska who had, for quite some time, been involved in the distribution of illicit press material.

The summer of 1898, when Wojciechowski wrote about his exhaustion, proved especially difficult for the PPS. Malinowski was in London and Piłsudski went to join him taking a copy of a confidential memorandum written by Prince Aleksander Imeretynski for publication.

This was one of the showiest and most successful propaganda actions of the PPS. After the death of Tsar Aleksander in 1894 his son Nicholas II was crowned and signs of liberalization emerged in the Polish politics of the new Tsar. The dismissal of the hated general-governor of Warsaw, Josif Hurko, and the appointment in his place of Paweł Szuwałow and in 1897 of Prince Aleksander Imeretynski, raised a political campaign in circles loyal to Tsarism, in expectation of the benefits which would flow from collaboration. In 1897, Tsar Nicholas arrived in Warsaw. He gave his permission for the building of a monument to Adam Mickiewicz, the great romantic poet, and allocated one million roubles donated to him by loyalists to build Warsaw Polytechnic. These gestures were intended to underscore a new attitude towards the Poles.

It activated the conciliationists assembled around St Petersburg's patriotic *Kraj* (the homeland) circle, later members of the Realistic Politics Party. Edward Michajlowicz Jaczewski, director of the governor-general's office had maintained contact with them. It was he who, in preparation of a policy paper advocating a change of political course in the Russian sector, approached the conciliationists. Those responsible for the preparation of this material, under the political supervision of Eustace Dobiecki and Erazmus Piltz, were the Reverend Prelate Zygmunt Chełmicki, Ludwik Straszewicz, Leopold Kronenberg and Count Stanisław Łubieński.

Material produced by them formed the basis of a confidential memorandum sent by Prince Imeretynski to the Tsar. This pointed to the necessity of introducing new reforms in order to cut the ground from under those whom he described as the 'uncompromising part of Polish Society'. He spoke of the conciliationists with disrespect, describing them as 'a weak trend'. He also advocated peasant land reform, the organization of popular libraries to counter socialist propaganda, the reform of methods of teaching the Polish language in elementary and middle schools, the introduction of the Catholic religion into school curricula, the setting up of miners' pension funds, and the establishment of the Polytechnic in Warsaw. Only the last proposal was to be accepted.

The Tsar's vehemently anti-Polish response appeared as minutes on the memorandum. The opinions of ministers with an interest in Polish affairs were similarly recorded. The memorandum and its enclosures fell into the hands of the PPS by circumstances as fortunate as they were unusual. Bohdan Dębicki, a member of the St Petersburg organization of the PPS, had a cousin who, in the course of settling various official matters in St Petersburg offices, took advantage of the services of a certain Długołęcki. He was a professional intermediary, who not only knew whom and how much to bribe, but also had civil servants paid for by himself in various offices. They passed on to him any information he required and occasionally helped him in settling official business. When Dębicki was visiting his cousin one day he met Długołęcki there reading aloud from a Russian document. He soon discovered that the material had come from the Tsar's office and concerned Polish affairs. Under some pretext he managed to get the papers from Długołęcki for a few hours, made copies and delivered them to the CKR.

In the summer of 1898 Piłsudski took these with him to London. The documents were published in an edition of 2000 copies under the imprint of the PPS. The pamphlet, consisting of the Tsarist document prefaced by a long essay from Piłsudski, was entitled 'Secret documents of the Russian government concerning Polish Affairs' (*Tajne dokumenty rządu rosyjskiego w sprawach polskich*). After a number of months a second 2000 copy edition of the pamphlet appeared, this time printed in Kraków. In 1899 over 1000 copies were smuggled to the Russian sector.

All this was a tremendous success for the PPS. It refuted the arguments of the conciliationists and showed the aims and intentions of Russian politics in a light that dispelled any illusions and gave spectacular proof of the strength and capabilities of the PPS. Obtaining top secret Tsarist documents, transporting them over the border and publishing them was an impressive achievement. This was a very important aspect of the whole affair: in circumstances of deepest conspiracy spectacular action won considerable public support. This applied to the publication of those documents, the continuous and regular publication of *Robotnik*, and the regular and continuous delivery of propaganda material. These were measures of the strength and capabilities of the party, giving it tremendous political capital and reinforcing the myth of PPS power.

As an organization, however, the party was still weak and small in numbers. It had little or no opportunity to expand its activities and any such move was regularly and quickly reversed by demoralizing arrests. The penetration of workers' centres by police spies was widespread and brought results.

The most important problem for the PPS was the permanent lack of members. Because of arrests or flight abroad, leading activists were only ever briefly effective. The PPS could not afford to finance illegal activists (maintaining the trinity on the CKR was a big enough problem), yet only such people could work effectively.

Even so the party leadership was not over-concerned about party membership. They believed that a successful uprising would depend more on a well-organized cadre party with the widest possible social support than on a mass party. This would involve wide ranging propaganda to sensitize the masses for action at the appropriate moment. Hence the great emphasis placed by the leadership of the PPS on publication and distribution. And besides, building up the party would, in the nature of things, have had to give priority to the struggle for the improvement of the condition of the working class which meant confronting the whole problem of class economics. It was thought that this would not produce any real gain and would only sap the party's energies.

In January 1899 Alexander Malinowski returned from London as an illegal activist. Another arrival to the Russian sector was Kazimierz Roźnowski, who had come to take over the task of printing *Robotnik* from Wojciechowski. In May, Wojciechowski coedited the 31st number of *Robotnik* with Piłsudski and in mid June escaped to Kraków. After Wojciechowski's departure, Piłsudski and Roźnowski printed the next number of *Robotnik* in Wilno and in the autumn the printing press was transferred to Łódź.

There, Piłsudski and his wife (using the name Dąbrowski) rented a first-floor four-roomed flat. Roźnowski lived separately but visited each day. A domestic was engaged for appearance's sake; a four-roomed flat without one would have aroused suspicion. But there were other complications. The domestic was not initiated into the secret of her employer's activities and this created the necessity of additional secrecy.

In 1899 the SDKP was reconstituted. Instrumental in this was the 22-year-old escapee from exile in Wiacka, Feliks Dzierżyński. (Lenin's future head of internal state security, *Cheka*, attended the same school as Piłsudski in Wilno. Ed.) Towards the end of the year, on his initiative, a meeting of Polish Social Democrats from the Kingdom of Poland and Lithuania took place in Wilno. Arrests in February 1900 (among those imprisoned was Dzierżyński and one of the organizers of SDKP, Antoni Rosół) weakened the nascent organization but did not destroy it. In August of the same year the party held a rally in Otwock at which its name was changed to Social Democracy of the Polish Kingdom and Lithuania (*Socialdemokracja Królestwa Polskiego i Litwy – SDKPiL*). Regional organizations grew in Łódź, Radom, Częstochowa, Białystok, in the region of the Dąbrowa Basin as well as in Lithuania. The PPS had lost the monopoly of the workers' movement in Russian-occupied Poland.

The economic crisis at the turn of the century and the natural disasters which affected agriculture caused a marked rise in political radicalism and in social unrest. The loss of face by advocates of conciliation and the tightening of control by the authorities heightened this discontent. Tsarism replied with repressions, with arrests and with the expansion of the police apparatus. In 1900 the Warsaw head-quarters of the Police Department was joined by the Section for the Protection of Law and Order and for Public Security, namely *Ochrana* – the secret police. The number of police spies and provocateurs was increased and special police units were introduced in factories.

During the night of 21–22 February 1900, after a six-year run of production, the illegal printing operation of *Robotnik* came to an end. At 3 a.m. police broke into Piłsudski's flat in Łódź. They had found the address on Wschodnia street by tailing Aleksander Malinowski, who had arrived in Łódź on party business. He was supposed to go on to Dąbrowa, where, after the assassination of a provocateur, the local organization of the PPS was in danger. On 21 February he left Piłsudski's flat with Roźnowski and was arrested at the railway station.

During the search of Piłsudski's flat the gendarmes discovered, to their great surprise, the printing press, nine printed pages of the 36th number of *Robotnik* and four pages in preparation for this issue, as well as party seals, handwritten material and correspondence. The haul was enormous.

Immediately after Piłsudski's arrest, Sulkiewicz, Sachs and Roźnowski discussed how best and how quickest to publish the 36th number of *Robotnik* in London and at the same time started to organize a printing works in Poland. But immediately after Sulkiewicz had posted a letter to Wojciechowski concerning these matter, Sachs and Roźnowski were arrested; now on his own Sulkiewicz had a difficult time in Wiezbołów, anticipating arrest any moment having left his passport with the solicitor Kruszewski whose flat had been searched by the police. However, the passport went unnoticed lying on the window sill.

At the end of March 1900 Wojciechowski returned to Poland for a short time and agreed with Sulkiewicz that one more number of *Robotnik* would be published in London and that at the same time he, Wojciechowski, would arrange the purchase of a new printing press. On 20 April he delivered the 36th issue of *Robotnik* to Sulkiewicz. It was dated 20 April 1900. Their aim was to create the impression that the party had a second press at their disposal and that the paper was being published in the Russian sector.

In May, Sachs was released on bail. He immediately left for Galicia. Wanted by the police and known to many agents, his operations had become greatly restricted within the Russian sector. For Piłsudski there was no hope of bail. In mid April, he was transferred from police cells in Łódź to confinement in pavilion X of Warsaw's Citadel which held political prisoners. This put paid to any hopes of escape or rescue. But Sulkiewicz and Gertrude Paszkowska did not spare any effort to spring Piłsudski. First it was necessary to find a way for Piłsudski to be transferred out of the Citadel and it was decided that he would simulate insanity, an illness which could not be treated in a prison hospital. On 15 December Piłsudski was moved from the Citadel to the mental clinic of Nicholas the Miracle Worker in St Petersburg. Soon after, Maria Piłsudski was released from prison and ordered to live in Wilno under police supervision.

In the psychiatric hospital, Piłsudski was placed in an isolation ward. He was separated, though not very successfully, from other patients. Staying in the weird environment of the hospital and observing the extremely brutal attitude of the nursing staff towards patients was, for Piłsudski, an extremely traumatic experience. He was also much weakened physically by simulating illness, by the refusal of meals, in Warsaw. The next three months must have been a most difficult time for him; it was not until March 1900 that the St Petersburg PPS organization managed to get into contact with him through a Dr

Sylwanowicz, a Pole, who worked in the hospital and who was connected with the party. Organizing his escape was difficult and preparations lasted a few months. In the end all went according to plan. During the night of 14–15 May 1901, Piłsudski escaped from hospital and a month later was in Galicia.

CHAPTER THREE

Pragmatist

In contrast to Tsarist Poland, Galicia – part of the Habsburg empire – was an oasis of freedom. Polish literature flowered luxuriantly and a theatrical renaissance flourished at a time when the national classics were forbidden in Tsarist Poland. In schools and universities national history was taught and the work of the Kraków school of history sparked lively debate. Much else was discussed, including art, especially that of the bohemian *avant garde* and also politics. Arrivals from the Russian sector were often offended by the sympathies of the Galicians whose gaze seemed fixed on Vienna and they were amused by the niceties of social life and irritated by its formality and presumptuousness. Yet, as soon as made, these criticisms evaporated in the atmosphere of freedom.

The young rebelled against the status quo, against submission to reality. News of romantic conspirators, coming from the Russian sector, fired their imagination and re-kindled their resolve for action. Freedom fighters were embraced by the young with an adoration which was almost idolatrous. And they were viewed with an equal measure of mistrust by the older generation.

Political life pulsated in Galicia. The Polish Social Democratic Party of Galicia and Teschen-Silesia was strong enough to have succeeded in sending its own representatives to the Vienna Parliament, and the Polish Peoples Party, founded in 1895, which played a significant role in the villages, also had an important say in Galician politics. The latter was, however, dominated by Conservatives whose political position had not yet been threatened in any way. Theirs was a particular brand of Conservatism, quite enlightened, rather than backward looking. They understood that reform was needed, that the proverbial poverty of Galicia demanded policy changes and that nationalist conflicts in East Galicia could be solved only by compromise on all sides.

For more than four months Piłsudski breathed the Galician air. The contrast with the Xth Pavilion, the mental clinic and the difficulties connected with his escape was most striking. No wonder that, despite calls from Jędrzejowski, Piłsudski was in no hurry to go to London. Eventually, however, he went there arriving in the British capital on 19 November after a short stop in Katowice and Poznań. Throughout his stay in Galicia Piłsudski had maintained contact, by letter, with

Jędrzejowski, who kept him informed about the PPS. He also gained a great deal of information after his escape from his escorts (Sulkiewicz, Perl and Prauss) and from several PPS activists in Galicia. But he was best informed in London through access to much material and correspondence.

One particular source worthy of mention was a memorandum from 'Leon' (Bolesław Czarkowski), posted to London in the winter of 1902. He was a member of the CKR, one of the most active workers of the PPS in the Russian sector and very well informed. In his assessment the PPS was in 'deep crisis in all spheres of its activities'. He complained that when he had started to reorganize the party's activities into workers' circles it became evident to him that nothing could be done because there was 'no equation between intent and realization' and the situation seemed to be beyond anyone's control. There was complete lack of organization and outdated rules which led to 'chaos and demoralization'. The intelligentsia were absent from the workers' circles, party literature was in short supply, the transfer of material crossing the frontier was badly organized and funds were in short supply and poorly distributed.

Piłsudski resented Czarkowski's allegations. In a letter to Jodko on 11 March 1902, he described a 'redundant criticism', a discovery of 'America long discovered' which gave the impression of a watertight case when it was in reality 'full of holes'. Yet Czarkowski was nearer the truth than Piłsudski dared believe. The crisis which affected the PPS was not just the mere product of a temporary breakdown but had deep rooted causes which he would find out for himself after his return to active work in Tsarist Poland. In London and out of direct touch with PPS matters, he refused to accept Czarkowski's analysis.

Piłsudski returned to Poland at the end of April and in June participated in the sixth congress of the PPS, in Lublin, where a complete overhaul of party structure, into regions and functional departments, was hotly debated. According to Piłsudski's plan the CKR would be convened twice a year and would consist of regional representatives, the editor of *Robotnik* and representatives of the committee for foreign affairs.

His proposals met very strong opposition from a number of party activists from within the country, especially Feliks Sachs and Adam Bujno. In the event, a compromise was agreed upon by which membership of the CKR was enlarged and its executive committee now included Czarkowski and Bujno as well as Piłsudski. This ensured that the political command of the party remained in the homeland. At least formally.

This first, sharp, dispute and its virtual rejection of the Piłsudski plan, marked a new stage in the internal situation of the PPS. The monopoly of authority exercised by a small group (Piłsudski, Stanisław Wojcie-chowski, Aleksander Sulkiewicz, Aleksander Malinowski, Bolesław Czarkowski, Bolesław Jędrzejowski and Witold Jodko) was being challenged. A more prominent role within the party was increasingly being played by its younger members who held quite a different view of the tasks ahead for the PPS from those of their seniors. Disagreements about organization and about political authority in the party, were reflections of a much deeper divergence of opinion of which, at the time, even the participants in the debate were not yet fully aware.

It concerned the interpretation of the PPS slogan: 'The struggle for independence'. In articles published in *Przedświt*, Witold Jodko, Bolesław Antoni Jędrzejowski, Stanisław Grabski and Tytus Filipowicz advocated fighting for independence by force of arms, a struggle organized and directed by military conspirators loyal to the cause – a national uprising of the working class, led by the PPS. However, its aim was not to build a socialist system, but to create a democratic republic, which would, over time, turn to socialism. This was a clear and unequivocal retreat from a class position and it prompted the polemics of those activists, like Kazimierz Kelles-Krauz, Feliks Sachs, Marian Bielecki and Adam Bujno, who held to the inseparability of national and class aims of the PPS.

The aims of the PPS also concerned Lenin. In an article published in 1903 as 'The national question in our programme' he stated that although 'the rebuilding Poland before the fall of capitalism is improbable, it cannot be said that is impossible. That is why Russian social-democracy does not . . . rule out the Polish having as its slogan a "free and independent Polish Republic" even though the probability of its realization before the victory of socialism is entirely negligible'. The programme of Russian social-democracy 'demands only that a truly socialist party does not demoralize the consciousness of the proletariat, does not obfuscate class struggle, does not deceive the working class with bourgeois-democratic slogans and does not disturb the unity of the current political struggle of the proletariat. On this depends the whole essence of the matter, and only under such circumstances shall we recognize self determination'. In Lenin's view, the PPS was trying in vain to make a separate case for itself by alleging that self-determination and the right to struggle for a free and independent republic was being denied it by German or Russian social-democrats. 'Such is not the case but in denying the importance of class in the struggle, in confusing the issue by chauvinism, in upsetting unity in the continuing political struggle – this prevents us from seeing in the PPS a true workers' social-democratic party.'

Piłsudski, of course, had no intention of being a member of 'a truly social-democratic workers' party'. Moreover he was prepared to do anything to prevent the PPS ever becoming such: because his aims were different.

The leadership of the PPS was in difficulties. The new situation really required a new course of action. The loss of monopoly by the PPS, a renewed interest in political activity by the intelligentsia and the working class, and stronger pressure from within the party for the realization of its class aims all came as a surprise to them. When it came to preparations for the May Day (1901) celebrations, they did little and restrained the popular activities of the party which, with the benefit of hindsight, could only have had negative results – loss of influence and loss of a potential clientele.

From about the year 1900 it was obvious that power was slipping away from the party leaders. Material factors, such as the arrests of Piłsudski and Malinowski, speeded up that process. Wojciechowski wrote, in a letter of this period, that the former 'CKR dictatorship' no longer existed and that this was a sign of change taking place within the party.

In contrast to the years 1892–1900, when Piłsudski would very seldom, and then only briefly, leave the country, after 1902, when he recommenced active political work in the field, his stay in Galicia was prolonged for various reasons. In the main these related to family matters. Through marriage to Maria he became a stepfather to 12-year-old Wanda, to whom he was very attached and whose death in 1906 affected him greatly. Maria herself, after escaping from Wilno, was wanted by the police and could not, without risk, appear in the Russian sector. In the circumstances Piłsudski decided to transfer *Przedświt* and the foreign committee of the PPS from London to Galicia (accomplished in 1903) where he wanted to organize the party's central leadership. His plans materialized only in part.

It appears that Piłsudski's unwillingness to work in the Russian sector came from his dislike of the role of agitator. It is significant that, among numerous reports about Piłsudski's activities in this, as in the previous period, there is not a single report mentioning his activity among workers. Piłsudski was not suited to speaking to large gatherings. The activities that he was used to and enjoyed most were writing and editing and also inspiring and directing people. This work could equally well be done from the territory of Galicia.

The international political situation now became more and more threatening. In the Far East, a Russo-Japanese conflict was brewing. In Russia, influential circles pressed for war, believing that only through war was it possible to stop Japan's territorial ambitions and, in the face of growing social tensions at home, victory in a small war would play a very positive role.

Piłsudski observed the growing conflict with great interest. At the end of January 1904, together with Jodko and Jędrzejewski he decided to approach the Japanese envoy in Vienna, Viscount Nabuoki Makino, with an offer of cooperation.

On 6 February 1904 Japan broke diplomatic relations with Russia. Two days later Japan attacked the Russian Pacific fleet and forced it to take shelter in Port Arthur. On 10 February Russia declared war on Japan.

On 13 February Jodko informed Aleksander Malinowski that a letter had been dispatched to the Japanese envoy in Vienna containing a general statement proposing cooperation between the PPS and Japan, and a request for talks. It was planned to form a legion in Japan composed of Polish prisoners of war and volunteers from America, as well as to obtain funds from the Japanese for intelligence and sabotage work in the Russian sector.

Makino had no intention of getting involved with a 'representative of the strongest party' and left Jodko's letter unanswered as he did with a second dated 21 February.

At about the same time (25 February) Jodko despatched a letter to London in which he advised Tytus Filipowicz to get in touch, through Michał Woynicz (a well-known antiques dealer in London sympathetic to the PPS) with the British government and with the Japanese Embassy.

During March and April meetings took place between Tytus Filipowicz and Colonel Taro Utsunomiya, the Japanese military attaché at the London Embassy. The latter made it clear that, while he was prepared to sign an agreement concerning intelligence and sabotage activities, he was not empowered to take any political decision with regard to the formation of a Polish Legion, or to support a Polish case at a future peace conference. Eventually, at the beginning of May, there emerged the proposal that representatives of the PPS travel to Tokyo at the expense of the Japanese government.

On 2 June Piłsudski arrived in London and after a few days left with Filipowicz for New York. He stopped, for a short while, for talks with Aleksander Dębski, one of the founders of the PPS long settled in the USA, and then journeyed via Chicago to San Francisco, and by boat to Yokohama, arriving during the night of 9–10 July. The next day, Major Saburoh Inogaki arrived and took the Poles to Tokyo where they were accommodated in a small hotel. In rather amusing circumstances they met James Douglas who had been in Tokyo over a month. He was a colourful personality who originated from Scotland but was brought up in a Polish environment in the Ukraine and was secretly associated with the PPS whilst working for Roman Dmowski's rival National Democracy (*Endecja*) party. Suffice it to say that he went to Tokyo as the correspondent for the *Endek Słowa Polskiego* (Polish Word) which was published in Lwów and he reported on his activities to the PPS through Jodko and Malinowski.

Douglas had been informed of the schedule of Piłsudski's and Filipowicz's trip to Tokyo but forgot the date of their arrival and spent the day with Dmowski instead. That afternoon, when on a walk with Dmowski to his horror he spotted Piłsudski and Filipowicz riding in an open carriage. He tried to avert Dmowski's attention from them but Piłsudski stopped the carriage and walked towards Dmowski. Douglas did not know that soon after their arrival Piłsudski and Filipowicz had noticed Dmowski's name and the name of his hotel in the newspaper *Japan Times* and were *en route* to pay him a visit.

Piłsudski and Dmowski met on 14 July. Nothing is known about what amounted to the longest conversation, between themselves, in the life of the two political rivals but is clear that close social contact between them was possible despite the unbridgeable political gulf. Years later Dmowski wrote of the encounter in Tokyo: 'I tried to find out from both leaders of the PPS what they intended to achieve by an uprising in the Kingdom and how they envisaged its consequences. I tried to convince them, that what they wanted to do was nonsense and a crime against Poland but I failed in my attempts and in reply received a long winded tale full of muddled platitudes uttered with enormous self-confidence'. Piłsudski left no similar report and although we have no details concerning their talks the texts of the memoranda presented by them to the Japanese government are known.

Soon after his arrival in Tokyo, Dmowski submitted two extensive reports concerning conditions in Russia and about Polish matters in general and then a third just before his departure, when he had failed to gain the promised audience with the minister of foreign affairs. Dmowski tried to convince the Japanese that while it was indeed possible to stir up local disturbances, such uprisings would not be in Japan's interests because they would be immediately and cruelly suppressed, allowing the Russians to withdraw a large number of forces from the Russian sector and to transfer them to the Far Eastern front. Dmowski reasoned that after the inevitable suppression of the uprising there would follow a social collapse which would be to the advantage of Russian circles wishing to secure peace for themselves in Poland under Russian occupation.

In his memorandum of 13 July, Piłsudski began by discussing the diversity of nations in Russia, distinguishing between the historic nations (Poles, Finns, Georgians and to an extent Armenians) and those outside this category (Lithuanians, Byelorussians and Latvians). Of them all, Poland represented the strongest anti-Russian nation. The political aim of the PPS was 'to break the Russian state up into its main constituent parts and to bring independence to those countries forcibly merged into the Russian Empire. We consider this to be not only the fulfilment of the cultural aspirations of our country in seeking independent existence, but also a guarantee of its existence, because, deprived of its conquests, Russia would be so weakened as to no longer threaten or endanger its neighbour'. Carefully avoiding definite commitments, the memorandum further discussed the future direction of PPS policy and the possibilities that could lead to a Polish-Japanese alliance.

The Japanese General staff rejected Piłsudski's and Filipowicz's offers, interested only in intelligence and sabotage action. This it agreed to subsidize to the tune of around £20,000 (remitted monthly until the end of the Russo-Japanese war by the Japanese military attaché in London) together with some arms, ammunition and explosives. Set against hopes with which the Polish party approached their Japanese mission, this was not much. But, if we realize that this assistance was exclusively at the disposal of Piłsudski's group, then it counts for more and it undoubtedly made Piłsudski's group entirely independent of the CKR and gave it the freedom to conduct its own politics.

Yet it must be admitted the Piłsudski-Filipowicz mission ended badly. Dmowski could, perhaps, claim success in managing to paralyse the activity of his political rivals. In any event, it seems that the Japanese had never had any intention of engaging in exotic affairs with Poles. They were not needed because the war resulted in a series of successes for the Japanese army. The political aim of Japan was not the destruction of Russia, only the limitation of its appetite for territory in the Far East. Resilient Japanese imperialism would not tolerate competition. The only Polish contribution of any interest to Japan was reconnaissance, and its political involvement in Polish affairs was undesireable as a potential complication in future peace negotiations.

At the end of July, Piłsudski and Filipowicz left Tokyo and sailed for Canada, Piłsudski returning to Kraków in September. The long journey proved to be a waste of time. Obviously it widened Piłsudski's horizons. He came into contact with the USA and Japan but it would appear that this made little impression; Piłsudski was generally very closed to foreign influence. Outside Poland he mostly felt very uncomfortable and never enjoyed travel to distant places. A comparison of the influence of the Japanese trip respectively on Piłsudski and on Dmowski is rather telling. Dmowski wrote: 'I could not have foreseen that one expedition to the Far East would tell me more than the greatest thinkers in Europe today'. For Piłsudski the Japanese expedition was no greater intellectual inspiration than for the average tourist.

The time was not however right for tourism. Too many events of great moment were taking place in the Tsarist Poland.

By mid-1904 it was obvious that hopes for the transformation of the Russo-Japanese war into a European conflict had failed. At the same time, the sudden growth in radicalism among workers proved that more often than not the PPS was caught unprepared for their impulsive, spontaneous manifestations, and was being left behind by events. This was clearly felt by party workers at grassroot level who were in touch with popular opinion. The gulf emerged in discussions by the CKR in March and in August. Piłsudski's absence had impeded change; he had left behind him 'the old ones', as those members of the executive who still wished to control the party along established lines were known. But this was no longer possible due to the growing political isolation which now threatened them with loss of influence in the party. Between the 17 and 20 October a meeting of the CKR took place in Kraków, the old guard still believing that they held a clear advantage.

It is perhaps advisable, when attempting to understand political shifts within the PPS, to try to avoid over-simplification in applying any such category. Distinct groupings can be discerned on the wings of the executive but, in the main, their divergences were recognized as tactical rather than ideological. On concrete issues many positions were held. At times these could be contradictory. Yet the majority of the CKR members occupied central positions – on some questions supporting the right wing, on others the left wing of the party.

It is essential to underscore a further point. During 1904 'the old ones' were quite obviously losing their monopoly of power in the party, or rather, despite insistent efforts, had failed to achieve this monopoly. But at the same time they dominated the rest of the party by remaining an organized group and by retaining control of the main organs of party activity: The Executive Committee, Foreign Committee, *Przedświt* and *Robotnik*. The left wing of the party had an increasingly greater influence in local organizations and, in practice, it led the activities of the PPS in the Russian sector, but it was atomized, not organized.

At the Kraków meeting, it was widely accepted that tactics had to be dramatically improved. In his opening speech Piłsudski assessed the situation as 'serious'; there was no clear policy though 'expectations of change and hope for improvement are widely held'. At a moment in time, when 'upheaval is possible, we are silent and do great harm to Poland's cause. We should not now be silent! Politics are not mathematics. It is impossible to calculate and foresee everything'. Passivity amounted to negative policy. Piłsudski feared that if no change were effected then, in the event of the downfall of Tsarism the CKR would be 'too late'. He urged that a 'change of tactic is essential, even if this tactic were to lead to an insurrection, steeped in blood. This would be less costly than our lifelessness today the organization must be prepared for change'.

By preparedness, Piłsudski meant the rebuilding of the fighting units within the organization. Indeed, the Warsaw groups had already instructed Bronisław Berger (alias Kuroki) and Walery Sławek to organize groups of fighters whose job would be to protect demonstrations although they had not yet been equipped with fire arms. Both the 'old ones' and 'young ones' agreed to the need for an expansion of the fighting units though they did so for different reasons. In the opinion of the latter, a fighting organization would exist to protect mass movements whereas the former saw the possibility of creating, within the framework of the party, a multilayered, hierarchical, conspiratorial organization.

The announcement, by the Tsarist authorities, of the mobilization of reservists, significantly intensified tension in the Russian sector. On 28 October 1904, the Warsaw organization of the PPS organized an anti-mobilization demonstration. About 200–300 participated before the march was dispersed by Cossaks. Some dozens were injured though workers had demanded, for quite a time, that the demonstration should not be left vulnerable to a charge by the Cossacks and the police. On 10 November there was a mutinous outbreak of rioting by 1200 reservists at the Petersburg station in Warsaw. It was brutally quashed.

In such a climate and in the light of the party's new tactics, a demonstration on Grzybowski Square was planned for Sunday 13 November. The *Ochrana* (secret police) had been warned about the coming demonstration by an informer. In the courtyards by Grzybowski Square and its surroundings, Cossacks and police took up their positions. Attempts were made to hold back crowds from the square, but without success. By the afternoon the square and its neighbouring streets were full of people. An appeal by the police for the crowd to disperse went unheeded. At 1 p.m. when people began to leave the church beside the square, the sister of Stefan Okrzeja, a leading member of the PPS fighting organization, approached a group of 60 militants and removed from under her blouse a red flag with the inscription 'PPS: Down with war and Tsarism! Long live a free Polish nation!'. Okrzeja raised the flag and intoned the anthem '*Warszawianka*'. The procession then started in the direction of Bagno street. At that moment, from a nearby gate, there ran out a detachment of a few dozen policemen. Charging the crowd with sabres, they forced their way towards the standard. As one of the policemen reached for the standard the militants began to fire their weapons. The shooting was chaotic and not very accurate, but it was enough to force the police into retreat. After a moment's hesitation, mounted police dispersed the crowd. About 20 militants remained with the standard and, firing their arms, managed to escape; 413 were arrested. A large number of demonstrators took refuge in the church. After several hours they obtained from Karl Nolken, the police chief, an assurance that they would not be harmed and they left the church. Despite the promise about 250 more people were subsequently arrested.

As demonstrators were still gathering on the streets close to the square, shots were fired in the direction of military and police. New marches began to form. Spontaneous demonstrations erupted at various points throughout the city. Its citizens were angered and excited. There were 6 killed and 27 wounded. Military and police casualty figures were not disclosed.

The impact of this demonstration was enormous. Never before had effective resistance against the military and police taken place on such a scale. It had enormous propaganda value and, at the same time, the barrier of fear of the military and police had been breached.

Expression of popular discontent followed in other centres. There were demonstrations in Radom, Ostrowiec, Ćmielow, Kalisz, Sosnowiec, Łódź and Pabianice. In a few places bridges and railway lines were damaged by dynamite, preventing transport of mobilized forces. In Częstochowa a bomb was thrown at the monument of Tsar Aleksander II. The wave of organized and spontaneous demonstrations, often transformed into armed uprisings, spread throughout Kingdom Poland in December 1904 and January 1905. News of these, very often exaggerated, spread fast into areas where peace still reigned. A general and political strike was fermenting. This was the birth of a revolution.

On 22 January 1905 a demonstration of approximately 150,000 Petersburg workers, organized by the priest Gapon, marched towards the Winter Palace carrying portraits of the Tsar and church banners. The throng intended to hand the Tsar a petition, approved at factory meetings, containing demands for an eight hour working day and for the democratization of the state, freedom of speech, freedom of the press, the right to strike, the right to organize unions, equality before the law and a Constituent Assembly. The demonstration was essentially peaceful in character. It was an expression of faith in the 'good Tsar' surrounded by 'bad officials'. But the Tsar had no intention of being a 'good Tsar'. The demonstration was greeted by a salvo of shots and Cossack sabres.

It was a massacre on an unprecedented scale. On the square before the Winter Palace about a thousand people lay scattered dead with many more wounded. Church banners were dyed with blood changing them to red standards.

In Russian occupied Poland news about the Petersburg massacre quickened the development of the strike movement. The workers parties (PPS, the Bund and SDKPiL) were caught unawares and were overtaken by a spontaneous mass movement. In their appeals, they proclaimed a general strike which in a few days paralysed the Kingdom.

The January-February strike had a multiple meaning, but first of all it demonstrated the power of the working class. Small in comparison with the whole population (less than four per cent) it managed nothing less than to bring life to a standstill. On the streets of towns and villages there crowds gathered, intoxicated with freedom and power. Every revolution is the product of a mass consciousness. The strike of January-February was a milestone in the growth of this consciousness.

These events brought into relief the basic contradictions between the 'old' and the 'young'. For the 'old' the general strike confirmed the possibility of realizing their programme of an anti-Tsarist uprising with the working class as its main force, but, at the same time, they were decidedly against connecting the action of the Polish proletariat with the activities of the Russian working class. The political aims of the Polish and Russian proletariats were, in their opinion, different. The 'old' responded with aversion to the class programme of the 'young'. They attempted to bestow a national character upon the workers' demonstration, so as not to alienate other social classes with a common interest in the overthrow of autocracy and the attainment of republican, democratic and national freedoms. Yet, the role of 'old' in the party was ever more clearly diminishing.

Between 5–7 March 1905, the Warsaw Workers' Committee and the so-called Central Bureau of the PPS organized the seventh party conference. This was done without permission of either the Executive Committee or the Foreign Committee. The conference agenda consisted of three items: party tactics, membership of the CKR, and organizational matters. Discussion concerning party tactics, concentrated on two main problems: 1) whether the main purpose should be the preparation of armed insurgency units, or whether it should be directing the peoples' movement during revolution and 2) whether the slogan should be 'independence' or 'autonomy'.

With regard to the first, the assembly decided on a compromise. It did not support the insurgency programme and very strongly emphasized the interest in common between the Polish and Russian proletariat; but equally, it did not dismiss the possibility of the realization of armed insurrection in favourable circumstances. This is particularly clear in the brief given to the Conspiratorial-Combat Department. It was to direct mass street demonstrations, while at the same time being prepared, as a conspiratorial organization, to undertake the armed struggle at the appropriate moment.

As for the actual political programme, it was agreed that the party's slogan should call for a democratic 'Sejm' (Parliament) in Warsaw, and, for the present, to fight for autonomy, leaving 'independence' for the future. This was a fundamental change of programme since it meant that the party was giving up its current attempt to sever Polish territories from Russia (i.e. the insurgency programme) in favour of a struggle, in common with the Russian parties, for the democratization of the Romanov Empire.

Equally important were organizational decisions to increase the role of middle party management by introducing a mechanism of control over executive action. Elected to the CKR were: Jan Rutkiewicz, Henryk Minkiewicz, Adam Bujno, Walery Sławek (a future Polish Prime Minister), Aleksander Malinowski and Józef Piłsudski, the latter on the condition that he would be active in the Kingdom.

In sum, the VIIth assembly was an unmitigated disaster for the 'old ones', symbolized in their loss of leadership. First reactions were impetuous. In connection with the assembly's dismissal of Leon Wasilewski from the Foreign Committee, Jodko-Narkiewicz and Jędrejowski resigned ostentiously. Their hope was that, in consequence, the VIIth assembly would be regarded as illegal, thus causing a split. At a previous point in the conference Stanisław Jędrzejewski and Aleksander Malinowski had threatened the party with as much. But Piłsudski was against a split – realizing that, at that moment, it would have meant a complete defeat of the 'old ones', whose influence in the party was minimal. All they had left at their disposal was the printing works of *Przedświt*, because, following the arrest of Józef Kwiatek the assembly entrusted the editorship of *Robotnik* to a 'young' Jan Strozecki. Piłsudski therefore willingly accepted mediatory action by Kazimierz Kelles-Krauz. Linked by the strong bonds of a common past with the 'old', Kelles-Krauz was without doubt ideologically closer to the 'young' and, above all else, he was afraid of a split, believing that the divergences were of secondary importance, arising partly from personal factors and partly as a result of the methods used by the 'old' rather than being fundamental differences over the party programme.

This mediation resulted in a joint meeting of the old and new Foreign Committees and was to bring positive results to the 'old'. More immediately, a split was avoided and the 'old' formally submitted to the resolutions of the assembly. Three months later, Kelles-Krauz was dying of TB, aware that a crisis in the party had been prevented. But was he aware that differences were only partially resolved? That a split was unavoidable?

A distinct growth in the radicalization of the masses came with the May Day celebrations. In Warsaw, the PPS organized only local and district demonstrations; the SDKPiL organized central demonstrations. The army used firearms against a crowd numbering several thousand. In the ensuing massacre, 37 people were killed. Many more were wounded, officially 35 but, as usual in such a situation, a number of the injured avoided contact with the ambulance service and the hospitals. That same day there were armed clashes in Łódź and in the Dąbrowa Basin and demonstrations spread into some rural areas.

During May and June social tension tightened; strikes, meetings, spontaneous marches and demonstrations organized by workers' parties became part of the political climate of the Kingdom. Attempts by the authorities to stir up anti-Jewish feelings as a means of rechannelling this tension met with decisive opposition from the workers. At the end of May the workers of Warsaw undertook, spontaneously, to clear the city of thieves, bandits and saboteurs. There were casualties, but the city was cleared of such anti-social elements. Similar action took place in other cities.

Of these, Łódź stands out for the number of strikes, meetings and marches that took place. On 18 June a 5000 strong march was attacked by Cossaks and by the army. Five marchers were killed. Two days later a crowd of about 20,000 took part in their funeral. The majority of factories went on strike. The next day, at dusk, a huge demonstration (officially given as 70,000) filled the streets of Łódź. The army again used fire arms. They killed 31 and wounded hundreds. This was 21 June, the day before Corpus Christi, when, from morning, workers attacked any policemen and Cossaks appearing on the streets. That evening the first barricades appeared. The day's outburst was spontaneous and surprised the workers' parties.

On 23 June a strike paralysed the whole of industrial Łódź. On the streets over 100 barricades were erected. The Tsar ordered martial law. An unequal battle went on for two days. The workers were poorly equipped and badly organized, but the situation produced new leaders and organizers.

A few days before the June uprising in Łódź a meeting of the Executive Committee of the PPS took place near Warsaw, initiated by the Warsaw Workers' Committee and the Press Section. Debates began on 15 June and ended on 17 June, almost a day before the events in Łódź, events which apart, perhaps, for their sudden ferocity and scale, could have been predicted. With respect to the lead up to them there had

never before been such intense displays of mass feeling. The terror
deployed by the authorities brought results opposite to those intended;
it intensified resolve and awakened solidarity.

To a certain point it is possible to repress the masses using police and
army, but once that moment passes, terror fuels the fire. Inflamed
passions, for a while held in check, explode into larger flames. Strikes,
meetings and mass demonstrations, generate the consciousness of
strength and a determination to fight. And this is what revolution is: the
culmination of demonstrations ever more powerful, ever larger and
taking in an ever wider terrain; the determination to fight which exposes
any attempt to stop these processes by force as futile. Revolution
consists of dozens or even hundreds of events, both large and small,
which amass into a new reality.

The council of the PPS assembled in this charged atmosphere, clear
distinctions emerging between the political platforms of the 'old' and the
'young'. Stormy debates peaked in clashes and sharp controversies and
the minutes of the proceedings reveal how speaker cut short speaker in
heaping criticism on members of the CKR: for their failure to pursue a
consistent line of policy as evinced in the absence of a cohesive ideology
for the party. The editorial policy of *Przedświt* was particularly
criticized in this regard and the council dismissed Jodko from the
editorship for initiating polemics with *Gazeta Ludowa*, the paper
published by the peasants' section of the party.

A discussion then ensued concerning the party's attitude towards the
revolutionary movement in Russia. The first to speak was Marian
Bielecki who presented the arguments from both wings of the party. The
'young' held that the Polish movement could only be part of a general
Russian revolution and nothing more; that autocracy in Russia would
not collapse under pressure from political movements in the borderlands
(*Kresy*) and that without the overthrow of autocracy no political
advance could be made. The 'old' contemplated the possibility of self-
determination and of independence from the Russian movement and in
working towards their goal of independence for Poland, treated the
Russian movement as just another external factor. Bielecki emphatically
declared his support for the 'young'.

Piłsudski took up the argument against Bielecki. He saw the issue as
concerned solely with the question of how best to further the party's
watchword of independence. He believed Polish independence an
unlikely outcome in the prevailing situation but affirmed that a struggle
shared with the Russian movement and aimed at the downfall of
Tsarism could easily lead to federation, so why not to independence?
Taken at face value his policy was in agreement with the attitude of the
'young', but in reality it could just as well lead to an alliance with

liberal-bourgeois Russian groups rather than with socialists and it still allowed the Russian revolution to be perceived as an extraneous factor.

As the debate developed the 'old' pointed to a weakening of the Russian revolutionary movement after events of January–February, and contrasted it unfavourably with the May Day celebrations in the Kingdom which were more widespread with workers' demonstrations driven by the very lack of national freedom.

At the end of the debate, the committee passed a resolution in favour of renewed struggle in the Kingdom through the deployment of armed groups. This was intended to lead to the intensification of repression, which would, in turn, catalyse an uprising. In Poland's struggle against Russia, such an uprising could promote national unity and a rejection of the class character of the struggle. This was Piłsudski's thesis.

Divergences which emerged during the June Assembly were partly confused by imprecise definition. The same words were used to mean different things. The term 'revolution' was used freely both by those applying it to the highest form of class struggle of the proletariat, and by those interpreting it as armed struggle against Tsarism. In the latter case the term revolution could be used both in the context of national uprising and in the context of a people's uprising and was far from precise. Even the concept of socialism was variously understood – from Mickiewicz's formula of social justice to a theory of scientific socialism, with all the consequences arising from that.

Until 1904, these were theoretical differences, which genuinely separated party members but which were possible to reconcile within the bounds of the party. The revolution of 1905 changed this situation. While the main form of party activity continued to be the publication and distribution of political material together with the creation of a cadre organization, the lack of precision over policy and differences in interpretation did not have a direct bearing on events. But when the movement became a mass movement, when the party had to take decisions regarding concrete situations, when theoretical quarrels had to turn into resolutions on immediate action, then change was inevitable. Revolution sped up polarization within the party and within society.

On 20 October a strike which began at the Moscow railway works soon grew into a general rail strike which became the signal for a general strike throughout Russia. On 25 October a strike paralysed the railways in the Kingdom and then became a general strike. 'Brave Poland' – as Lenin wrote – 'again stood in the strikers' ranks, as if to deride with powerless anger enemies who imagined that they could destroy her with their blows, but who only strengthened her revolutionary powers'.

The first reaction of the Tsarist authorities was to attempt to crush the strike by force. Demonstrating crowds were dispersed with salvoes, killing many and wounding many more but this method was no longer effective. On the contrary – it encouraged the masses to even greater opposition. A political solution was now essential. On 30 October the Tsar's constitutional manifesto was proclaimed. It offered 'the inviolable principle of citizens' freedom on the basis of real personal immunity, freedom of conscience, freedom of speech, freedom of association' adding, 'no law can be enforced without the approval of the State Duma (Parliament)' and promised 'worker and peasant representation in the Duma'.

The Russian and Polish proletariat replied to this constitutional manifesto with a strike, demanding a general amnesty and the proclamation of a democratic republic. Despite these events the manifesto had its intended effect. It polarized the political opposition. The bourgeoisie and the lower-middle classes, hitherto paralysed by the brutishness of the Tsar's policies were now so terrified at the scale of the revolutionary movement and of its programme of social reform as to recover the will for political action. The National League, together with the traditional groups of advocates of conciliation began to organize manifestations of gratitude, and to point out the political nonsense of further strike action. The National Workers Union, led by the National League and founded for the political purpose of throwing the workers movement into disarray, undertook anti-strike action which went as far as the murder of active members of the workers' left-wing organizations.

The workers of Warsaw were to discover the value of the Tsar's assurances of freedom soon after the proclamation of the manifesto. Workers marches were dispersed with the same brutality as before – on 1 November the army fired at demonstrators on Bank Square. Nine were killed. A little later mounted Cossacks charged a crowd on Theatre Square. They hacked to death over 40 people. Severe clashes also occurred in other areas of the Kingdom.

In this renewed cycle of working class protest and repression by the state, political action by the nationalists (predominantly *Endeks*) gave succour to the authorities. Demonstrations, religious and patriotic in character, intended to draw supporters away from the workers' parties, were organized with the permission of the authorities. The right-wing press and nationalist manifestos surpassed themselves in hurling abuse at revolutionary movements. This was sword play with nationalistic slogans. A special edition of the Endecja's *Gazeta Polska* (Polish Gazette) warned, that if calm did not return, Prussian forces would march in. This Prussian spectre allowed the nationalists to gain strong support amongst the intelligentsia.

Piłsudski and the old guard responded to the crisis by concentrating their efforts on developing the Combat Organization. In Kraków a school for fighters was formed by Władysław Rozen (alias Barnaba). Over a hundred participants attended three courses each lasting four to six weeks. They were instructed in military drill, somewhat unnecessary for the purposes of the fighting squads but encouraging an *esprit de corps* to which Piłsudski attached great importance; in the use of arms (for which private shooting ranges were rented); in the principles of diversive action and in orienteering. Entrants to the first course were trained as instructors for subsequent courses, each of which ended with examinations.

A great quantity of arms were purchased and transferred to the Russian sector, where they were hidden in camouflaged stores, a dangerous task which was organized by Aleksandra Szczerbińska. Born in 1882, she lost her parents in childhood; her mother was about 40 when she died and had given birth to 12 children, only five of whom survived. Aleksandra was brought up by her grandmother. They lived very modestly on a small country estate. Through her grandmother, a strong personality, Aleksandra learned about patriotic traditions. After completing school she enrolled for a commercial course in Warsaw but the future prospects were limited for a young girl of slender means. In 1904 she joined the PPS. She worked in the party organization in Praga (a working class suburb of Warsaw) and at the beginning of 1906 she was entrusted with the organization of the arms depots. She met Piłsudski in May 1906, when she was 24 years old and Piłsudski 15 years her senior. As she recalled, he then appeared to her an elderly man. She changed her opinion of him when they met again at the conference of the Combat Organization in Kraków. As secretary to the conference she was in frequent contact with him.

Aleksandra was a very handsome woman with an unusual kind of beauty which was remarkable even in a photograph preserved on police files. She fascinated Piłsudski. In January 1907 she was arrested but released for lack of evidence. Shortly after, she travelled with a supply of arms to Kiev where Piłsudski was planning a bank robbery.

In Kiev Aleksandra and Piłsudski often went for walks together. Piłsudski talked of his plans for the future, of legislation he would introduce in a free Poland, about the founding of a Polytechnic in Łódź and the re-opening of the University in Wilno. On the lips of an illegal activist of a small organization, the Revolutionary Faction of the PPS was not an impressive force and all this sounded rather far fetched. But Piłsudski's burning ambition impressed her as indeed it had impressed Maria and earlier Leonarda who knew of his political yearnings through his Siberian letters to her. Piłsudski was a closed and secretive man, who revealed his innermost thoughts only to the women he loved. Aleksandra gives evidence of this aspect of Piłsudski's character in her memoirs and in fragments of Piłsudski's letters to her which she preserved.

During those Kiev walks, as Aleksandra recollects, Piłsudski 'told me that he loves me. I remember how surprised I was by his declaration. Up to that moment I had thought of him as an ideal friend, and suddenly something very unexpected happened. It was years later that I became convinced that friendship is the best foundation for love. For a very long time we knew nothing of the things considered to provide the basis of happy marriage. We lacked home, and peace, and security and had in their place, constant work, regular hardship, danger and insecurity about tomorrow. Our love endured all these, but equally important, outlived later years of peace and victory. For the time being , however, we had to wait. The first wife refused divorce'.

This departure from chronological sequence records important moments in Piłsudski's private life but let us now return to the problems of the Combat Organization. To the majority of the old guard it would become a vehicle for the rebuilding of their position in the party and, if this were to prove impossible, would be a support for themselves in case of a split. To others, hopes that the organization would provide an officers' cadre for future uprising now became realizable. This was the plan which Piłsudski was to work out more precisely and was to achieve in changed circumstances to which we shall return later. The plan was founded on the belief that in a future uprising Polish armed forces would have to oppose the Russian army. The mass of the workers was essential to the realization of this idea but they had to be organized and directed. The 'young' anticipated that the role of organizer and leader would be taken by the party. Piłsudski was only interested in creating a military organization or rather its surrogate.

The Combat Organization was in training for action when the occasion demanded. Such a moment would occur in the event of an exceptional weakening of Russia through revolution or in the case of a European war, in which Germany together with Austro-Hungary would be on the opposite side to Russia. In the first five years of the 20th century, a European war appeared to be a realistic prospect. Piłsudski gave it serious consideration. That is why, as far as he was able to, Piłsudski opposed the use of the Combat Organization in street action, a reluctance which also arose out of his disbelief in and fear of, the coming of revolution. In any event, Piłsudski attempted to separate the Combat Organization from events in the Russian sector. This was not easy. He was under pressure from two sides from the 'young' of the CKR and from the Combat Organization itself.

Faced with a pronounced ebb in the revolutionary tide the 'young' insisted that party activity should focus on agitation and that the Combat Organization should ensure the safety of agitators. They condemned the policy proposed by the old guard of intensifying terrorist and partisan action. For his part, Piłsudski now put all his energies into what may be called 'expropriation'. Three such raids were executed without CKR permission. On 20 October a robbery was committed at the post office near Włocławek; three days later there was another at the railway treasury office in Radom, and on 8 November a similar attack was made on the station in Rogów near Łódź. The third took place not only without the permission of the CKR but against its specific instructions.

The IXth PPS conference, attended by 58 members, was convened in Vienna. Proceedings opened on 19 November 1906. The course of the debate was somewhat predictable with Piłsudski and the old guard clearly taking up a compromise position, while the left wing tried to turn to its favour the explosive differences building up within the party over the previous two years. Feliks Sachs proposed a motion of censure, which was seconded by Horwitz and Koszutska against members of the Combat Organization and all who had showed solidarity with them and stating that in the light of the basic differences over the party's programme and by consciously breaking the CKR directive they had 'placed themselves outside the PPS fold'.

This motion was voted on twice. In the first round it was rejected because a majority of the conference were against putting the blame on the old guard for attempting 'to separate the revolutionary movement in Poland from the movement in the Russian state as a whole' and for attempting to 'bestow upon it, as a last resort, the character of national uprising'. This clause was eventually set aside as a tangential issue. The motion was again put and gained 28 votes with only 11 delegates voting against it and 2 abstentions. The split in the party became an accomplished fact.

The outvoted group published a 'Declaration of delegates resigning from the 9th Assembly of the Polish Socialists' Party'. It contained 10 points setting out the minority position. They were of course intended as an appeal for the support of party members by presenting the minority as the party's only radical force and by pointing out that the position of the minority was consistent with resolutions of previous party meetings.

It would, however, be a mistake to try to define the ideological and political programme of Piłsudski and his close collaborators in terms of statements made after the split. In the struggle for support true intentions were concealed in language and argumentation suited to the audience; an intense political battle was engaged in through the manifesto – hence the 'olds' apparent radicalization of language and policy. In their publicity material from this period, the word 'revolution', which also appeared in their party name, was used wherever possible, similarly the terms 'class interests', 'proletariat' etc.

The PPS-Revolutionary Faction was founded in Kraków, the destination of the minority group immediately after they left the forum of the Vienna assembly. It was at the Kraków conference that the name 'Revolutionary Faction' was adopted and a new CKR elected, consisting of: Witold Jodko, Stanisław Tor and Feliks Turowicz. In continuing with established machinery, if only in name, the old guard wanted to show that they did not accept the split as final. On the contrary, there were now two factions within the party, which, in favourable circumstances, could be united. Of course this was not possible, but it gave the PPS-Faction a very convenient argument in the contest against the PPS-Left.

Despite all its hopes and efforts, the Faction did not gain the wider support of workers' organizations. The two largest (Warsaw and Łódź) declared in favour of the Left. The Faction obtained support from Częstochowa and from a section of the Dąbrowa coal basin organization, and of course from the Combat Organization, although some of its local sections supported the PPS-Left.

Declarations of support depended on many factors, amongst which, matters of policy did not always take priority. Much depended on which of the groups had better contact with the local organization before the split and also on how the proceedings of the IXth Assembly were reported to the regions and districts. This depended on whose publications first reached the organization in question. Finally, many of those who declared themselves for the Faction, did so because the Left wing of the party had removed the independence slogan from the party manifesto. In this way, the PPS-Revolutionary Faction came into existence. From the start it was a party which was politically heterogeneous, as indeed was the PPS-Left. Moreover, the split marked the end of the process of polarization within the executive of the PPS though it was only one more stage in the process amongst the party's grassroots support.

Immediately after the split, priority was given by the new leadership of both PPS parties to questions of organization and propaganda; each was after the greatest possible support from the party masses. In March 1907 the first convention of the PPS-Revolutionary Faction took place. It was called the Xth Assembly, again to emphasize continuity. The assembly accepted a programme proposed by Feliks Perl and Witold Jodko and made changes in the CKR to included Tytus Filipowicz, Władysław Mech, Stanisław Jędrzejewski, Michał Sokolnicki and Niedzysław Dąbkowski; Piłsudski did not stand for election. He made a speech at the assembly, but was not directly involved with the organization of the PPS-Faction, partly because he was primarily concerned with the Combat Organization and partly because he was caught off balance by the speed of change.

Very little reliable information has survived about Piłsudski during this period. It does appear, however, that he went through a deep crisis, typically marked by a sharp decline of activity. Both the split and the conflicts which had preceded it profoundly shocked him. These events had, in some measure, undermined the work of almost 15 years of his life. All his plans and aspirations had collapsed. The PPS-Revolutionary Faction had survived, but nobody realized its weakness better than Piłsudski. Moreover, he knew that the Faction was only the relic of an old conception. The opportunity, which had occurred during the PPS revolution, to direct the masses of the workers' party on the path to a successful uprising, had been lost. There was nothing to suggest that what had happened to the PPS would not happen again, to the Faction, if ever the revolutionary situation were to repeat itself. Nor that the mass movement would refrain from taking a direction unacceptable to Piłsudski. A new plan of action was needed. But Piłsudski did not have one.

Piłsudski's psychological crisis deepened with the death, in 1906, of Wanda, the daughter of Maria Piłsudska from her first marriage. He was very attached to his stepdaughter. Wanda's death and Maria's illnesses placed a considerable strain on his marriage. It was at about this time Piłsudski met Aleksandra Szczerbińska and fell in love with her, further complicating the situation. There was also the question of his physical condition. He had never enjoyed the best of health and now developed a heart complaint with a fear of TB returning. He was physically exhausted and this deepened his depression. As is often the case, his state of mind was not without influence on his physical condition.

And there was something else. On 29 September 1906, a few weeks before the split, Piłsudski and Jodko had had a discussion with Col. Franz Kanik, chief of staff of the 10th Corps in Przemyśl. According to Kanik's report to the Chief of General Staff, 'They introduced themselves as members of a branch of the Polish Socialist Party and offered us their intelligence services ... against Russia in return for certain ... services from our side'. These amounted to: 'help in obtaining arms; toleration of a secret arms depot and of party agents in Galicia; and in the event of intervention by our monarchy, an end to repressive measures against Austrian reservists and against revolutionaries who would take part in the fight against Russia. To learn more I listened, without expressing any opinion, to the end of what both gentlemen had to say. Apparently, the party has at its disposal 70,000 armed men in the Kingdom, and in the case of open warfare it is capable of mobilizing 200,000'. Numbers were of course, to put it mildly, grossly exaggerated. At this time the PPS had 50,000 members, of whom no more than 5,000 were armed. This was few weeks before the split and at the time Piłsudski and Jodko could only count on a few thousand party members rather than tens of thousands. But this cloaking of the real situation was essential and, more importantly, impossible to check by the other side.

The deepening rift between Austro-Hungary and Russia, primarily in the Balkans, made armed conflict between Poland's oppressors appear possible. In any event, the situation was in crisis and the heightening tension made the Piłsudski-Jodko offer to Austria-Hungary all the more attractive, especially to the military. They would gain a network of informers in the Kingdom at a very low price. However, it meant involvement with the Polish question and supporting Polish wishes to change the status quo. Neither political nor military circles in Austro-Hungary were interested in that and mainly for this reason, the Chief of General Staff dismissed the offer.

Although Piłsudski's first attempt to contact Austro-Hungarian intelligence ended in failure, something had been gained. PPS aims, as formulated by Piłsudski, were explained to military circles, a factor which played quite an important role in later activities. Not without importance either was that paths to future contact were open.

The deal offered to Austro-Hungarian intelligence by Piłsudski and Jodko was, in a sense, the consequence of the deal proposed to the Japanese. The fundamental difference was that in 1906 an offer of co-operation was made to one of the powers occupying Poland and, although it was against another oppressor, it thus remained ambiguous.

The offer should be analysed in political terms. It emerged from Piłsudski's evaluation of the international situation in which he envisaged an intensification of the rivalry between Russia and Austria-Hungary. In this context the political interests of Austria-Hungary, in their anti-Russian aspect, were convergent with Piłsudski's political aims. It was essential to convince the armed forces of this and to obtain their support for his activities in Galicia. Though political support from Vienna would have been equally effective, this was not possible because Piłsudski was not in a position to offer anything of advantage to the politicians. He could nevertheless offer valuable intelligence to the military. It was a risky ploy, if only because its disclosure would further compromise Piłsudski's position within the PPS. Therefore the circle of the initiated among Piłsudski's collaborators was very narrow. This was one of the most closely held secrets.

Piłsudski's conception of the struggle for Polish independence rejected the route through social revolution in Russia. Revolution there could be the ally of a Polish national uprising only in as much that it could contribute to the internal weakening of Tsarism. Based on this assumption, the Polish uprising was realizable in only two ways. Firstly, in the event of revolution in Russia, a possibility which Piłsudski had dismissed; or alternatively through Russian involvement in a conflict such as the Russo-Japanese war. This war had revealed the enormous weakness of Russia; a giant with feet of clay. But the theatre of that war was rather far removed from Polish territories. In the event of conflict with Austria-Hungary or against its German allies the battle zone would run through Poland. In this situation Austria-Hungary would become, according to Piłsudski, the natural ally of a Poland active against Russia. It would thus make sense to consider the decision to contact Austro-Hungarian intelligence in this context and also as a logical follow on to earlier attempts at contact with Japan. If linking of the Polish cause to the proletarian revolution in Tsarist Russia were rejected, the only alternative was to seek support for it amongst the countries opposing Tsarist Russia. Of course, another possibility existed – that of loyal co-operation with Russia in the hope of gaining, for that price, legal and political concessions in the Russian sector. This conception was that of Roman Dmowski's National League.

Political circumstances apart, Piłsudski's decision to offer assistance to the Austro-Hungarian intelligence service was pragmatically sound. Since 1904, Galicia had been the base for subversive activities directed at the Russia sector. The editorial office of *Przedświt*, the office of the Foreign Committee of the PPS and Piłsudski himself were all located in Galicia. Centres of military training were organized there and weapons and propaganda publications were shifted to the Russian sector via Galicia. It was also the base of the political command of the old guard. For all these reasons it was very important to ensure that the clearly justifiable interests of the police were neutralized. In this the military authorities would have proved most helpful, but Piłsudski and Jodko's offer was turned down. The Chief of Staff could not yet see the necessity of involvement in the Polish cause. The possibility of gains looked rather chancy and did not bear any relation to the political price, a situation which was soon to change with the intensification of conflicts between the European powers.

Meanwhile, from Piłsudski's point of view the situation went from bad to worse from one month to the next. The Combat Organization in the Russian sector disintegrated as a result of mass arrests and through a collapse in morale because of the failure of the revolution. The political influence of the PPS-Faction suddenly began to shrink, though in this regard the party was no different from others within the workers' movement.

Of more immediate interest to Piłsudski, conflicts were growing within the remaining Combat Organization. It was being said, ever louder, that this unit restrained the activity it was set up to promote and that it had to re-assert its presence in some extravagant action. The fact that Piłsudski had so far not taken part in any engagement (even the bank robbery in Kiev ultimately proved impossible to mount) also created ambiguity.

The *impasse* in party matters also worsened financial difficulties. The Combat Organization, with its complement of a dozen or so illegal activists, was costly to maintain. Printing activities, aid for the families of imprisoned militants, bribes to help them to freedom, all consumed substantial sums. To meet costs a number of expropriatory measures were organized. Three of them were successful, but, in all, brought not quite 40,000 roubles, which just about covered debts and the department's running costs. That is why, when the Kiev action collapsed, Piłsudski began preparing, as he wrote to Jodko, 'to grab something bigger with all our remaining strength'. That meant organizing a large enough action to yield a sum of money sufficient to solve the organization's financial problems for a longer period of time.

It became apparent that such a project would be easier to realize in Lithuania where, so far, such actions had not yet been undertaken and where, in consequence, the alertness of the authorities was minimal. Piłsudski decided on an attack on a mail train. Bezdany, the second station beyond Wilno on the Petersburg track, was the chosen location. Prystor left for Wilno for reconnaissance and on his return assured Piłsudski that such an action had a reasonable chance of success. Piłsudski decided to lead it, thereby killing the rumour that he was trying to save his own skin. Preparations began. Prystor travelled to Wilno with his wife and Piłsudski with Aleksandra Szczerbińska. The general plan of action had to be adapted to conditions on the ground. Preparations lasted quite some time. At first action was projected for the beginning of 1908, then for Easter, then for summer. During the preparations Piłsudski made several trips to Galicia. Once more he attempted to make contact with Austrian intelligence, but again to no avail.

Preparations were drawn out because Piłsudski was not in a hurry. He felt happy in Wilno and it was important to him that he was with Aleksandra. This was, in a sense, their honeymoon. At last they could spend longer together. It was psychologically difficult to cut short these moments of joy and make the decision to undertake action which might result in death through a fight or on the gallows.

When, at last, a definite time was set for action, Piłsudski was fretful of the possibility that he could get killed and wrote a letter to Feliks Perl. 'I fight and die only because I cannot live in the shithouse that is our life. It is an *insult* [underlined in the original] – do you hear me? It insults me as a dignified, unenslaved human being. Let others play at growing flowers, or at socialism, or at Polishness, or at whatever in this shithouse. I cannot! This is not sentimentalism, not procrastination, not a route to social evolution or anything else. It is ordinary human dignity. I wish to win. And without a fight and a fierce fight at that, I am not even a wrestler, but merely a beast of burden beaten with stick or whip. You understand me I presume? Neither despair, nor self-sacrifice guide, but the will to win and to prepare for victory. My final idea, which I have had no chance to develop anywhere yet, is the necessity in our circumstances to develop our physical strength . . .'

The deadline for the raid at Bezdany was set for Saturday 19 September 1908. It was to involve 19 fighters, divided into three groups. The first six, under the command of Tomasz Arciszewski, were detailed to throw a bomb under the mail carriage and neutralize the military escort. The second group, of four, led by Piłsudski, had to take over the mail carriage and seize the money. The third group, of eight, under Walery Sławek, had to occupy the railway station, destroy the lines and immobilize the railway officials and passengers. The 19th member of the raiding party was in charge of the *bryczka* (chaise) for delivering arms and explosives and for later transporting the money. Piłsudski's group had what was relatively, the easiest assignment, which suggests, together with what has already been mentioned, a mistrust of his practical fighting capability.

The majority of the group were in Wilno though six, chosen from amongst the Kraków émigrés, waited with their leader, Czesław Swirski, in Warsaw. They had to leave by the morning train, meet Sławek in Grodno, receive their firearms on the train and, after the train stopped in Bezdany, take up positions planned in advance. Swirski's group left Warsaw on the morning of the 19 September. The remainder marched out from Wilno in small groups. Two of these lost their way and reached Bezdany just half an hour before the arrival of the train. At the same time the *bryczka* (chaise) bringing arms and explosives, was delayed, reaching its destination a quarter of an hour before the arrival of the train. In this situation and against the advice of a number of the raiding party, Piłsudski decided to postpone the action.

This decision was very risky since there was no possibility of notifying the Warsaw group of it; they were travelling to Bezdany on the train to be attacked. Instructed that the signal to start the raid was to be the explosion of the bomb immediately after the train had stopped at

Bezdany, they were to leave the train on the side opposite the platform and take up positions there. This they did. Unfortunately no bomb exploded and nothing appeared to be happening at the station. So they leapt back onto the train, thinking they were at the wrong station. At the next station they performed the same manoeuvre. They were exceptionally fortunate that their extraordinary behaviour did not arouse suspicion.

The raid on Bezdany station was postponed until the following Saturday, 26 September.

In later years the Bezdany raid played a significant role in the myth which was to be built, with his connivance, around Piłsudski. It was presented as the greatest achievement of the Combat Organization and as an example of strategic genius and leadership. This had very little in common with the truth. The Bezdany raid was no different to those undertaken earlier. Neither in organization nor in result. The 200,000 roubles seized was a lot of money, but it was only 30,000 more than the Opatów raid of 28 July 1905, led by Mirecki. Nor was the Bezdany action outstanding in the number it involved – 17, in comparison to 49 in the Rogów raid. Nor was it carried out with exemplary efficiency; only a portion of the money on board the train was taken and the getaway was rather chaotic. But since it was the only raid in which Piłsudski took part it came to be held up as a paradigm. This was of course much later because directly after the action the Combat Organization convened a special committee (Aleksander Prystor, Michał Sokolnicki and Gustav Danilowski) to investigate what had gone wrong.

At the beginning of October Piłsudski was in Kraków and went on to Zakopane where he joined in the organizational work in founding the ZWC (*Związek Walki Czynnej*), the Union for Active Struggle.

The origins of the ZWC may be found in the failure of revolution and conclusions drawn from this by activists of the PPS-Faction. Mention has already been made of Piłsudski's new political plans. He was not alone in these. In the first 1908 issue of *Przedświt*, Bolesław Antoni Jędrzejewski (alias Baj) published an article entitled: 'Concerning co-ordination at home'. Baj stated that in becoming a mass party, which was a great exaggeration, the PPS-Revolutionary Faction could ally with the non-proletarian parties, such as the middle class party, the *Endecja*. He was, of course, presenting a future perspective; in essence his thesis came to the following conclusion: there existed party political interests but also superior national interests in the name of which it was possible and necessary to co-ordinate party action.

Piłsudski had, simultaneously, thought of creating fighting units within the party and of coordinating the activities of these organizations to achieve a common goal. Despite their differences, the respective conception of Baj and Piłsudski were very close; they were based on the same premise of widening their sphere of influence beyond the socialist movement and building a broader base not defined by criteria of class alone.

The realization of these ideas came with the creation of the ZWC at the end of June 1908. Further work on organization was postponed over the summer holidays and it cannot be said that the ZWC idea met with wide support. In November 1908 it had 64 members, and in 1909, after a year's existence, 147 members – 105 in Lwów, 36 in Kraków and 6 in Borysław. These were not impressive numbers. Yet, in this case, it was not numbers which mattered but the fact of the association coming into being at all.

On 5 October 1908, Emperor Franz Joseph announced his intention to incorporate Bosnia and Hercegovina into the Austro-Hungarian Empire. This was in breach of the Berlin Congress of 1898 and led to a serious European crisis. Russia saw the Austro-Hungarian move as a direct threat to its interests in Serbia and Serbia lodged a firm protest in Vienna against the annexation of Bosnia and Hercegovina and ordered mobilization. Austria-Hungary replied by mobilizing its forces. It seemed that war was only days away. Germany declared that in the event of armed conflict she would come to Austria-Hungary's support. This restrained Russia, who withdrew support for Serbia. A crisis had been averted.

These events had great significance in shaping Polish political opinion. They revealed quite clearly that political processes occurring in Europe during the previous decade had led to an entirely new power structure. Political co-operation amongst the partitioning powers, so typical in the 19th century, was a thing of the past. The new era, expressed in the formation of military-political power blocs (the states of central Europe and the Entente) pitted the partitioning powers against one another and created a real prospect of war between them. Just how real a prospect, was shown by the 1908 crisis. War did not break out then, but it was widely recognized that Europe came very close to it. It was also recognized that the crisis was resolved only because of the fear of war and that all the reasons which brought it so close to breaking out still existed.

The crisis of 1908 hastened the Poles into shaping the so-called 'orientation programmes'. Consideration of Polish interests *vis-à-vis* the partitioning powers in the event of conflict between the latter had long appeared in Polish political literature. Yet such forays into future policy were, to some extent, theoretical and seemed so abstract as to minimize their potential worth. With the formation of power blocs at the turn of the century, the anticipation of conflict between the partitioning powers became a little less abstract but it was the 1908 crisis which revealed its reality. Suddenly, a Polish political literature developed which focused on the possibility of war. Opinion was split. The revolutionary movement, treating war as the outcome of capitalist class interest, took a decidedly anti-war stance. This became the common policy of the entire Second International, although time would reveal that only its revolutionary wing would remain loyal to it. In opposition were those who saw in war a chance to realize their political aims but they were not united in their view of how to exploit that opportunity.

Setting small differences aside, one could say that two 'orientation' programmes were formed: one for Russia and one for Austria-Hungary, or in other words, a pro-Russian and an anti-Russian stance. The development of these policies was made difficult by the slender amount of information each camp had at its disposal. Poles in Galicia appeared to be the best treated, but Austria-Hungary was in alliance with Germany whose anti-Polish policy brooked no trust. Supporting Russia could, possibly, in the event of its victory, offer the opportunity of uniting all Polish territories, but the situation in Poland under Russian occupation cast doubts on this.

Neither of these solutions was perfect, each harbouring within itself serious dangers and many unknowns.

The years 1909–1912 saw Piłsudski give a series of very lively lectures, in two closely connected fields of enquiry: the January uprising and military history. Piłsudski did a great deal of reading, reference to which is clearly visible in his lectures. The same period gave shape to the general foundations of his politico-military ideas. They were as follows. The growing hostility between blocs of European powers would lead to armed conflict, which, irrespective of the location of its outbreak, would spread onto Polish territory. Considering the strategic position of Kingdom Poland, the line of Russian defence would be the Vistula and Narew. Proof of this was the construction, by the Russians, of fortifications along this very line – Dęblin, Warsaw, Modlin, Pułtusk, Rozan, Ostrołęka, Łomża, Osowiec. This meant that Russian plans did not envisage defending that part of Kingdom Poland situated on the left bank of the Vistula. The assignment of defensive Russian detachments there would be for the sole purpose of conscription and evacuation.

This line of thought led Piłsudski on to further conclusions. The outbreak of war between the occupying powers would cause a sudden outburst of patriotic feelings. In the right circumstances these could be harnessed and paramilitary preparations in Galicia were being undertaken for that purpose; they were to fulfil an agitatory role and were to contribute to the organization of cadres of a future Polish army. The entry of Polish units into the Russian sector on the outbreak of war would create a mass inflow of volunteers, or perhaps even an uprising. Though small at first, these units would became a human mass which would transform itself into the Polish army. Its main source of officer material would come from the paramilitary organizations trained in Galicia.

Leaving aside, for the moment, the question of how realistic this conception was – the answer was provided in the first days of the war – it is fundamental to understand that it determined Piłsudski's political actions from 1909–1910.

In this context, the PPS had only an auxiliary assignment and then only in the preparatory period. Even so, if the conditions for the realization of his plans arose, then the connection between Piłsudski, the military organization and the party would raise an awkward problem; it would give initial developments a party gloss instead of the national dimension he wanted. But the problem would arise only at the outset, during the preparatory stages, when the PPS was in fact needed.

It is difficult to ascertain in just how much detail the conception introduced above was worked out in his mind. However, it seems that Piłsudski had formulated it only in general terms, leaving the rest to the course of events. His approach was always pragmatic; he had a clear aversion to theoretical analysis.

The ZWC had, as early as 1910, formed paramilitary organizations on the basis of an Austrian law which allowed the organization of rifle clubs (*Schutzen-Vereine*). These organizations were known in Kraków as riflemen and in Lwów as riflemens' associations. Both, as secret units, came under the command of the ZWC.

This move undoubtedly facilitated the growth and development of paramilitary organizations. Besides the riflemen and riflemens' associations there also came into being Polish riflemens' squads: the makings of a secret Polish army led by the nationalist-independence camp. Talks between ZWC and this Polish army had been carried on since 1909, but without result. Activists of the nationalist-independence camp viewed the ZWC with distrust, afraid of its radical socialism, and above of all of becoming subordinate to it. This fear of losing independence by giving party colour to the military movement, strongly pervaded the thinking within this camp. It also explains the wish of each group for independence from the National League.

Although some cooperation between riflemens' squads and riflemen units was possible, without political agreement this amounted to little more. Piłsudski and his close associates were well aware of this. Hence the emphasis on the question of coordination.

On 25 and 26 August there took place in Zakopane an 'assembly of irredentists', so-called. It was convened by Władysław Studnicki in close co-ordination with the PPS. As part of its programme, Piłsudski delivered a lecture about the state of preparation for an armed struggle. He placed emphasis on the reluctant, distrustful and disdainful attitude of the Polish nation towards Polish armed movements: 'Not only has martial thinking declined among us, even the thought of an independent Poland has disappeared from the agenda of cultural assemblies, disappeared even among Socialists. The nation is ailing and has lost heart. The older generation treats members of military organizations with a tolerant but sneering smile, as if they were lead soldiers'. In his summing up, Piłsudski came to the 'very pessimistic conclusion that the present (poor) state of the organization could not be otherwise and would remain so whilst it had neither moral nor material support from the people. The question of the armed struggle was of fundamental importance to Poland's irredenta'.

The Zakopane assembly of irredentists was a first step towards the closer coordination of paramilitary organizations especially since the formation of the PSW whose purpose was to broaden their political base. Yet the political opportunities so created proved to be ephemeral. That is precisely why Piłsudski, hoping for success, attached such importance to creating them – especially in the initial period when he participated in sessions of its executive.

A few months after the assembly in Zakopane, the international situation changed drastically. In October 1912, the first Balkan war broke out.

On 10 November, at the Vienna residence of Hipolit Sliwinski, a meeting took place which resulted in the formation of the Ad Hoc Committee of the Confederated Independence Parties, KTSSN. (*Komisja Tymczasowa Skonfederowanych Stronnitctw Niepoleglosciowych.*) In the chair was Włodzimierz Tetmajer. Piłsudski had earlier mooted the formation of the new committee.

In a letter to Gierszyński, written on 15 November, Jodko stated that two measures had been agreed upon in Vienna. Firstly, in the light of recent events, the creation of a body which would have overall authority to organize and co-ordinate an immediate armed response and to provide immediate guidelines to its constituent parties. Secondly, the committee would, for the time being, grant a supervisory authority over the creation of a fund and organization for military purposes.

A further element in this letter is particularly important – the formulation of the committee's policy. In the event of war it was to transform itself into a national government. Thought of such a development kept alive the tradition of Polish independence. It had entered the minds of PPS activists during the Russo-Japanese war and during the revolution. Earlier still it was imprinted on the thinking of the Polish League and echoes of it are soon found in contemporary literature and publications.

In the autumn of 1912, when it seemed that a European confrontation was not years, nor even months but only weeks away, the first stage of this plan had been realized in the establishment of the committee. In this sense the Vienna conference had enormous significance.

It does not seem particularly necessary to discuss the history of the KTSSN. Nor is possible to omit it completely. Most worthy of note was the period of the first few months, when the committee took shape with the outbreak of war in prospect. The committee was the urgent product of an urgent moment, after which Piłsudski and his close associates manoeuvred for political gain, as quickly as possible and for as much as possible. Jodko became secretary of the KTSSN, enabling Piłsudski's associates to play a decisive role on the committee. At its first meeting Piłsudski was appointed Chief of Command of squads and units of riflemen. Bearing in mind that Sławek was secretary of the Polish military fund, the tendency of Piłsudski's group to get hold of all key positions, is apparent.

We have introduced here the notion of 'Piłsudski's group'. It does seem that this period saw the establishment of specific arrangements between Piłsudski and his closest associates. Until the outbreak of revolution, Piłsudski was one of the party's leaders. His authority stemmed from years in exile, a significant role in forming the PPS in the Russian sector, and, for an illegal activist, a very long experience in leading the party. A successful escape magnified his prestige, but during the revolution his position was undermined. The leadership of the PPS slipped from Piłsudski's hands and he found himself, together with the old guard, in political isolation. Yet this did have its compensations in that his authority now grew among them, especially as his ideas appeared practical in reality. Slowly, out of a partner in common political activities there emerged a leader.

Movements of a paramilitary type enhanced that tendency. In the PPS, age difference and position in the hierarchy were not as clearly marked as in the riflemen's organizations. These mainly attracted the young, who, against all appearances, are particularly inclined to create structures of authority. A leader was created on the basis of voluntary submission to him. And by cloaking him in a mist of the myth of active battle against the oppressor it gave the process added impetus.

Operative too were Piłsudski's personal characteristics: ability to keep his distance, power to impose his own ideas, enigmatically expressed, so that even when his expectations did not materialize there remained the conviction that he was right after all. This was reinforced by Piłsudski's elastic pragmatism, thanks to which he could very quickly adjust in changeable situations.

This growth in Piłsudski's personal authority had impact on his closest associates who then built on it among the young rank and file, whilst at the same time becoming ever more subordinate to him. This was a very slow process in which it is difficult to identify any turning points. Rather more visible are its consequences. Ever more clearly Piłsudski played the leading part and his closest associates filled the role of his personal staff. In 1912 this situation had become obvious. The staff might change, but the mechanism of operating through a narrow group of the most faithful, remained a characteristic one for Piłsudski to the end of his life.

On the eve of the outbreak of war the following belonged to Piłsudski's group: Jodko, Sławek, Sosnkowski, Wasilewski, Kukiel, Sokolnicki and Jaworski. This was not a formal group, it did not meet together, it did not undertake any resolutions etc. Its members consisted of a circle of people connected by common activity and through the person of Piłsudski whom they still called 'Ziuk', but who became increasingly the 'Commander' (Kommendant).

Piłsudski's group now came to represent political power. The squads and riflemen's units comprised, in a period of a dramatic rise in tension, about 10,000 members. Although these are official statistics and are therefore bound to be inflated, precise figures are in this instance less important than general scale.

However, in this context, a rather unusual situation developed. The strength and influence of Galician groups represented on the committee was easy to verify, but the size of illegal groups from Kingdom Poland in which an element of mystery always played its part, could not be verified. In reality the PPS was at this time a fiction, but on the committee it appeared an important political party. The Peasant Union, formed, through the inspiration of Piłsudski's group, by Konstancja Klęmpińska was a microscopic organization without importance. Somewhat larger, but not much, were the political groups of the independence-nationalist camp.

However, in some situations even fiction can play a discernible political role. The names of parties can themselves determine the trumps in the political game. In the autumn of 1912, anticipating the approach of war, Piłsudski did not attach much importance to the actual strength of the groups answerable to the committee. Much more real to him was the alliance of units and of political groups within it, giving the outward appearance of a political platform broader than that afforded by the PPS and riflemen's units and associations. The outbreak of war meant the possibility of transforming the committee into a national government which, Piłsudski hoped, would provide political support for a fast growing Polish army.

CHAPTER FOUR

The Commander

On 28 June a successful attempt was made at Sarajevo on the life of Archduke Francis Ferdinand, the successor to the Austro-Hungarian throne. His wife died with him. The threads of this conspiracy could be traced back to Belgrade, the capital of Serbia and the days immediately following were full of tension. But the calm response from Vienna reassured Europe. Tension melted away; it seemed that the incidents in Sarajevo would not further influence the course of European events and politicians set off on their vacations.

Piłsudski treated the Austro-Serbian incident no differently. News of the assassination in Sarajevo reached him on the evening of 28 June, in Lwów, at a meeting of officers of the riflemen's associations. It did not cause any change of plans and it was agreed that a second officer course should be held at the end of July.

No one realized just how critical the secret talks between Vienna and Berlin were. The Austrian envoy in Belgrade handed an ultimatum to the Serbian government on 23 July. It was formulated very assertively and clearly threatened Serbian sovereignty. This was, for public consumption, the first signal that the situation in Europe was beginning to change. But still people could not accept the likelihood of armed conflict. On 25 July the Serbian reply was published. In general it accepted Austrian demands, but did record certain reservations. These appeared relatively unimportant and the anxiety caused by the ultimatum began to recede. Piłsudski, likewise, assessed the situation in this way. But it was a mistaken assessment. Just a few days later war broke out. Armed conflict between the military blocs of the powers was generally foreseen in Poland. But the outbreak of war at that particular moment surprised everybody, though it created certain opportunities for Piłsudski. He had long since prepared a plan of action.

On 2 August Piłsudski obtained Austrian permission to mobilize detachments of riflemen, within Austrian Poland. He was also informed that on the outbreak of Russo-Austrian conflict these were to be deployed against the enemy in the direction: Miechów-Jędrzejów-Kielce. This was a considerable change of plan since it had been expected that Polish units would enter the Russian sector through the Dąbrowa Basin whence Piłsudski had already sent reconnaissance parties. The change in the direction of operations now meant that Piłsudski's formations were to enter rural areas where the political influence of Polish detachments, especially those with allegiance to the PPS, was slight; future events demonstrated precious little enough support for Polish arms in the region around Dąbrowa.

On 3 August a cadre company was formed in Kraków composed of 144 members, drawn mainly from the officer training schools of the riflemens associations, under the command of Tadeusz Kasprzycki. Over the next two days the cadre company, camped in Kraków's oleander groves, awaited further orders. These were issued during the night of 6 August and at half past three in the morning the company marched in the direction of Slomnik and Miechówa.

Piłsudski remained in Kraków for the meeting, that same day, of the Commission of Confederated Independence Parties (*Komisja Skonfeder-owanych Stronnictw Niepodleglosciowych – KSSN*) at which he announced the formation in Warsaw of a national government, requiring from the High Command acceptance of its authority. To this he had agreed and in the certainty of 'a race against the Prussians to Warsaw' he asked the KSSN to accept this in a *fait accompli*. The committee unanimously empowered Piłsudski to initiate military steps, declared its support for urgent and close cooperation with the national government and agreed to keep secret for three days the decisions taken at its meeting.

But there was no 'national government'. From beginning to end this was an illusion created by Piłsudski. It had a dual purpose. First of all there was a need to attribute authority for armed action more widely than merely to the committee which, itself tended to be re-garded as a socialist enterprise, which Piłsudski wished to avoid. The national government was to raise military activity above party affairs and, significantly, this would also increase Piłsudski's authority enor-mously.

The entire gamble was based on the premise that the Kingdom would greet Polish detachments entering its territory with enthusiasm and massive volunteer reinforcements and that entry into Warsaw would be quickly achieved. Hence Piłsudski's statement about a race for the city against the Prussians. He calculated that if he entered Warsaw at the head of a Polish army, the fiction of a national government would become a reality. Hence too the three-day secret. It was not only a question of time in which to form a national government but above all time to mobilize as large as possible an expedition of young riflemen from Galicia. Piłsudski must, of course, also have anticipated the reaction of the Austrian authorities to the declaration of a national government. He judged, however, that in the course of those three days, the greater part of the riflemens' detachments would find themselves on Kingdom territory ahead of the Austrian army and that, in the event, the stance of the Austrian authorities in the face of an accomplished fact would not have dangerous consequences.

Undoubtedly, what drove Piłsudski to act as he did was the reaction of Poles in Galicia, and especially in Kraków, to the outbreak of war in Europe. Almost every memoir records widespread patriotic enthusiasm. The war between the partitioning powers for which generations of Poles had prayed was now a reality. The entire tradition of romantic literature, the weighty influence of Wyspiański and of 'Young Poland', the deep yearning for Polish independence – all this came to the fore in these August days. Kraków was in the grip of rampant patriotism.

The same people who had recently scorned the young riflemen, now became their warmest supporters. No one paused to consider what might be the political consequence of the direction Polish action had taken. These reflections were to come shortly, but in these first days of August the atmosphere of enthusiasm predominated. Even Feliks Kon, the famous activist of PPS-Left and a formidable critic of Piłsudski, had come round in support of Piłsudski's action. This was indeed an important measure of the feelings which had gripped Kraków.

The young men who marched out from the city's oleander groves at dawn on 6 August and whose detachments moved into the Kingdom in subsequent days, experienced even stronger feelings of patriotism. Years of preparation, years of playing at soldiers now acquired real meaning. Yet, with the exception of the cadre companies, the men were armed with ancient, single shot carbines, and were in fact without uniform. Future *ulans* (cavalry) carried their saddles on their backs; horses were to be obtained only later, in the Kingdom. Yet all these deficiencies were mere details in the great mission promised to them by history. How great, then, must have been their shock on entering the Kingdom to be greeted by mistrust and often by enmity.

Piłsudski's plans collapsed. The Kingdom did not come up to his expectations; it did not supply the volunteers he had counted on. Cadre divisions remained cadre divisions only – they did not grow into an army. Nor was there a swift march on Warsaw. Russian strategists did not intend, as Piłsudski had expected, handing over the western portion of the Kingdom without a fight; especially not Warsaw. The Tsarist army had prepared an offensive in the direction of Lwów-Kraków and it obviously could not expose its right flank. Moreover, Warsaw was an important railway junction of considerable significance in Russian plans. Consequently Piłsudski's detachments were barely able to reach Kielce and they were soon rebuffed from there.

Thus the two fundamental tenets on which Piłsudski's plans were built proved to be mistaken. This much became clear in the course of several days following 6 August. Not only to Piłsudski, but equally to the Austrian authorities. From their point of view the entire enterprise soon lost its purpose; the entry of Piłsudski's detachments did not cause an uprising to explode in the Kingdom, it did not delay or prevent mobilization to the Tsarist army and it did not create any diversionary action. Numbers of riflemen remained small (about 2500) and therefore constituted a force of no military significance, except in creating difficulties to local commanders.

So much more had been intended. The expression of Austrian willingness for organized Polish formations, in Polish uniforms, under Polish command made sense as the price paid for a massive influx of volunteers in the Kingdom. When this did not materialize the situation became increasingly uncomfortable for the central authorities in Vienna who were now playing the game over the map of Poland without gaining any actual advantages from their support for Piłsudski.

Thus, on 10 August, the decision to bring down the curtain on the riflemens' show was taken. The next day Władysław Sikorski, Piłsudski's close colleague at the time, drew up a memorandum, addressed to the high command of the Austrian army. He proposed the formation of an infantry corps of Polish volunteers, the Polish Legions, responsible directly to the Austrian high command. Polish political support for the corps was to be provided in an understanding to be reached between the KSSN and conservatives.

During the night of 12 August Piłsudski was summoned to Kraków for talks with the Austrian authorities. Colonel Nowak, in charge of Polish affairs, issued him with an ultimatum demanding that he should decide over the next 24 hours, either to the dissolution of the riflemens' detachments or to their amalgamation with the nearest formation of the Austrian army to come under Austrian command. This meant that Polish riflemen would have to wear the same black and yellow bands and swear the same oath as the Austrians.

This was a complete disaster for Piłsudski. Little wonder that, as he later stated, he threatened to shoot himself in the event of the Austrian proposals being carried out. All his plans were failing him and all the years of preparation now seemed purposeless.

Meanwhile, important political discussions were taking place in Kraków and Lwów. Conservatives and democrats sought ways of following up Piłsudski's initiative. They realized that to remain on the sidelines could lead to loss of influence in Galicia and, most of all, to loss of their monopoly in representing a pro-Austrian orientation in Vienna. They were also distressed by Piłsudski's unilateral attempt to create an apparatus of authority in the Kingdom. As a result, all the main political groupings in Galicia accepted, each for its own reasons, the need to form a united political platform. On 15 August a meeting of representatives of all Galician parties took place. A committee was formed to work on a manifesto setting out the organizational principles of joint political representation.

A secret meeting also took place behind the scenes between conservatives, represented by Jaworski, Starzewski and Rosner, and the KSSN represented by Daszyński, Sokolnicki and Sikorski. The representatives of the KSSN agreed to dispense with the notion of a national government. They also agreed to dissolve the Polish Military Fund (*Polskiego Skarbu Wojskowego*) and the KSSN, agreeing to replace it with an organization, which would limit its activity to Galicia. They themselves demanded only one thing – the maintenance of Piłsudski's position.

This meeting was of very great importance, not so much for the decisions taken, but as the beginning of a close political alliance between conservatives and supporters of Piłsudski, for whom much was at stake. The alliance gave Piłsudski a new lease of life; his Galician activities had gained him conservative support, which in the course of the next two years would prove itself to be the most important factor in his bid for political leadership. The understanding with the conservatives also helped rid Piłsudski of the socialist image which he wore with increasing awkwardness.

As a result of these secret talks a body called the Supreme National Committee (*Naczelny Komitet Narodowy* – NKN) was formed on 16 August. Its function was to command and control the military, economic and political organization of Polish armed forces which were now to be grouped into two Polish Legions, one in western and the other in eastern Galicia.

The NKN came to be accepted by all Galician parties. It was the product of compromise, born out of the exceptional situation existing in the second half of August. But this was a situation which began to change soon after the formation of the NKN, which in the form decided on 16 August, was very short-lived. Nevertheless, the formation of the NKN and the agreement of the Austrian authorities to the organization of the Legions rescued Piłsudski; though only placed in command of the First Brigade, Piłsudski's appointment was surely a success when compared to the real threat of his political demise.

On 22 August Piłsudski posted a bulletin in Kielce giving news of the formation of the Supreme National Committee. Certain aspects of this order are very characteristic of a new propaganda message put about by the Piłsudski camp. The Legions and the NKN were the result of the efforts of the riflemens' associations, 'the bravest and most energetic' patriots who had shouldered the initiative and responsibility of leading by example 'for the cause of independence in the Fatherland'.

Yet the actual threat to the future of the riflemens' units was known to only a few of Piłsudski's closest associates. Perhaps this was just as well since to the majority of riflemen the unfolding events were incomprehensible. The shock caused by the lack of interest of their compatriots in the Kingdom left a permanent mark on their psyche. Dreams were shattered and faith undermined when cold mistrust met the willingness of the young soldiers to make the highest sacrifice. All this had far-reaching consequences. The shock obliterated old divisions and created a new *esprit de corps*. Beliefs were now born not only of feelings of abandonment but also out of a sense of mission. Though composed later, the marching song of the First Brigade evokes a feeling which had already been born in August 1914. Its last verse, which continued to be sung throughout the inter-war years, contained this chilling refrain:

> We no longer need recognition from you,
> Neither your words, nor your tears.
> The days of seeking your compassion are ended,
> To hell with you!

Reflected here was a mood, which grew darker with time, of hatred for the people and the nation. Against all reason, a belief was born amongst the legionnaires that they alone stood on the side of right. They could not understand the devious ways of politics. They could not understand why, as soldiers of the national government, they now had to subordinate themselves to the Supreme National Committee (NKN) and why they had to swear an oath of allegiance to the Austrian Emperor, even though his title, referred to him amongst other things as the 'King of Poland'. But neither did they wish to understand, believing instead that 'The Commander knows what he is doing'. This thought eased their minds and provided all the explanation they required.

Such boundless trust in Piłsudski, which developed into a cult of the leader, was for the majority of riflemen and later for the First Brigade, a substitute for a political programme. They saw in their Commander the personification of their cause – the fight for independence.

The cult of 'The Commander' freed men subordinate to Piłsudski from responsibility and from moral qualms. There was a price to pay for such mindlessness, the full measure of which became apparent in the difficult days ahead when the Commander was interned at Magdeburg.

For many riflemen and, later, for many members of the First Brigade the cult was the product of bewildering change reinforced by feelings of rejection, brought on by the lack of political support from fellow countrymen. The cult was, further, actively promoted by Piłsudski himself. He recognized and valued its political utility.

From the very beginning of its existence he did not intend to support the Supreme National Committee (*Naczelny Komitet Narodowy* – NKN). Its formation may have saved him from defeat, but he did not consider its further development as likely to suit his own plans. He immediately encouraged the formation of an alternative political base, the Polish National Organization (*Polska Organizacja Narodowa* – PON) and sought a political understanding with Germany.

These moves can easily be explained. Piłsudski sought status in a position of political strength. Hence the importance to him of a military following. Clearly, the actual strength of several thousand untrained and poorly armed youths against armies a million strong counted for very little. But the legions had a political potential which he was careful to cultivate. Piłsudski conscientiously fostered their feeling of alienation. He was later to describe the legions as 'ghettos'. This epithet applied most clearly to the First Brigade. With the passage of time it formed its own style of existence, its own norms of behaviour; it became a closed society with its own system of values.

This ghetto-like community contained people of differing temperaments, various levels of intelligence and variety of moral standpoints. Sociologically, the most numerous group within the Brigade were members of the intelligentsia. In a political sense, the mind of the legion – let us call it that – contained an ill-defined idea of independence which was tinged with radicalism. It represented a symbiosis between the socialist and the romantic tradition of Polish nationalism. The First Brigade believed in a particular brand of radicalism which united a socialist past with a colourful, romantic and aristocratic tradition. Their political platform was founded on emotions and therefore lacked stability; with the passage of time not much would remain of their dreams of a socially just Poland. What did remain constant, from the first months of the war, was the Brigade's belief in its own superiority over the rest of Polish society and in its messianic role.

In early September Piłsudski ordered Jodko and Sokolnicki to establish the Polish National Organization on the territory of the Kingdom then occupied by the central powers. Piłsudski's aim was to deal politically with the Germans through the PON. Its personnel included the most able representatives of Piłsudski's group who had, not long since, worked together in the KSSN. On 14 September during a meeting at Sławek's home, Sokolnicki proposed sending a delegation for talks to Berlin and to Hindenburg's headquarters.

A decision on this proposal was not reached there and then. But talks on the subject continued between Michał Sokolnicki, Władysław Sikorski, Artur Śliwiński and Stanisław Downarowicz. They were

concerned about the situation in which the southern flank of the eastern
Austrian army was in retreat whilst in the north, German armies
effected lightning successes. Two other items of information added
urgency to their discussions; firstly, that the Germans were about to
organize an administration in the newly occupied Kingdom; secondly,
that certain political circles in Berlin were inclined towards political
contact with Poles. It was decided that Jodko and Sikorski should leave
for Berlin and Sokolnicki for Hindenburg's headquarters. Sokolnicki
never managed to reach Hindenburg. Jodko and Sikorski did make
contact, but with low ranking officials in Berlin. The talks were a farce.

On return to Kraków, the PON deputies met with Captain Luders,
the official in charge of the political department at the HQ of the IXth
army. The first talks between Jodko and Sokolnicki (who had replaced
Sikorski) and Luders took place on 30th September. Luders proposed
collaboration over intelligence gathering, and agreement on this led to a
discussion of the request that the PON should recruit for the ranks of
the Polish Legions. The request was granted. Several days later on 10
October yet another concession was granted by the Germans. The PON
was to be permitted to participate, to the strength of one infantry
battalion and one cavalry squadron, in the battle for Warsaw. However,
Piłsudski rejected the offer. He intended to get permission to march an
entire regiment to the capital. The German General Staff turned this
plan down, fearing it would cause problems with the Austrians and not
wishing, for obvious political reasons, to sanction the presence of a large
number of legionnaires in Warsaw. In the event the issue receded from
view as the German offensive was held up by the Russians.

The more serious setback for the PON was that it was not able to gain
public acceptance. Mistrust of the German forces in occupation was
reflected in public perception of the PON. German brutality, as
demonstrated in the destruction of Kalisz, confirmed their worst fears. It
was also clear that the political influence of the PPS, which constituted
the main support of the PON, was minimal in the region of Dabrọwa. In
these circumstances the leadership of the PON decided to begin talks
with the NKN.

Here too there were problems. At the inception of the NKN two
sections, the western and eastern, were formed. They were intended by
Piłsudski's group as the political back-up for the western and eastern
Legions respectively. Within the eastern theatre of operations the
decisive political role was played by the Galician *Endecja* in alliance
with the parties of the centre and the right. All these parties had joined
the NKN out of fear of political isolation but, from the very beginning,
pursued an independent line as in their attempts to check the growth of
the eastern Legion. Indeed the defeat of the Austrian army in Galicia,

the surrender of Lwów and the retreat in the direction of Kraków considerably eased matters for the *Endeks*, Piłsudski's great rivals.

Through forced marches the eastern Legion managed to retreat, via Sanok and Jasło, to Mszany Dolnej where a crisis erupted within its ranks. This appeared to be caused by the wording of the oath of loyalty, but in reality the eastern Legion disintegrated for lack of morale. Out of its remnants was formed the third regiment, which together with the second regiment was, at the suggestion of the eastern section of the NKN, directed by the Austrian High Command to the defence of the Carpathian passes leading into Hungary. The Galician *Endeks* had thus scored a double success in witnessing the downfall of the eastern Legion and the weakening of Piłsudski's position since it was now impossible to unify the second and third regiments of the Legion with his first.

Further setbacks hit the NKN. On 24 October a group of conservatives, which included the princes Witold Czartoryski and Andrzej Lubomirski, publicly announced their decision to withdraw from the committee.

The NKN now found itself in a most awkward political situation. The aristocratic secession reduced its political base to a coalition of democrats, socialists and Krakówian conservatives together with some peasant representation. At the same time the formation of the Polish National Organization (PON) revealed that socialists – with the support of progressives and peasants – were conducting a political campaign which aimed to marginalize the Supreme National Committee (NKN) by reducing its support to Krakówian conservatives and democrats. Needless to say, success in this would have extinguished the political aspirations of the founders of the NKN which is why the committee so readily agreed to the proposal of talks with the PON. Let it also be said that the political leaders of the NKN did not know and had therefore not taken into account, that an understanding between the competing bodies was just as essential for the PON which had itself ceased to exist, as revealed in the course of negotiations on 22 November in Vienna.

The dissolution of the PON was a particularly damaging blow for Piłsudski. It was, after all, his second political defeat in the course of the last few months. Not, perhaps, as threatening to his political future as the fact that his plans proved inapplicable during the first months of the war, it was, nevertheless, to complicate his political manoeuvres.

Piłsudski had banked on the Germans but was badly let down by them and even more so by the disastrous response to his call to arms in the Kingdom. Nor was his standing much different in that part of the Kingdom still in Russian hands. Here, the Polish Military Organization, (*Polska Organizacja Wojskowa* – POW) formed in Warsaw on Piłsudski's initiative, was developing but weakly. His commission to

Artur Śliwiński, in the second half of September, to form a national government also floundered; admittedly this initiative resulted in the formation of a Union of Organizations for Independence, but this meant nothing because, in practice, the union had no influence.

In this situation the NKN remained Piłsudski's only springboard for future political activity. Evidence of the importance which he now attached to the committee is apparent from the second half of November when he left the front in order to supervise the amalgamation of the PON and the NKN, and again later from 18 December when he arrived in Vienna and stayed for several weeks for talks with activists of the NKN. At the time of this second journey the first regiment of the Legion was upgraded into a brigade. Almost immediately it engaged the Russians in a bloody battle at Łowczówki. The legionnaires fought splendidly. As distinct from soldiers of the Austro-Hungarian army they were a formation of volunteers with strong motivation to fight; their lack of training was rapidly made up by experience in the field.

Piłsudski was important to the NKN, which, in turn, was essential to him. There was therefore nothing strange in them easily coming to an understanding. This was driven by varying intentions and different aims, but these would play a role only later. For the moment the agreements reached ideally suited Piłsudski. Sokolnicki took charge of the Secretariat and Sikorski of the Military Department of the NKN. Two of Piłsudski's close co-workers were well placed, occupying the most important positions on the Executive Committee.

Besides, Piłsudski had little scope to conduct politics in any other way than in tight alliance with the conservatives. As long as Warsaw and the greater part of the Kingdom remained in Russian hands, so long was Piłsudski politically restricted. But, however tight the alliance made with the conservatives at the turn of the year 1914, it was not, as we shall see, long lasting. At the same time it had a significance far greater than the hastily improvised political collaboration would suggest. Certain paths which Piłsudski was subsequently to use in his political activities were thereby cleared. Contacts, which he would often use, were made then and remained available to him in the future. Most importantly, the barrier of mistrust towards Piłsudski which had existed in conservative circles, because his career had caused them so much unease, was now broken. It was now recognized that Piłsudski's socialism was a thing of the distant past and that in social policy he was much closer to Krakówian conservatives, who recognized the need for reform, than to socialists. This was to have great significance in later years.

Thus Piłsudski had attained the broadening of his political base for which he had worked since 1908. But at the same time the situation was not propitious for further political gains. Gambling on Germany had not paid off; the military successes of the Russian armies in Galicia and the Kingdom, very much narrowed his field of political activity. Also, for him to engage personally in the affairs of the NKN did not make much sense, especially as he had trusted men in place. That is why, after his Viennese success, Piłsudski returned to the First Brigade at the front.

Piłsudski had hoped, most of all, to achieve something which did not come until later, a link-up between the Legions' various groups. In almost every one of his numerous letters to Jaworski he returns to this matter. However, the Austrian authorities did not have the slightest enthusiasm for the union. The grouping together of several thousand legionnaires and handing them over to the political influence of Piłsudski or to the First Brigade was out of the question for the Austrian authorities. From their point of view the First Brigade caused difficulties enough. Relations between the First Brigade and the Austrians were never easy. Though the Austrians were not without fault in this, Piłsudski intentionally drove the two sides to conflict. He understood that the re-awakening of animosity toward the Austrian army would establish an important element of unity for the First Brigade in off-loading frustrated feelings.

Contemporary diaries and later memoirs provide many examples of the unco-operative and even hostile attitude of the First Brigade towards the Austrian army, to which it was, after all, attached. A rather paradoxical situation developed whereby the Austrians and Germans, the latter to a lesser degree, were treated as enemies. This is not difficult to explain as an expression of feelings amongst the legionnaires. They understood the purpose of the war, the object of their sacrifice, less and less. They wanted to fight for Poland, but they fought for Austria. Hence the frustration which often surfaced in a wave of ill-feeling toward the Austrians.

Piłsudski actively encouraged this sense of apartness in his subordinates, not only in relation to the Austrian army, but also to the two other brigades of the Legion. Apartness heightened the sense of identity and strengthened the internal bonds of the First Brigade. Piłsudski realized full well that his political strength depended on the First Brigade, on its loyalty, its belief in him and in its own mystique.

Throughout the first half-year of 1915 Piłsudski remained with the First Brigade within whose ranks he was carefully cultivating a following. He consciously chose to wear the plain grey uniform of his fellow riflemen towards whom he adopted a paternalistic attitude. They addressed him directly as Commander, but amongst themselves they talked of him as 'the old man'. At the time he was approaching his fifties. He was older than the youngest legionnaires by 30 years; he was

1   *Student:* Fourth Year, Secondary School, Wilno, 1880

2 *Party Activist:* In London with fellow PPS representatives attending the fourth Congress of the Second International, 1896. *L to R* – Ignacy Mościcki, Bolesław Jędrzejowski, Bolesław Miklaszewski (standing), Józef Piłsudski, Aleksander Dębski, Witold Jodko-Narkiewicz

3 *Legionnaire*: December 1914. Autographed print produced for propaganda
purposes

4   *Inner Circle:* Warsaw 1917. *L to R* – Julian Stachiewicz, Tadeusz Kasprzycki. Józef Piłsudski, Michał Sokolnicki, Walery Sławek, Bolesław Wieniawa-Długoszowski

5 *The Commander: Visit to Wilno*, 1919

6 *At the Belvedere Palace:* Józef Piłsudski with President Gabriel Narutowicz, December 1922

7 *Insurrectionist:* Piłsudski with General Gustaw Orlicz-Dreszer after meeting President Wojciechowski on the Poniatowski bridge, Warsaw, 12 May 1926

8 *Minister for Military Affairs*: Member of Kazimierz Bartel's (on Piłsudski's left) cabinet, formed on 15 May 1926

9   *Holiday maker:* Piłsudski playing patience in the garden of his villa at Funchal, Madeira, December 1930

10 *Father and Daughters:* Piłsudski with Wanda and Jagoda, Warsaw, August 1932

11   *On Parade:* Piłsudski's last military review, Mokotów Field, Warsaw, 11 November 1934

12 *The Mourner:* Piłsudski bidding farewell to his sister's (Zofia) coffin en route to Wilno from Warsaw, 6 February 1935 (three months before his own death, 12 May 1935)

older than the corps commanders and from his Chief of Staff by 20 years.

The first year of war witnessed far-reaching changes of personnel within Piłsudski's inner circle. Those who, up to the outbreak of war, constituted Piłsudski's most trusted staff began to play a progressively smaller role in the decisions taken by Piłsudski. Sokolnicki and Wasilewski worked in the General Secretariat of the NKN, Sikorski together with Kukiel in its Military Department and Sulkiewicz served in the Legions as a NCO and did not have a political role. Jodko was prevented by Piłsudski from wider involvement in politics and Jędrzejowski had died in March 1914. From the old team of Piłsudski's close collaborators there remained close to Piłsudski only Sławek who now joined a new, tightly knit, group of trustees comprising: Kazimierz Sosnkowski, Artur Śliwiński, Edward Rydz-Śmigły, Julian Stachiewicz, all, apart from Śliwiński, officers of the First Brigade.

German success, at the beginning of May 1915, on the Russian front near Gorlice, and the subsequent German thrust from the north forced the Russians to retreat. The occupation of Warsaw by the central powers, which was crucial to Piłsudski's plans, was imminent. But when the German army entered Warsaw on 5 August they did so without detachments of the Legion, which put paid to Piłsudski's hopes of a triumph from which all else was to follow. Yet, in the event, it does not appear that this was such a setback for him. On the contrary, it was, in a certain sense of benefit to him.

A year previously Piłsudski had counted on public enthusiasm, which was to be evoked simply by the appearance of the Polish army, to call for independence. In the summer of 1915 he was well aware that support in the Kingdom for the Legions was low; they were a further limit to his political influence there. That is why he now settled on a radical change of political plan. Piłsudski decided to halt recruitment to the Legions, a decision which caused sharp conflict with the Military Department of the NKN, particularly with Sikorski, and a weakening of ties with the NKN.

Piłsudski believed that he could not risk the political future by another inevitable display of weakness and that in order to gain support in the Kingdom his policy was to gain political leverage *vis-à-vis* the central powers. This line of thought had further ramifications. Recognition for Piłsudski's cause in the Kingdom could only be gained through the hostility of Polish society toward the central powers, through conflict between the Legion and the central powers.

In this respect, the absence of the legions during the entry of the German army into Warsaw was, in a certain sense to Piłsudski's advantage; he had thereby avoided confronting the Legion with public opinion in the capital. Nevertheless, he himself decided to go to Warsaw and arrived there on 15 August. Piłsudski's supporters gave him a reasonably noisy reception. A demonstration was organized outside the Hotel Francuski where he was staying. The show of support was not very big, but sufficed in getting the German authorities to order Piłsudski to leave town. One up for Piłsudski in terms of his new game plan. He had somehow to convince public opinion in the Kingdom that he was serious about Polish sovereignty in his conduct of politics, that he was independent of Germany and Austria-Hungary. He could do this in only one way, by dramatically worsening relations between the central powers and the NKN. Removed from Warsaw, he moved to his estate at Miętno near Garwolina, and then on to Otwocka, from where he conducted a lively, fortnight long political campaign. Its aim was to prepare for the political crisis which he had initiated with his decision to stop recruitment to the Legions, and with his activation of the Polish Military Organization (POW) which was to play an extremely import-ant role in his plans.

The new policies adopted by Piłsudski evoked opposition even among his closest allies. Sokolnicki remembers that he was not convinced about the soundness of the Commander's move and advised Piłsudski that he was committing serious errors in 'succumbing to the destructive influence of the Kingdom'. Such warnings had an effect. It does appear that it was Piłsudski's uncertainty as to the reaction of his own collaborators to his moves which now halted the new policy. But of course it was not only that. He also required time to form a military *cum* political base in the Kingdom. Hence the Polish Military Organiza-tion (POW).

Piłsudski now directed all his energies into the building up of this secret organization. He was determined to extend its activities within and beyond the Kingdom. To this end officers from the First Brigade, together with civilian political activists, especially members of the PPS, transferred their services to the POW and energetically set about furthering its development.

The central powers avoided taking any decision over the question of Poland. They took into account the possibility of having to make a separate peace with Russia and of course any concession to Poles would weaken their position in such an eventuality. This silence on the part of the central powers, in the face of such concrete administrative moves as the division of the Kingdom into two spheres of occupation, placed Piłsudski and the Legions in an ambiguous political situation which must have given rise, among legionnaires and within society, to questions about the purpose of Polish arms.

Until the occupation of the Kingdom by the central powers a reply was easy but with Warsaw in their hands and without a word about their future intentions it became progressively more difficult to reply to this question. The Legions appeared to be simply a formation of Polish volunteers fighting at the side of the central powers against Russia.

Piłsudski very quickly grasped the political implications of the legionnaires' dilemma and this was one reason why he was soon to consider the dissolution of the Legions, which had, he believed, in the circumstances, accomplished as much as could be expected of them. Recalling this period many years later, Piłsudski was to say that he saw the year from August 1915 to July 1916 as a lost cause. And this is a correct assessment. In fact, from August 1914 events had rather worked against Piłsudski.

He had sensed success in just two matters. In the autumn of 1915 every unit of the Legions found itself to the north of Wołyn and this fulfilled a basic condition in his long-held wish to unite the Legions. There was also his attempt to gain a following in other brigades. Whilst he could be certain of the First Brigade, he knew that the two remaining brigades of the Legion were suspicious of him. In building up their loyalty to him, Piłsudski had to set aside, for the time being, his intention of dissolving the Legions. Instead, he devoted his time in Wołyn to gaining political influence in their brigades, and had some success in doing this.

April 1916 saw Piłsudski involved in the formation of a Colonels' Council within the legions. This was, in essence, a vote of no confidence in the high command and in the Military Department of the NKN.

In memoranda sent to the NKN and to the Austrian military authorities, he now also demanded three further developments. Firstly, the formation by the central powers of a Polish government. Secondly, the 'legionization' of the Legions, that is to say the removal from them of Austrian officers and the nomination of a Legion officer as their commander. Thirdly, the liquidation of the Military Department.

The formation of the Colonels' Council was an act of great significance for Piłsudski. It allowed him to intervene directly in the politics of the Legions and, in so doing, to overcome the ill-will shown to him by the Second Brigade. In this he had greater success amongst soldiers than among officers. As an act of insubordination it demonstrated that Piłsudski had decided to risk a confrontation with the command of the Legions and with the Military Department. However, there was no adverse response from above to the Colonels' Council. Consequently, Piłsudski decided to force the issue. He resigned. His resignation was accepted almost two months later on 26 September 1916.

The announcement of Piłsudski's departure caused an acute crisis. Legionnaires were forced for the first time in the history of the Legions and in a situation beyond their comprehension, to take a political decision. Until then the Commander had done their thinking for them; now he had abandoned them. Uncertainty and insecurity spread through the Legions. There were instances of suicide. Men who had been dedicated to the cause for over two years and prepared to suffer further for it were now saying that those who had questioned the need for such sacrifice were right all along. The Commander himself first came to these same conclusions.

These feelings intensified because the week before the news of Piłsudski's resignation was given out, the Austrian authorities announced the reconstitution of the Legions into an Auxiliary Corps. (*Korpus Posiłkowy*) Though it was permitted to display Polish standards and insignia, the Austro-Hungarian authorities remained silent over its future purpose in terms of Polish independence.

The crisis in the Legions was prevented from doing further damage to morale by events which suddenly altered the political situation. On 5 November 1916 the governor-generals of Warsaw and Lublin issued a joint proclamation announcing the intention of both Emperors to support the creation, on territory under Russian occupation, of an independent Polish kingdom with a constitutional government and with its own army.

Piłsudski reacted to the news in two letters which were widely distributed in the form of leaflets. In a letter dated 5 November 1916, addressed to Col. Rydz-Śmigły, he ordered legionnaires to withdraw any offers of resignation which had been prompted by the crisis. On 6 November, he wrote to the Rector of Warsaw University, Józef Brudziński, leader of the Polish delegation which had conducted talks in Berlin in October. Piłsudski told him that a soldier, unless he was a mercenary, owed loyalty to the government which provided him with legitimate leadership and that he would return to his duties the moment the authority of a Polish government became a reality.

Though the offer was clear, Piłsudski's situation was hardly straightforward. There was a real threat of Piłsudski being marginalized at the very moment when a Polish state was taking shape and forming its army. He feared that others, such as Sikorski and Józef Haller, the commander of the Second Brigade, would take his place. That is why the immediate aim of Piłsudski and his associates was not to miss out on the opportunities offered by the decree of 5 November.

However, the situation again changed rather quickly. It soon became apparent that the declaration of 5 November did not bring the central powers the results they had intended; instead of a rush of new recruits to the colours, Poles responded with reserve and mistrust. Clearly, something more was called for if recruits were to be had. Piłsudski saw his chance. He decided to go to Warsaw where he had a long discussion with Beseler, the German commander. In a report to Bethman-Hollweg, the German Chancellor, Beseler described Piłsudski as 'not over clever, personally self-assured but fractious, lacking military expertise, a dilettante and a demagogue capable of an almost hypnotic influence over his circle, especially on the PPS and POW'. But Beseler did not dismiss the possibility of using Piłsudski to help with the formation of a new army.

This indeed was the subject of a long memorandum, dated 26 December 1916, sent by Piłsudski to Beseler. He made three main points. Firstly that an army had to be formed as quickly as possible and it had to be as large as possible. Secondly, that it should be given first class training. Thirdly, that recruitment had to be based on a campaign which popularized the idea of an army. This task required cognisance by the authorities of certain psychological characteristics of the Polish nation, namely, that Poles were distrustful of any bureaucracy and always preferred to undertake every job themselves without having to co-operate with officialdom; and, that because Poles did not constitute an organized nation, feelings outweighed reason in matters of policy. Hence the trick in governing Poles depended on rousing the appropriate feelings. That was precisely why, according to Piłsudski, the recruitment drive had to be conducted with Polish assistance through the legions in direct contact with paramilitary organizations and with the help of civil-political agencies, such as the regional committees he had long favoured. Involving the legions would require fulfilment of a number of conditions which included: 1) The legions to come under the orders of the Provisional Council of State (*Tymczasowa Rada Stanu* – TRS) which was being formed. 2) A declaration to be made authorizing the formation of the first Polish corps. 3) The use of officers from the legions to organize the corps. 4) The appointment of popular and experienced men to lead it. 5) Acceptance of the principle that soldiers should not interfere with internal policy. 6) Removal from official contact with the public and from propaganda activity all officers who had not been to the front and who only represented political functions of the army and these officers to be categorized as army officials. 7) The establishment of officer schools with priority given to non-commissioned officers from the Legions.

These points, taken from Piłsudski's long memorandum, are essential to the understanding of Piłsudski's political plans especially as he now advocated a return, in changed circumstances and hence in modified form, to the plan which he tried to realize in August 1914, namely to have the Legions as cadres in a future army led by himself. He was, of course thinking of his own charismatic appeal when he wrote of the need to place a popular and experienced man at its head. Furthermore, he based his faith in paramilitary organizations on his pre-war experience in Galicia and his proposed use of provincial committees signalled the genesis of a new political structure. His views on officers who had not fought at the front were aimed at the elimination of the military department of the NKN.

Beseler would have had to be very naive if he had not guessed at Piłsudski's intentions. Of course he had and that is why he turned down Piłsudski's suggestions, giving as his reason for doing so his intention of devoting all his energies to organizing the recently announced 'Provisional Council of State of the Kingdom of Poland'.

This met for the first time on 15 January 1917. It was composed of 25 members, drawn from both occupied territories, viz. territories occupied by the central powers and by Russia. However, since it was only meant as a political gesture promoting increased recruitment, its actual powers were negligible. Beseler himself realized that, as a political gesture, the Council of State was insufficiently attractive in itself to thaw the cold mistrust of Poles in the Kingdom and so he promoted the appointment of a regent. In this he was, for the time being, unsuccessful. Conceding too little too late was characteristic of the central powers, especially the Germans, in their dealings with Polish society, to which an appeal was now made for a million recruits. Failing to overcome Polish hostility, they also failed to get the results intended by their policies.

Piłsudski was appointed *raporteur* of the Military Commission to the Provisional Council of State (TRS) and, in a move meant to underline his loyalty to it, the entire membership of the POW, numbering some 10,000, placed itself at the disposal of the Provisional Council. This was entirely a propaganda gesture because the POW continued to operate as a secret organization. However, Piłsudski tried hard at first to engage in the work of the Council. His aim in this was to get acceptance of the proposals he had made in his long December memorandum to Beseler. He was aided by his closest collaborators, Śliwiński, Sosnkowski and Kasprzycki and worked in association with the independence parties in mounting a broad propaganda campaign in favour of the Council. Wishing to extend its mandate beyond Beseler's narrow terms of reference, the propaganda referred to the Council as a surrogate Polish government.

However, the passage of time revealed that the authorities did not intend to treat seriously the institution they had created and that Polish plans for a share in government stood no chance of being put into practice. Even those who greeted the formation of the Provisional State

Council with optimism were soon disappointed and it became increasingly difficult to justify.

Then came the February revolution in Russia. The abdication of the Tsar and the declarations of the Petrograd Council of Workers and Soldiers Deputies as well as those of the provisional government substantially altered the political situation in favour of Poland. The Petrograd Council stated that Poland had the right to full independence, without any conditions or limits. Two days later the statement was repeated by the provisional government, this time with two fundamental conditions: a future independent Poland was to embrace a military alliance with Russia and was to agree to changes in the boundaries of the Russian state. Despite these conditions the provisional government, under the direct pressure of the Petrograd Council's declaration, recognized Poland's right to independence. This meant that although it was possible for Poles to justify political collaboration with the German occupants up to March 1917, from April 1917 this was not the case – especially as a marked decline in living conditions together with news of events in Russia precipitated mass radicalization in occupied Poland.

These events forced a revision of existing plans; Piłsudski was, yet again, in a political *impasse*. He had fully engaged in the activities of the Provisional Council, which led him into a blind alley and caused a marked drop in his popularity. After the Russian Revolution he sought a way out of an increasingly unprofitable situation. He now decided to engineer his own dismissal from the Council of State and the tone of his speeches at its sittings became sharply critical. But Piłsudski was frustrated by new developments in his attempts to create a crisis. On 10 April Beseler was given direct authority over the Legions as Commander-in-Chief of an emergent Polish army, the object of much Polish effort in the Provisional Council from the moment of its formation. Piłsudski could not bring a crisis to a head at this particular moment, especially as it coincided with his efforts at forming two secret organizations, A and B.

The first was intended as an umbrella organization to gather together the leaders and influential activists of left wing parties. The second was to do the same on the right. Independent of each other, both were supposed to be subordinate to Piłsudski. Because of the opposition of the *Endecja*, organization B did not materialize. Organization A did, although it was dealt a severe blow by the arrest of Piłsudski (of which more below) and of Sosnkowski, who co-ordinated its formation. Eventually, organization A became the political nerve centre of Piłsudski's camp and was to play a key role during Piłsudski's internment.

Between April and May 1917 Piłsudski's political conduct was most hesitant. Perhaps he hoped that an agreement with the Germans was still possible; that they would become more flexible over Polish policy. Yet, if this was his hope, it was countered by the sudden and universal intensification of hatred towards the occupants.

Sensitive to the sudden rise in social tension, Piłsudski's now saw an opportunity to extricate himself from the Provisional State Council (TRS). Herein lay the origins of the crisis within the Legions in July 1917, when those legionnaires who were not citizens of Austria-Hungary, were told to swear an oath of loyalty to the dual monarchy. Although its wording was actually much more acceptable than the wording of the oath made in 1914 Piłsudski was, nevertheless, determined to exploit the issue of loyalty as a way out of his dilemma; he made the oath an issue of principle in the context of Polish independence by insisting that the only Polish army that could be formed would be a Polish army with the Commander at its head.

The problem was, however, that the Germans had already decided against the formation of any such army; they had stopped trying to raise a million new recruits from the Kingdom. The Russian Revolution had removed the threat on the Eastern Front and there was now a real possibility of an end to the war with Russia. As for the war on the Western Front, here Polish recruits from the Kingdom could not be used, especially not after the advocacy of the Polish cause by the American President and not after a start had been made in the formation of a Polish army in France. German policy towards Poland changed; it was no longer a case of raising recruits but of guarding its rear by ensuring the security of Polish territories. This was to be achieved by administrative and political means, which meant that the German authorities were most careful to ensure that decisions concerning Polish affairs depended solely on them.

In these circumstances Piłsudski's demonstrative actions did not have the desired effect. In fact the outcome was the opposite of that intended. A wave of arrests surged through the membership of the POW, particularly affecting those legionnaires who did not have Austro-Hungarian citizenship. They were interned in camps at Beniaminów and Szczypiorno. Those who admitted to Austrian identity were partially recruited into the Austrian army and partially into the Polish Auxiliary Corps, under the command of General Zygmunt Zieliński. Legionnaires who actually took the oath joined the Polish Military Force, PSZ, constituting the *Polnische Wehrmacht* answerable directly to Beseler.

The arrests crippled the functioning of the POW for many months, especially when during the night 21–22 July 1917, Piłsudski and Sosnkowski were themselves arrested. After short stays in a number of prisons Piłsudski was taken to the military prison of Magdeburg, where he was held in strict isolation until August 1918 when he was joined by Sosnkowski.

After the arrest and exile of his youth and his incarceration following the raid on *Robotnik*, Piłsudski found himself in prison for the third time, this time in German hands. Though conditions were tolerable, Piłsudski bore prison badly. He was in poor physical and psychological state, the latter caused not only by loneliness but also by family complications. Alexandra Szczerbińska gave birth in February 1918 to their daughter Wanda. Piłsudski tried desperately to see them both but personal contact was refused. Wanda was born when Piłsudski had turned 50. Two years later Jagodka was born. He became very closely attached to both. This almost dry and introverted man became increasingly brutish with age but, with respect to his daughters, was the gentlest, the most charming, the most loving father. Did he only joke, when he said that Wanda should be the Queen of Poland?

If in a personal sense his stay in Magdeburg bore down cruelly on Piłsudski, at least in a political sense it yielded enormous dividends. It broke the *impasse* in which Piłsudski found himself after the outbreak of the Russian Revolution and it gave him an excellent way out of an ambiguous but increasingly damaging reputation for collaboration with the Germans. Piłsudski was now portrayed as the victim of injustice, a symbol of the struggle for freedom, a martyr. With every passing week and month of his stay in Magdeburg Piłsudski grew in political stature. His popularity led him inexorably to leadership of the nation. Of course, none of this would have occurred without an intensive propaganda campaign. This was carried out with great panache by his co-workers whose activity reflected popular emotion and it bore fruit because it fell on fertile soil.

The fact that Piłsudski was isolated and that he had no opportunity of political dealings was equally in his favour. He could not engage in damaging political contests. He could not be identified in any way with the Regency Council formed in September 1917 to represent 'the highest authority in the Kingdom', nor with its succession of governments, nor with the Polish Military Force. As each of these institutions compromised themselves in the public mind so Piłsudski's political capital grew. Time in prison was on his side. He was able to regain his old reputation and emerge from his political meanderings with a renewed strength of purpose and sense of direction; imprisonment gave him a status he had never held before.

CHAPTER FIVE

Head of State

On 10 November 1918 (a day before the armistice) Piłsudski and Sosnkowski, released from captivity, arrived at Warsaw station at about 7 a.m. They were met by Prince Zdzisław Lubomirski, representing the Regency Council, and by a small group of POW activists headed by Adam Koc. Lubomirski seemed very agitated and expressed his concern to Piłsudski about mounting social tension in the country. Sensing the threat of revolution and recognizing that, in the eyes of society, its position was compromised, the Regency Council wished only to hand authority over to Piłsudski as quickly as possible. He hesitated, wanting first to find out more about the prevailing situation at home and abroad.

Events were moving fast. Within four days of Piłsudski's arrival, the Germans had completely abandoned Warsaw. They had been assured by Piłsudski of a safe retreat across Poland. Before they left they had endowed him with the title of Chief of State.

In Paris, the National Polish Committee (KNP), had been in operation for over a year. Dominated by the *Endecja* and led by Roman Dmowski the committee was recognized by the allies as officially representing Polish interests. In eastern Galicia battles raged on between Polish and Ukrainian forces. They had begun with the Ukrainian capture of Lwów during the night of 31 October and early hours of 1 November. Ukrainian superiority soon became apparent.

Within Kingdom Poland the situation was complicated by the speed of events. In Lublin, which Piłsudski wanted to visit but was persuaded not to, the first Council of Workers Delegates (*Rada Delegatów Robotniczych* – RDR) in Poland was formed on 5 November. Its membership included the SDKPiL, PPS-Left, PPS and Bund. Two days later a Provisional Government of the Peoples' Republic of Poland, with Ignacy Daszyński as premier, was announced in Lublin. (Daszyński was leader of the Polish Social-Democratic Party in Austrian-occupied Poland. As a member of parliament in Vienna, he was a man of considerable political experience.) Soon after this, a workers' council and a Red Guard were formed in Dąbrowie Górniczej and more workers' councils sprang up in all the larger centres of the Kingdom.

In Kraków, authority had, since the end of October 1918, been exercised by the Polish Commission of Liquidation (*Polska Komisja Likwidacyjna* – PKL). Like the National Council of the Principality of

Cieszyn and other such bodies, the PKL was in effect an independent organ of Polish local authority. In Warsaw the Regency Council, led by Władysław Wróblewski tried to fulfil a similar role. In Poznań a Military Council was formed on 10 November. The next day it was transformed into a Council of Workers and Soldiers and was reorganized yet again on 13 November into a Polish-German governing body. Poznań also witnessed the emergence of the Commisariat of the People's Supreme Council, under the leadership of Wojciech Korfanty. This was entirely independent of German authorities.

Euphoria at the prospect of imminent independence and an explosive growth of political radicalism coloured life in village and town. The masses had great expectations of freedom while panic at the thought of revolution gripped the propertied classes. News of the outbreak of revolution in Germany heightened these feelings which were to play an increasingly significant role in the unfolding political drama.

On 10 November, while Piłsudski conferred with the Regency Council, the streets of Warsaw rang with revolutionary songs. Crowds waving the Red Flag demanded the removal of the compromised and reactionary Regency Council. These street demonstrations strengthened Piłsudski's position. He was given command of the army and on 12 November he publicly announced Regency Council willingness to favour the formation of a national government to which it would be prepared to hand over authority. Piłsudski further declared his intention to follow agreement with the Lublin government by consultations with representatives of all parties.

This announcement is very significant in understanding Piłsudski's plans. He did not wish to be the agent of either the Regency Council or the Lublin government. He hesitated from coming out directly against the Regency Council as this would have identified him with the independence parties of the left. He refrained from close contact with the Lublin government because he found its leanings to the extreme left repulsive. Waiting to see how things developed, Piłsudski wanted to retain a free hand in politics.

Eventually, a left-wing government led by Jędrzej Moraczewski and dominated by Piłsudski, came to power at the turn of 1918–19. It lasted just three months. Piłsudski then formed a government under the premiership of Ignacy Paderewski. This was a very skilful move. Paderewski was the Paris-based Polish National Committee's delegate in the USA and this prevented *Endeks* from coming out against him. Indeed, the *Endecja* must have been convinced of its own success. And yet Paderewski himself was not an *Endek*. He was the symbol of traditional, aristocratic patriotism, a person of right-wing views but not a public exponent of such views. The left, with some reservations, could accept him. He was after all a great and famous pianist. Fêted in Europe and America, he had *entrée* to the most exclusive salons. This had currency in internal and external politics and gave Paderewski the opportunity to normalize relations between Piłsudski and Dmowski's Polish National Committee in Paris. Piłsudski had made efforts in this direction ever since his return to Poland from Magdeburg.

However, for a variety of reasons his priority lay with the formation of the army. Piłsudski firmly believed that the army determined the strength of the emergent nation whose borders had yet to be fixed. It was indispensable in achieving his territorial aims in the east, of which more to follow. It was essential in securing internal stability. Moreover, he hoped it would secure his political base. Because Piłsudski refused, on principle, to involve himself with any political camp, the army played an especially important role in this regard.

The army was also important to him in furthering national solidarity; he hoped to remove political differences by the very process of its formation. This was not easy. The ranks contained men who had fought against each other at the front and those who not long ago had been regarded by many as traitors. It was in fact easier to heal division between those whom fate had placed on opposite sides in the war than for those who had started out together on 6 August but who later, during the crisis of loyalty within the legions, found themselves at loggerheads. Piłsudski knew full well that he could not form an army while relying on the First Brigade as his main support. This meant preventing Piłsudskiites from involvement in building up Poland's military strength, something which was incomprehensible to several of the Commander's closest collaborators.

During public appearances Piłsudski spoke out strongly for national consolidation and urged men to smooth over the lines of old division. He addressed his remarks particularly to legionnaires, to the old soldiers of the First Brigade and of the POW. After all, the strongest opposition to his policies on national solidarity came from within these circles. As pretenders to the leadership they could not come to terms with the thought of being treated on an equal footing with Sikorski or Zagorski or other despised officers from the Austrian army.

Meanwhile, the results of the elections to the Constitutional Sejm (Parliament), held at the end of January 1919, became known. They denied the possibility of independent government to any party or grouping. Although the right emerged as the strongest political camp it did not gain an overall majority; with 34.2 per cent of the votes it had 3.4 per cent more than the centre and 3.9 per cent more than the left. The results of the elections expressed a low level of working class consciousness and the superficiality of radical feelings.

On 20 February 1919, at the third sitting of the Sejm, Piłsudski announced his resignation as Provisional Head of State. The Sejm responded by inviting him to take office as Head of State until such time as the Constitution was agreed. Piłsudski accepted, subject to what was later called 'the small constitution', a decree defining the limits of authority of the Sejm and of the Head of State.

Piłsudski had thus accomplished the first stage of his plans. He had successfully led the process which had resulted in the formation of the Sejm while still retaining power. However, his authority was not as limitless as before the calling of the Sejm. He was now accountable to the people's representatives.

The result of the election, the poor response to the Polish Communist Party's (*Komunistyczna Partia Polski* – KPP) appeal for support, the organizational incompetence of the Councils of Workers Deputies in competing for power, the strengthening of state administration, the rebuilding of the army, the state take-over of control over the People's Militia (*Milicja Ludowa*) – all these factors dispelled anxieties, particularly among the propertied classes, of an imminent revolution. The growing conviction that the moment of revolution had passed strengthened the position of the centre and right, especially that of the *Endecja*. Admittedly, the Paris-based Polish National Committee had recognized the authority of the Warsaw government and had widened its own membership to include Piłsudski's delegates, but this did not signify that the *Endecja* was prepared to co-operate. Setting aside the fact that the nationalist camp saw in Piłsudski a most threatening competitor in the race for power, fundamental differences concerning the political future of the eastern territories of the emergent state made agreement impossible. In general terms, two contradictory concepts worked against each other. The Belvedere camp (as Piłsudski's supporters were now called, referring to the Belvedere palace, Piłsudski's official residence) advocated federation, the nationalist camp, incorporation. Dmowski envisaged the absorption, into the Polish Republic, of the entire provinces of Lithuania, Ruthenia and the greater part of the provinces of Volhinya and Podolia. He saw devolution of power to the regions only in terms of cultural and economic policy; political authority was to be highly centralized in all other matters.

Piłsudski adhered to the federal concept of which there were many variants. In general federalism claimed legitimacy through its long history; it held a traditional place in Polish political thinking. Throughout the entire period of the partitions it appeared and re-appeared in political programmes. The rebuilding of the union with Lithuania formed the key element in many of these.

(The link between Poland and Lithuania dates from 1389 when Prince

Jagiełło of Lithuania married the Polish Queen, Jadwiga. The Jagiełło-nian empire, which included lands stretching from the Baltic to the Black sea, inspired Piłsudski's eastern policy. At first Poland and the eastern borderlands or *Kresy* merely shared a monarch but by the end of the 16th century they had fused politically into a single Commonwealth (*Rzeczpospolita*). Its social, economic and cultural life, until the middle of the 18th century, was dominated by the Polish *slachta* or gentry into which the local aristocracy was absorbed, by a rapid process of Polonization. The Commonwealth went into decline in the 17th and 18th centuries by which time it came under Russian dominance. Poland was then partitioned between Russia and Prussia in 1772. The second partition, which also involved Austria, occurred in 1793. The third partition, by all three powers again, took place in 1795. This was followed by the incursions of the Napoleonic wars, resulting in increased Russian control of an even greater portion of Polish territory in the settlements after the defeat of Napoleon in 1815. Ed.)

However, events in the second half of the 19th century necessitated modification to the scope of Poland's eastern vision. The growth of nationalism and the development of a nationalist political movement in Lithuania and in the Ukraine placed a question mark over Polish federal plans. Polonization was seen as a threat by Lithuanian nationalists, and not without some justification. We must also take into account local social structures whereby the village was Lithuanian, Byelorussian or Ukrainian and the manor house, Polish. Equally important became the intensification of class conflict with its strong influence on the evolution of the national consciousness of the overwhelming majority of inhabitants of these lands.

An additional complication arose out of the fact that Lwów, as well as Wilno were towns which were unambiguously Polish in every regard. They were, however, surrounded by a non-Polish population, whose developing sense of national identity, particularly around Lwów, and less so around Wilno, conflicted with that of the Poles; the number of incidents of clashes between Poles and Ukrainians and Poles and Lithuanians grew in number, which did not augur well for plans for federation.

During the terminal stage of the demise of the Austro-Hungarian monarchy, a Ukrainian constitutional assembly met in Lwów on 19 October 1918, and announced the creation of a West-Ukrainian People's Republic. During the night of 31 October–1 November Ukrainian detachments overran nearly the whole of Lwów as well as the greater portion of Eastern Galicia across the River San. This territory witnessed several bloody fights between Poles and Ukrainians. Armed clashes also erupted along the River Dnieper between supporters of a bourgeois Ukrainian People's Republic, bolsheviks and Russian counter-revolutionaries.

Strong German detachments were stationed in Lithuania, during this early period in the formation of the Polish state and their presence prevented open Polish-Lithuanian conflict. However, political relations between the two peoples were very inflamed. On 1 January 1919, Poles in Wilno attempted to wrest control of the town from continued German occupation. This attempt at liberation was only partially successful. Four days later Wilno was occupied by detachments of the Red Army and power was taken in the name of the Lithuanian Peoples' Republic by a Provisional Government of Workers and Peasants. In February 1919 the Lithuanian Republic linked up with the Byelorussian Republic.

What of Polish interests? On 16 April Piłsudski made his first move to settle this question. He ordered the occupation of Wilno and of Wilno Province. By 21 April the town was in Polish control. The speed of the offensive may be explained by several factors. Piłsudski feared the occupation of Wilno by the Kowno (Kovno, Kaunas) government. Given that joint Lithuanian-German operations had been conducted in March against the Red Army and that Lithuanian forces, acting alone, were in evidence from the beginning of April, he wished not to be faced by a Lithuanian *fait accompli* in Wilno. Internal factors also played a role in the timing of Piłsudski's action. Firstly the Sejm was still on Christmas recess. The majority of Sejm members would have opposed the move and given priority to action in East Galicia. Secondly, Haller and his army was shortly expected to arrive from France. (Józef Haller commanded the second brigade on the eastern front. After the Bolshevik revolution he left Russian territory for France to take command of Polish troops in that country. He was promoted to General in 1920. Ed.) Fearing Haller's popularity, Piłsudski wished to reinforce his own public standing by a successful military and political *coup*.

The operation did end in military success but it did nothing to sway Lithuanian opinion in favour of federation with Poland. Voluntary union, a fundamental aspect of Piłsudski's federal policy had failed to materialize; there remained only the possibility of the direct incorporation into Poland of the occupied Lithuanian territories.

The achievement of Piłsudski's eastern policy depended not only on a solution of the Lithuanian problem but also on a satisfactory outcome of the Polish-Ukrainian conflict in Eastern Galicia. This war posed a threat to the right flank of Polish forces in the east by placing a considerable strain on the small and ill-equipped Polish army. It also made cooperation with Ukrainian nationalists, another key element in his eastern policy, very difficult.

Moreover, political pressures at home meant that Piłsudski could not allow a protracted solution to the Eastern Galician question. The Wilno expedition prompted an intense campaign by the *Endecja* against Piłsudski's designs in the east. The Lithuanian adventure came under particular criticism for taking place while battles were still being fought in Eastern Galicia. Indeed, Piłsudski had been under attack well before the Wilno expedition for not taking care of Eastern Galicia. Here everything was in a state of flux. However, we need to explain this complex situation, albeit it in the barest outline, in order to better understand Piłsudski's plan of action in the Ukraine.

Ukrainian statehood was being claimed simultaneously by three political formations: the Ukrainian Soviet Socialist Peoples' Republic, the Ukrainian Peoples' Republic (led by a 'Directorate' headed by Semen Petlura) and the Western-Ukrainian People's Republic in Eastern Galicia. The last two joined forces with the Whites (under Anton Denikin) and with Polish detachments, in opposition to the Red Army. It was in the interest of Piłsudski and of the Entente, though for different reasons, to try to end the Polish-Ukrainian conflict in Eastern Galicia and to arrive at a political understanding between Poland and the Ukrainian People's Republic.

For the Entente, and especially for France, the ending of the Polish-Ukrainian conflict was a step in creating an anti-Soviet coalition, all the more necessary in view of the Red Army's evident success in the north and in the south from the beginning of 1919. But despite close involvement by the Entente, negotiations conducted then failed to result in a ceasefire.

Instead, the conflict escalated when Piłsudski took charge of a renewed Polish offensive in Eastern Galicia on 14 May. Polish armies were very successful and moved quickly forward but after just 13 days, because of very strong Entente pressure to limit Polish conquest, Piłsudski halted the offensive. Only a small portion of Eastern Galicia remained in Ukrainian hands.

In Paris, where the shape of Poland's frontiers was being considered, the peacemakers debated the future of Eastern Galicia at length. In fear of greater Bolshevik conquests allied permission was given, on 25 June, for Polish forces to occupy territory up to the river Zbrucz. This was conditional on a final decision on this portion of Galicia being made at a future date. On 28 June, Piłsudski again took matters into his own hands and started a new offensive and by 18 July had pushed Ukrainian forces out beyond the Zbrucz. In the main these Ukrainian forces were responsible to the Directorate. This made agreement with Petlura and Piłsudski more likely. With detachments of the Ukrainian People's Republic supported by the Red Army on the one side and a serious threat from Denikin's forces on the other, there was no other choice; the end of military activity against Polish forces allowed the Directorate continued existence. Let us also add that when Denikin refused to recognize the Directorate, France recalled its military mission from Petlura's headquarters.

On 9 August Petlura wrote to Piłsudski, proposing an understanding and co-operation against the Red Army. On 1 September a Polish-Ukrainian truce was signed and a line of demarcation between Polish and Ukrainian forces agreed. This cleared the way for political negotiations which were started in Warsaw by an Ukrainian mission led by Andrzej Liwicki.

There now remained the question of Polish-Soviet relations, especially Piłsudski's position *vis-à-vis* the Russian counter-revolution. The rather complex set of problems associated with this aspect fundamentally shaped Piłsudski's eastern policy.

When Piłsudski, as Commander-in-Chief of the Polish Army, notified the allies of the birth of the Polish State on 16 November 1918, he did not copy the message to Soviet Russia. This omission undoubtedly aroused Russian mistrust. But one ought not to over-emphasize its significance because Soviet Russia was not at the time recognized by any European state and the Polish gesture meant only that Poland saw itself linked with the Entente. Nevertheless, in the context of the outbreak of revolution in Germany and in the hope of extending the revolution into western Europe, the Polish problem had two important aspects for the Soviet authorities: the reborn state was seen by them both as a barrier to the spread of revolution and as a state with which the Soviet authorities had to attempt to normalize relations regardless of Poland's socio-political configuration.

The first diplomatic contacts between Warsaw and Moscow were made on 26 November when Leon Wasilewski, the Polish envoy, presented Georgii Chicherin, the Peoples' Commissar for Foreign Affairs, with a note protesting against the internment of personnel of the Polish embassy and against the arrest of a number of other Polish officials. In his reply Chicherin stated that nobody had been arrested. A lengthy exchange of messages ensued, in the course of which Chicherin raised the issue of normalizing relations with Poland and proposing an exchange of diplomatic representatives. The Polish side emphatically rejected the Soviet initiative.

Piłsudski did not want an understanding with Soviet Russia for a number of reasons. In company with most European politicians he did not believe in the durability of Soviet authority and thought that normalization of relations with Moscow would make more difficult the realization of his eastern policy. Undoubtedly he also feared the revolutionary tendency in Poland; it was easier to weaken it by presenting the new Russia as an enemy of Poland and, taking into account the policy of the Entente towards revolutionary Russia, as an enemy of the West.

As already mentioned, Polish forces found themselves in conflict with detachments of the Red Army in the second half of February, 1919. But this did not result in the breakdown of political contacts between the two states. At the end of March a special delegate of the Polish Government, Aleksander Więckowski, went to Moscow. He conducted negotiations with Chicherin to the end of April when the talks broke down because of the Wilno expedition. Nevertheless Chicherin had at the time declared that the Soviet government was willing to continue negotiations whenever the Polish government halted its 'provocative activity against the Soviet republics'.

Talks were re-activated in June by the Bolshevik agent, Julian Marchlewski. After escaping from Germany (where the revolution had been defeated) he went on his own initiative to Moscow, first conferring with officials in Warsaw, in an attempt to resolve the Russo-Polish conflict. He conveyed the message to Lenin that Poland would not pursue her activities on the Eastern front if the frontier question could be settled through unofficial negotiations and with the assurance that the Red Army would not cross the agreed boundaries. After talks with Lenin, who briefed him fully on territorial questions and gave him plenipotentiary powers, Marchlewski returned to Poland on 10 July. He was taken to Białowieza, for talks with Aleksander Więckowski who had been sent there by Piłsudski. It was agreed between them that official talks about an exchange of captives were shortly to begin under the aegis of the Red Cross, and that these talks could eventually lead to peace negotiations.

At about the same time Piłsudski tried to discover the strength and aims of the Russian counter-revolution. This was not difficult because White generals did not hide their intention to reinstate 'a single and undivided Russia'. They were also prepared to promise a favourable response to the question of recognizing the Polish State, within ethnic boundaries, but only following victory over the revolution. This statement together with the positive support of the Entente for the rebuilding of 'Greater Russia' made Piłsudski very uneasy because such intentions cut across Polish interests and, if realized, would extinguish his eastern plans. Piłsudski came to the conclusion that he would not therefore support the White generals. He felt that relations with the Reds were more worthwhile for Poland, believing that the situation in Russia would, sooner or later, lead to the downfall of the Bolsheviks and to such a weakening of Russia as to enable him to successfully effect his eastern policy without having to concede anything to the Whites.

Consistent with this line of reasoning and despite strong British pressure, Piłsudski avoided co-operation with Denikin. However, in September 1919, as a concession to the Entente powers, Piłsudski sent General Aleksander Karnicki and Jerzy Iwanowski to Denikin's head-quarters. He also considered sending General Eugeniusz Michaelis to Kolchak. But he refused Denikin a Polish offensive, which could have been an extremely serious blow for Soviet Russia.

On 11 October talks started between representatives of, respectively, the Russian and the Polish Red Cross. The Soviet delegation was headed by Marchlewski who quickly resumed with Ignacy Boerner the negotiations he had started with Więckowski, who had died in the meantime. On 3 November Piłsudski entrusted Boerner with a message for Marchlewski. He gave his word, as Head of State, that Polish forces would not advance beyond currently occupied positions and advised the Soviet side to withdraw by 10 km in order to create a neutral belt. If this were done and if all Communist agitation in the ranks of the Polish army were to cease and if Petlura's forces were no longer attacked by the Red Army, Piłsudski said that he would be prepared to send his plenipotentiary for talks with Lenin.

Boerner added that he had Piłsudski's permission to state that Poland was not and did not wish to be Europe's *gendarme*, that the only principle on which policy was based was that of Polish state rights and that this did not include supporting Denikin in his fight with the Bolsheviks. Marchlewski departed for Moscow, to present to Lenin the conditions set out by Piłsudski.

Piłsudski's aim was not, however, to conduct peace negotiations as became clear on 26 November when Boerner handed him the Soviet government's reply, brought back by Marchlewski, accepting in essence all the conditions presented to it and suggesting further negotiations. Piłsudski declined from further talks and shortly afterwards ordered Boerner to break off negotiations.

This was because the military situation in the east had changed markedly. The Red Army had given Denikin's forces a sound thrashing which lifted the White threat to Moscow. In Siberia Kolchak was rapidly losing ground and only weeks separated him from certain defeat. White Russia was lost. It had stopped existing as a military and political power of any consequence. What Piłsudski had feared was the restitution of old Russia and this was no longer a threat. Changes in policy towards Russia by the Entente also came into effect about this time. Already in the spring of 1919, attacks made on interventionist detachments by the Red Army, prompted a decision to withdraw from direct military intervention in Russia. The tactic now adopted was of dividing Entente support between the forces of Russian counter-revolution led, respectively, by Denikin and by Kolchak. But because of the defeat of the White generals, nothing came of this plan. On 9 November 1919 the British Prime Minister, Lloyd George, declared that Great Britain would no longer intervene in the civil war. This instantly changed the policy of Britain and France towards revolutionary Russia. The French premier, Clemenceau, was able to convince Lloyd George, that Soviet Russia ought now to be isolated from other countries 'by a barrier of barbed wire'. But this was only meant as an interim solution. From the point of view of France, Poland now stood, as Piłsudski had foreseen, as the main bastion of French anti-Soviet policy. This opened up new opportunities for Piłsudski to realize his eastern policy. He also believed that Soviet Russia had been so weakened by civil war that she would have to accept the outcome of that policy, in which case Piłsudski would ignore offers of peace from Moscow.

Negotiations with Petlura were, however, pursued. In mid March 1919 the bases of a political agreement and a military convention had both been agreed. On 21 April a political agreement was signed to the effect that 'The Polish Republic recognizes the Directorate of the Independent Ukrainian People's Republic with Simon Petlura at its head as the supreme authority of the Ukrainian People's Republic.' This sounded grand, but in reality it conceded little, because Petlura's armies were already beaten, and Petlura himself was in Poland. He was entirely dependent on the Polish government and had a taste of what this implied when he and his ministers were arrested for 24 hours for being too obstinate in the course of negotiations. From Piłsudski's point of view Petlura and his government represented nothing but an embellish-ment of Piłsudski's policies in the east.

As these depended heavily on the use of armed force, his energies were now directed at organizing a new command structure which would enable the Polish armies, which were spread along four fronts to be accountable directly to a supreme command. In April Piłsudski was appointed First Marshal of Poland. He immediately approved promo-tion of a great number of his men up through the ranks and on 25 April went on the offensive against the Red Army.

Even before the Polish offensive the Red Army had started to withdraw. Meeting no opposition, Piłsudski stopped the offensive after the occupation of Zytomierz, believing that the enemy's armies would concentrate in defence of Kiev. However the Soviet command did not intend to engage in battle in conditions from which it could not benefit; far from preparing the defence of Kiev it ordered its evacuation. In this situation further delay made no sense for Piłsudski. He gave the order to occupy Kiev on 8 May. The previous day Polish patrols had entered the town meeting no resistance. Two days later the bridges across the Dneiper were captured and its eastern bank secured in defence of Kiev.

What was presented to the public as lightning military success was, in reality, a thrust into emptiness; the object of the offensive, the defeat of the Red Army, had not been achieved. On the contrary a threatening situation had resulted for the Polish army. A week after the occupation of Kiev, Soviet detachments went on the offensive in Byelorussia. This forced Piłsudski to transfer a portion of his forces from the Ukraine to the South-Eastern front. Though the hurriedly improvized Soviet offensive in Byelorussia was quickly halted and a portion of lost territory regained, the Soviet offensive of 26 May on the weakened Ukrainian front required the use of reserves. But there was a lack of reserves and a lack of adequate railways in this region which meant that the means to transfer armies to where they were most needed was limited.

Deficient leadership, especially in its underestimation of the strength of Soviet cavalry bearing down on Kiev, exacerbated the vulnerability of the Polish armies. After stopping Semion Budienny's first charge, the Polish High Command made the mistake of believing that another cavalry attack on a strong defensive position would also result in its defeat; only a few days later Budienny broke through the defences and swept to the rear of the Polish armies.

If that is how the military situation stood in the first days of June, Piłsudski's political aims in marching on Kiev had fared no better. On 26 April Piłsudski's and Petlura's orders of the day were broadcast to Ukrainians: Polish armies were about to enter the Ukraine to liberate it from alien hordes and would remain in the Ukraine until such time as rightful Ukrainian authorities took charge.

No reference was made of social policy. And not surprisingly. Behind the Polish army the Polish gentry returned to the Ukraine, brutally re-imposing their traditional privileges. Their behaviour even forced the military high command to issue an order on 12 May which stated that it was not part of military policy to re-establish the rights of Polish landowners.

Piłsudski's intentions in the Ukraine are in many ways analogous to his plans relating to the Polish Kingdom before August 1914. As then he held to the belief that the entry of military detachments would be sufficient to find wide social acceptance. This would express itself in a massive influx of recruits. In 1914 the Polish army had been expected to rise in this manner. In 1920 the same was to apply to a Ukrainian army. In both cases great store was set by the occupation of the capital. In both cases public enthusiasm was expected to be generated simply by cries of independence.

In both cases this plan went completely awry, though of course for different reasons. The entry into the Ukraine of Polish detachments was treated by the people as being on a par with German and White (Russian) military occupation. The Ukrainian peasant, who had been given land by Soviet authorities and from whom this land was now being confiscated by Polish occupants, did not even have to consider on whose side to place his sympathies. The reception of the Polish army was hostile. Petlura himself was seen as a bankrupt politician, unable to gain wider influence in his country. The number of recruits he had attracted barely made up the two divisions with which he had entered the Ukraine from Poland. Plans to form six Ukrainian divisions, to enable the transfer of Polish armies from the Ukraine to the White Russian theatre, collapsed completely.

In the course of the month-long Polish occupation of the Ukraine, it was possible neither to create a Ukrainian state nor to call a constitutional assembly together in Kiev, clear evidence of the hostility of the Ukrainian masses towards Piłsudski and Petlura. Moreover, the unlikeliness of Piłsudski realizing his political hopes was compounded by the fact that his idea of creating a Ukrainian state was accepted neither by the majority of the Sejm nor by the Entente states. Even France, so ready to support the liquidation by Poland of Soviet authority in the Ukraine, was, because of its concern for the position of the Whites, opposed to the formation of a Ukrainian state. If Polish actions were intended to gain speedy mass support from the Ukrainian people by a *fait accompli* which was later to be justified, they failed miserably. The Ukrainian masses did not give Piłsudski their support. This political failure together with the failure of his military aspirations made the future of Piłsudski's eastern policy look decidedly unpromising. Yet he felt sure that the actions he, Petlura and the Polish government had taken in recognition of the Ukrainian People's Republic provided sufficient justification for the Kiev expedition. In this belief he was not to be disappointed.

On 18 May Piłsudski returned to Warsaw from the Ukrainian front. Premier Leopold Skulski hailed him as a victorious leader. A special mass was said at the Church of St Aleksander and a special meeting of the Sejm was held in his honour. There, the Marshal of the Sejm (Speaker), Wojciech Trampczynski made a speech welcoming Piłsudski's return 'in a triumphal victory which would forge the political unity of Polish society'.

The tone of these speeches matched the enthusiasm of the street. The conquest of Kiev was greeted as success in a great military tradition. Polish society, crushed by years of captivity and hardship, felt the need of lightning success, of an affirmation of its own strength. Even those who usually prided themselves on a realistic view of policy threw caution to the winds. And the voice of those who were against the aggression in Polish policy, against its unmistakable class character, reached only a few in those days of euphoria.

While Piłsudski was being showered with flowers on the streets of Warsaw and even as the crowd unharnessed the horses from his carriage to haul it themselves, a new Soviet offensive in Byelorussia forced Polish armies to retreat. And though, as we have noted, positions previously held were in part retrieved, the advances of the Red Army meant that the Soviets had regained the operational initiative.

June brought further Polish reverses. The piercing of the Ukrainian-Polish front by Budyenni's cavalry forced the army of General Rydz-Śmigły to vacate Kiev during the night of 10–11 June. A general retreat now began and in the second half of the month Polish armies reached the line from which the Kiev expedition had been launched. The retreat continued.

On 4 July Soviet armies re-commenced their offensive on the Lithuanian-Byelorussian front. It was not possible to stop it at the line of the trenches constructed by the Germans during the First War. Soviet detachments occupied Mińsk on 11 July, Wilno on 14 July, Grodno on 19 July, Białystok on 28 July and took Brzesc-on-the-Bug on 1 August.

In the shadow of these reverses, the Sejm approved an order calling for a Council of National Defence (*Rada Obrony Państwa*). Its membership included: the Head of State as chairman, the Marshal of the Sejm, 10 Sejm representatives, the Prime Minister, three members of the Cabinet nominated by the government together with three representatives of the military nominated by the Commander-in-Chief. It had the power to make decisions on all matters related to the conduct of war and the making of peace. The council signified a considerable slimming down of Piłsudski's authority. Until that moment his powers as Head of State and Commander-in-Chief were virtually limitless.

Meanwhile Poland's military situation worsened day by day. The glory of gaining Kiev melted away suddenly, especially as all attempts at halting the Red Army ended in failure. Piłsudski's eastern policy, embodied in the expedition to Kiev, no longer met with popular support. The majority no longer understood why Polish blood was being spilt in the Ukraine or why Soviet peace proposals had been rejected. Polish successes in the first period of the campaign had undoubtedly led to the growth of Piłsudski's popularity and to an extension of political credit to him by a wide public. However the events of June and July not only exposed the illusory nature of Piłsudski's plans but also showed his actions as a threat to the very existence of Poland.

Discontent grew equally fast in the army. Experienced and well-trained officers bridled at Piłsudski's style of leadership, so full of wasteful contradictions and harmful personal intrigues. While Piłsudski was successful, these feelings had little significance, but as he was forced onto the defensive more and more military subordinates started to ask whether or not they were the victims of their Commander-in-Chief's dilettantism.

On 24 July the Council of National Defence formed a coalition government with Wincenty Witos (leader of the Peasant Party) at its head and (Socialist) Ignacy Daszyński as vice-premier. It was supported by all parliamentary parties, from the *Endecja* on the right to the PPS on the left. Two days earlier the government which had been replaced had turned to the Soviet government with a proposal for a ceasefire.

On 30 July, Białystok, which had come under Red Army occupation, witnessed the emergence of a 'Provisional Revolutionary Committee of Poland', formed by activists of the Polish Bureau of the Central Committee of the Russian Communist Party (Bolsheviks). It included Julian Marchlewski, Edward Próchniak, Feliks Dzierżyński, Feliks Kon and Józef Unszlicht and commenced its work immediately by organizing a local administration.

From the beginning of August Soviet detachments crossed the Bug. The war now entered ethnic Poland. This caused a marked shift in public opinion. The threat to Polish independence drew everyone together. The government cry, 'Fatherland under threat' quickly produced wide support.

During the first days of September a plan for a counter-offensive was hatched. Various possibilities existed. First, to regroup around Modlin and Płońsk for an attack in the north-east, which would mean engaging with the strongest concentration of the Red Army. Second, an offensive from the locality of Karczew along the Warsaw-Mińsk Mazowiecki highway with the aim of relieving the defence of Warsaw. Third, to launch an attack at the junction between the northern and southern Soviet fronts, thus creating a strategic threat which would force the enemy's armies to retreat.

Piłsudski opted for the third plan of action. It promised the greatest prize but carried the greatest risks. So much depended on being able to amass an adequate force for the attack in good time. Since there were no reserves this would inevitably weaken other sectors of the front. Much also depended on maintaining the defence of Warsaw. Enemy forces were already in evidence in the capital's hinterland and if this infiltration continued, Warsaw would stand little chance of holding out for any length of time. Equally important was the ability of General Władysław Sikorski's army, positioned to the south of Warsaw, to undertake offensive actions against the main strength of Mikhail Tukachevsky's forces. Failure in any one sector would upset the whole plan and this would mean military catastrophe.

On 6 August Piłsudski ordered the first manoeuvres for the battle ahead. The choice of date was not accidental. On this day, six summers ago, a cadre company had marched out of Kraków's oleander groves thus initiating Polish involvement in the Great War. This was a symbolic date and Piłsudski had a feeling for symbols. He also believed in lucky dates.

The re-grouping of forces had commenced. On 12 August Piłsudski left Warsaw for Puław, where he took command over the formation of the attacking group. Before he left, Piłsudski explained to Witos that he felt responsible for Poland's predicament and could not bring himself to agree to talks with Soviet Russia. He even spoke of resigning as Head of State and Commander-in-Chief.

On 14 August Sikorski attacked from the region of Modlin in the direction of Nasielsk and Pułtusk and on 16 August the Polish offensive across the river Wieprz commenced. It encountered little resistance. On 17 August the Red Army started its retreat. Two days later Polish armies occupied Brześc-on-Bug followed by Łomża. On 25 August Piłsudski successfully held off a Soviet counter-offensive along the line running west from Grodno through Białowieze and along the length of the Bug. At the end of August a new Polish offensive began. It resulted in the occupation of Grodno, Lida, Slonim and Pinsk. On the south it reached the line of the river Zbrucz.

From 17 August, 1920, Polish-Soviet negotiations commenced in Mińsk. These ended on 2 September, when the decision was taken to continue them in Riga, where the two delegations met on 21 September. The Polish team was headed by Jan Dąbski. The Soviets by Adolf Joffe.

While these talks progressed, the Wilno affair, an indirect consequence of the 1920 war, blew up. Seeking the support of the Entente at the lowest point in Poland's fortunes, the Polish government had earlier agreed to return Wilno to Lithuania. Soon after this decision had been taken Lithuania broke the peace treaty it had made with Soviet Russia in which the independence of Lithuania with Wilno as its capital was recognized. Then, at the beginning of August, retreating Soviet detachments handed Wilno back to Lithuanian control.

Piłsudski, however, simply could not leave it at that. Not only from the point of view of personal sentiment and ties of feeling, which undoubtedly played an important role in explaining his actions, but also for political reasons. If he wished to remain as leader he could not afford to allow the public to see failure at Kiev repeated in the loss of Wilno, a juxtaposition made by the political press of his opponents. Indeed, Piłsudski had already, in the second half of August, started making preparations for the occupation of Wilno. This had to be done by subterfuge because such action could not have been formally sanctioned. A pretext had to be found. A 'rebellion' would be staged among troops from the region wanting to rid Wilno of Lithuanian and Bolshevik control.

General Lucjan Żeligowski was given the leading role in this action. He had at his disposal around 14,000 soldiers, most of whom were from the area. They were to be reinforced by around 65,000 soldiers of the second and third armies.

Piłsudski told him that, after its conquest, Wilno and its region would come under the authority of a Provisional Governing Commission which was to control a territory to be designated Central Lithuania. This new name for the ancient land of historic Lithuania signalled a renewed commitment to the federal principle. Central Lithuania together with ethnic Lithuania (with its capital in Kaunas) and Byelorussian Lithuania (with its capital in Mińsk) was to comprise a tripartite state tied in with Poland. This hope was equally as unrealistic as other Polish federal concepts.

At daybreak on 8 October Żeligowski's divisions began their march on Wilno. On entering the city in the early hours of the following afternoon these 'rebels' were greeted with great joy by the populace. Żeligowski, who had had misgivings about Piłsudski's scheme immediately asked to be released from service in the Polish army.

Three days after the occupation of Wilno, a preliminary peace treaty between Poland and the Soviet Union was signed at Riga. It marked the end of a war that had started in February 1919. The final peace treaty, whose clauses differed little from those of the preliminary peace treaty, was signed in March 1921.

Piłsudski's conception of the shape of the eastern boundaries of the state, his eastern policy, was completely defeated. Even the construction of a Polish-Lithuanian federation proved a non starter. Contrary to expectations after the occupation of Wilno, relations between the two nations steadily worsened to a state of enmity. In the Ukraine, the idea of forming a state subject to Poland, burst like a soap bubble in the aftermath of the Kiev expedition. Piłsudski's hopes of drawing together the Baltic republics and Lithuania, in an anti-Soviet coalition, also foundered as did the hopes he had in the success of separatist bourgeois movements wishing to restore the nations of the former Romanov Empire. Piłsudski's intention to form a system of bourgeois nations around Russia was not to be realized.

This was an anachronistic concept, indicating a lack of understanding of social mechanics. It was born on the threshold of the 20th century, under the influence of the outburst of national consciousness in Central and Eastern Europe during the last decade of the 19th century. These processes were rather tightly bound up, though not always in a clearly visible manner, with the development of class consciousness in the masses and the shaping of programmes of social reform. The experience of the revolutionary period, 1905–1907, should have illustrated this well enough to Piłsudski. But it did so in part only.

The weakness of the revolutionary movement in Poland at the moment of statehood and the mobilizing effects of nationalistic slogans convinced Piłsudski of the possibility of countering calls for social reform by use of such slogans. Piłsudski did not value the great example of the Russian revolution, which linked a social programme with a programme of national self-determination. In constructing his plans, he operated in categories of thought typical of the ideas of the 19th-century concepts of the intelligentsia. The October Revolution had ploughed up the consciousness of the masses. It had created a new situation, which Piłsudski did not understand, and that is why he had to lose.

Poland paid a high price for Piłsudski's eastern policy, not only in the unnecessary shedding of blood and in war damage. Poland also lost any chance of friendship with the Entente and she forfeited territory in the west. Unable, because of commitments in the east, to help the rising in Silesia, Poland lost the plebiscite on the future of these lands. By the same token Poland's engagement in eastern affairs was not without influence on the plebiscites in Warmia and Mazuria.

The Riga peace treaty terms gave Poland eastern territories smaller than those proposed to her in 1919 by the Soviet government. Events in years to come showed that, regardless of which political coalition exercised authority, Poland was unable to establish good relations with either Byelorussians or Ukrainians living in its eastern territories. Constant conflict with this population attained the proportions of civil war which was a significant factor in weakening the Polish state.

As soon as the Polish-Soviet war had ended, Piłsudski was confronted by internal political and economic questions and he had no economic policy. Economic problems were alien to him. He did not understand them but rather made light of them. According to him, the capitalist system of private ownership and laws governing the market should operate independently of the state. Further measures were not called for and were indeed dangerous. Strange policy indeed for one whose youth had been shaped by the socialist movement.

Piłsudski also lacked internal political policy with respect to the complicated question of the national minorities and concerning the burning question of agrarian reform. He was also undecided about his own role within the state. The formula, arrived at in November 1918, whereby Piłsudski (as Head of State) would be above party politics and independent of the military did not work out in practice.

Undoubtedly he had made a success of organizing the army, but even this achievement was flawed. The generals, whom Piłsudski was unable to control politically, were not a well-integrated group. The officer corps presented a better case but here too there were problems. Generally speaking, Piłsudski was unable to mould the army politically.

This was important, in so far as having lost the means of exerting control through the army, Piłsudski emerged as a politician lacking an adequate political base. The Belvedere camp, loyal to the Commander, did exert great influence in such important aspects of state life as the military and foreign policy. But it was, at most, rather a small group. The Belvedere camp comprised only the PPS, PSL-Freedom (*Wyzwolenie*) and small groups within the intelligentsia. Activists of these parties provided him with only limited means of control. Exploiting them skilfully, Piłsudski nevertheless exercised care to remain independent of their parties rather than give his position clear political definition.

When attempts were made to form a broader base, it was always with reference to the tradition of the Legion. In Poland the ending of the war gave rise to the question of what to do with troops being stood down? The problem had arisen, but on a much smaller scale, in 1918. Now, the demobilization following the end of the Polish-Soviet war witnessed thousands of men lost in the unfamiliar circumstances of peace. Legionnaires were least able to adapt themselves to the new conditions. This was because the majority had been recruited from among the young intelligentsia. After nearly seven years spent in trenches, with their education curtailed, they were ill-suited to civilian life. There was no place for them in society. When the state was being formed and its administrative apparatus being staffed, they found themselves at the front. Returning, in glory, to civilian life, it soon became apparent to them that they were not needed by anyone, that their fate was a matter of indifference to their countrymen. This gave rise to intense frustration, to feelings of victimization and alienation. There were other, no less significant problems. In the Legions, and later in the army, these men had lost the habit of independent thought and the ability to take political decisions. ' "The Commander" knows best', was a formula which allowed them to survive one crisis after another, to navigate the meanderings of Legion politics and, later, of politics in the army.

After demobilization they stood helpless in the face of bewildering social and political problems; abandoned by 'the Commander' they had to find answers to dozens of questions hurled at them by an incomprehensible reality. Yet these frustrated, disappointed legionnaires, represented a large pool of political strength. Though bitter in their feelings toward Piłsudski for having abandoned them, they were, in the main still loyal to him and to the memory of war. Even those who had somehow settled back into civilian life held in their mind's-eye a vision of the war ever more beautiful and bright against the drab backcloth of their unfolding everyday life.

The relatively few legionnaires, some 20 per cent, who continued to serve in the army, could also be included as potential supporters of the Belvedere camp. The membership of this dynamic non-party formation naturally belonged to various political parties and groupings. The majority recognized the authority of the Commander without reservation; they were used to hierarchical forms of subordination. They had everything to gain, little to lose. The ambiguous ideology of independence, which helped to cement the Belvedere camp together, was easily transformed into an ideology, equally unclear and ill-defined, of the state. It addressed itself less to the intellect and more to the emotions.

Piłsudski's decision to find support among groups of legionnaires should be recognized as a logical consequence of the way the situation had developed for him. Wishing, as he did, to continue to play the dominant role, or even a shared role in the state, he had to adapt his behaviour to prevailing circumstances.

(The constitution of the Second Polish Republic was finally adopted on 17 March 1921. Modelled closely on the French system, real power lay with the legislature made up of a Sejm (lower house) and a Senate. Of the two the Sejm was vastly more powerful. The president, as titular Head of State, had the right to appoint the government but not to dissolve parliament. In this way Dmowski's National Democrats hoped to insure themselves against Piłsudski if he became president after the forthcoming elections, in 1922. The *Endecja* dominated the right in the spectrum of Polish politics. Theirs was basically a middle-class party, supported by white-collar workers and much of the intelligentsia – the dominant urban class. In the elections of 1921 and 1922 the party formed joint lists with the Christian National Party of Labour. This Catholic party gradually freed itself from dependence on the *Endecja* and in 1925 changed its name to the Christian Democratic Party (*Chadecja*). In the Centre was the Piast party, (PSL-*Piast*) led by Wincenty Witos and supported, in the main, by well-to-do peasants. On the left was the Liberation Peasant Party (*Wyzwolenie*), (PSL-Freedom) and the Polish Socialist Party (*Polska Partia Socjalistyczna*), PPS. On the extreme left was the Communist Party of Poland, [*Komunistyczna Partia Polski* (KPP). Ed.]).

Under the new constitution, the constrained role of the president did not give Piłsudski much scope for action. Nor, given the composition of the political spectrum, could he attempt to gain a majority in the *Sejm*. He could however undertake to try to create an extra-parliamentary political force. A legion-based group could constitute such a force which would give Piłsudski influence within the army, as well as in different areas of civilian life.

In 1922 it was possible to observe certain moves of the Belvedere camp which add up to make a logical whole. Firstly there was the publication of a weekly, *Głos* (Voice) and a monthly *Droga* (The Way) whose purpose was to exercise the ideological programme of this camp. Then, between 5–8 August 1922, in Kraków, a convention of legionnaires took place. Over 2500 attended, perhaps not so many in comparison with the overall number of those who went into the Legions, but one should remember that this was only the beginning of the formation of a political group which was based on a widely felt sense of solidarity, one which overrode the differences of the past.

Undoubtedly too, the shaping of the idea of creating a political base out of a Legion group, was influenced by the success of Italian fascism; the March on Rome, in 1922, gave a realistic perspective of how power could be gained through the efforts of a movement of former combatants.

In November, the elections to the Sejm and Senate took place. Compared to the constitutional Sejm a marked change had occurred in the political composition of the new parliament. The central groupings, dominant in the constitutional Sejm, lost 24 per cent of their seats, mainly to the parties of the national minorities which gained over 16 per cent of the seats, making up one fifth of the Sejm's composition. The parties of the left increased their seats by 5.5 per cent. The right gained the least with a 3.2 per cent increase in seats. By remaining in coalition with the *Chadecja*, it held 38 per cent of the seats. However, even taking into account the political defeat of the centre and left, this was however too little to form a parliamentary majority. That is why the *Endecja* placed such emphasis on winning the support of PSL-*Piast*.

To Witos, its leader, the alliance with the right seemed equally promising. The alternative for him could only have been an alliance with PSL-Liberation and PPS. But this coalition would still have been 14 per cent short of a majority. In any case, an understanding with PSL-Liberation was neither easy nor pleasant for Witos.

The alliance between the right and Witos became apparent during the election of the Marshals for both houses of Parliament when it secured Maciej Rataj as Marshal of the Sejm and Wojciech Trąmpczyński as Marshal of the Senate. However, when it came to the election of

President, *Endeks* and *Piasts* parted company. PSL-*Piast*, together with the PPS, PSL-Liberation and NPR, declared themselves for the candidature of Piłsudski. But the Head of State did not intend to stand for election as President. On 4 December he explained his decision to a mixed audience of ministers and members of both houses: the powers of the president were rather limited and his dependence upon the government rather great.

Taking note of Piłsudski's decision, which mainly satisfied the *Endecja*, both chambers of parliament came together as a National Convention on 9 December to choose the President. At the fifth vote Gabriel Narutowicz was elected. He had gained 62 votes more than the candidate of the right, Count Maurycy Zamoyski.

Shocked by the result, the right immediately started a bitter and intense political campaign against Narutowicz. This was not only a reaction against the defeat at the forum of the National Convention, but equally and perhaps mainly, out of fear for the future. It was determined that the majority which chose Narutowicz should not last long. If this momentary coalition of the left, the national minorities and some sections of the centre were to be perpetuated, then the political aspirations of the *Endecja* would become seriously threatened.

The campaign conducted against Narutowicz was no less intense after he took the oath as President. The right believed that there would still be a chance to force him to stand down if a government were not formed. This was a very real possibility in as much as the majority which had ensured Narutowiz's selection was of a temporary nature which was exactly why the right had started their campaign against Narutowicz in the first place. Newspapers carried articles increasingly critical of the President. Agitation in the streets was spread by word of mouth in terms which appealed to the instincts of the gutter. Prejudice and xenophobia ran amock. Narutowicz was accused of being a stranger for having spent long periods of his life in Switzerland and of being an unbeliever because of his liberal attitude towards religion, that is, of lacking commitment to the teachings of the Church. Throughout the campaign against him he was accused incessantly of having been imposed on Poland by the vote of the national minorities.

This seed bore fruit. On Saturday, 16 December (1922) Narutowicz returned the visit of Cardinal Kakowski before appearing at the opening of an art exhibition. He arrived there a few minutes after midday. As he was viewing one of the paintings three pistol shots rang out in quick succession. The President slumped to the ground. He died without regaining consciousness. The shots from the gun held by Eligiusz Niewiadomski had found their mark. The assassin was an amateur painter, a state official and a former member of the National League. He was acting independently, but the moral responsibility for this crime weighed heavily on the right.

In the course of the next few hours the future of the country lay in the balance. In accordance with the constitution, Maciej Rataj, Marshal of the Sejm, took on the mantle of President. Later that evening he formed a new Cabinet headed by Władysław Sikorski. Piłsudski, who would have been the assassin's victim had he stood for and gained the presidency, was appointed Chief of General Staff. His supporters immediately took advantage of the political crisis and of the explosion of anger among the masses against the right. Bogusław Miedziński, one of Piłsudski's closest collaborators, tells us that during the evening of that fateful day Ignacy Matuszewski, Adam Koc, Konrad Libicki, Władysław Włoskowicz, Ignacy Boerner, Kazimierz Stamirowski, and Henryk Floyar-Raychman all gathered at the headquarters of the General Staff. They dispatched trusted officers to the Ministry of Internal Affairs and police headquarters to await further orders. Because government had ceased to function nobody intervened to question the purpose let alone the propriety of these activities. What was being prepared, in agreement with the director of the Warsaw organization of the PPS, Rajmund Jaworowski, was 'a punitive action' against the right. This was a plot to liquidate selected activists of the 'national camp' and in its wake to bring in Piłsudski, at the head of the army, to restore law and order 24 hours later.

The infiltration of state institutions by Piłsudskiites on the night of 16–17 December and the preparation for a 'spontaneous' mass protest aimed at taking power. This would have been achieved at a moment when a large section of public opinion was in a state of shock over the murder of the President and even those who had submitted to the right-wing gutter propaganda would soon have regained their senses. Niewiadomski's repugnant plot was incompatible with Poland's entire political tradition. But these dozen or so hours would have been enough for a severe blow to have been struck. Piłsudski would have been in the process of restoring order with the help of the army and the perpetrators would have vanished under this cover. Piłsudski would have been seen as the one who saved the country from anarchy and the threat of civil war.

But the plot failed for two important reasons, firstly because Daszyński, the leader of the PPS, took a strong line against those members of the party who intended to participate and secondly because the plotters had failed to organize the means of carrying it out. Its true to say that even before the plot was first mooted, Piłsudskiites were taken aback by the course of events and were quite unprepared for them. They did not anticipate that the campaign against Narutowicz would end in murder, so they did not have a ready made plan of action for such an occurrence. This meant that they had to improvize. They infiltrated some national institutions, but that was not enough. Further moves required organized squads and the Piłsudskiites neither had these at their disposal nor had sufficient time to form them. They counted on the PPS, but Daszyński's decisive position ruled out such support. Moreover, there was lack of leadership. Piłsudski's role, which had been allocated and defined for him by the plotters, automatically eliminated him from active participation in the first stages of a *coup d'état*. Perhaps the news of Sikorski's premiership also contributed to the decision, taken during the night 16–17 December, not to go ahead with the plot.

Relations between Sikorski and Piłsudski were still good at this time. What is more, by giving the military portfolio to Kazimierz Sosnkowski and by agreeing to the appointment of Piłsudski as Chief of General Staff, Sikorski ensured that representatives of the Legion group were in key positions. Although Sikorski could in no sense be regarded to have belonged to the Piłsudskiites, they did rather well in the circumstances. They had been too slow off the mark. But they knew that on another occasion, at a moment of political impotence at the centre with crowds again out in the streets, the entry of Piłsudski onto the political stage, at the head of the army and hailed as the nation's saviour, could still be staged.

Sikorski showed himself to be an energetic prime minister. He convinced Rataj that it was necessary to introduce a state of emergency and, as his first official function, declared that if peace did not return to public life he would use the army without distinguishing between guilty and innocent. This bore a clear message for Piłsudskiites. As for the right, it did not intend to undertake any action. Above all else it wanted a return to normality, a state of affairs best embodied in Stanisław Stroński's article (in the right-wing *Rzeczpospolita*, a daily he had founded with Paderewski in 1920) entitled, 'Pray silence over the coffin'.

A National Convention was called by Rataj for 20 December; a president to be chosen once again. In the first ballot Stanisław Wojciehowski easily gained the required majority with 293 votes, against 221 for Kazimierz Morawski the candidate of the right. Wojciechowski was supported by the same parties, including the national minorities, as had voted for Narutowicz. When the results of the elections were eventually declared a shout addressed to the right came from the benches of the left: 'When will you kill him?'.

The right, however, now saw its chance of gaining power by a coalition with PSL-Piast. After the dramatic happenings of December, Witos displayed a very much stronger tendency to compromise with the right. He became convinced that the left was weak and that Piłsudski was too indecisive, all of which dissuaded him from seeking allies here. He also realized all too well the value that his party could be to the right, a value that had, after all, been significantly realized in the election of Rataj as Marshal of the Sejm and the election of Wojciechowski as President. However, as to further deals with the right, Witos was not in a hurry. He held back in order to raise his price, believing that the road for political advantage lay clear ahead.

Piłsudski, much less certain of how to proceed, kept silent. Wojcie-chowski's election had unsettled him. The President had been a close friend, a quarter of a century earlier, when together they had published *Robotnik* and directed the activities of the PPS. (See above.) Later they went their separate ways and the knots of friendship became undone. Wojciechowski became Minister of Interior Affairs in Skulski's cabinet. Contact with Piłsudski was renewed but the political differences between the two former friends were also revealed. Piłsudski had supported the candidature of Wojciechowski for the presidency and this clearly made room for collaboration. But did Wojciechowski want to involve himself in Piłsudski's struggle for power? Much depended for Piłsudski on a positive answer to this question. For the moment, however, Piłsudski had rather limited possibilities of political action. He had to wait on events.

The days of Sikorski's cabinet were numbered from the beginning. He could exist only as long as negotiations continued between the right and *Piast*. Though not in a hurry to strike a deal, Witos could not drag them out too long. The negotiations were nevertheless difficult because both sides had to make rather fundamental concessions. The peasant parties had to accept worse terms on agricultural reform than had been suggested by the agreement of July 1920. Yet they could take some consolation in the thought that it was better to have a more limited reform realized, than a better one left on paper. For its part, the right, whose clientele in great measure were landowners, had to agree some aspects of agrarian reform. This was not easy but was a price which had to be paid for an alliance with *Piast*. Negotiations dragged on but by the end of April a compromise was worked out. Opposition within the right meant that the eventual signing of the agreement was delayed to the second half of May.

On 24 May in the debate over the provisional budget, a proposal to cut out additional funding for the premier's office and for the Ministry of Foreign Affairs was carried. The government offered to resign, and President Wojciechowski entrusted Witos with the task of forming a new cabinet.

On the day Witos' cabinet was announced, Piłsudski moved out of his official residence to a villa in Sulejowek, a suburb of Warsaw. Two days later he resigned from the position of Chief of General Staff, but kept the chairmanship of the Inner War Council.

This body had been formed by presidential decree on 7 January 1921 and was to be responsible for the direction of military policy at the highest level. It was concerned with matters to do with preparation of operational war plans. Thus the decisions of the Inner War Council were binding upon the Minister for Military Affairs, who was in fact designated its vice-chairman. The Inner War Council's brief gave it the right to decide on all military matters; almost everything could be subsumed under the heading of 'war preparations'. The council not only overshadowed the Ministry of Military affairs but was independent of the government and, in consequence, of parliament. This was contrary to the spirit of the March Constitution and to the fundamental principles of the parliamentary system.

Clearly, there now arose the need to draft new regulations concerning the organization of the nation's highest military authorities. Correctly anticipating that it would lead to conflict with Piłsudski, neither Sikorski as premier, nor Sosnkowski as Minister of Military Affairs wished to undertake this matter. But Witos' cabinet had to undertake the task sooner or later. It could not tolerate Piłsudski in his position as chairman of the Inner War Council. Piłsudski was well aware of the government's feelings. At a press conference summoned on 24 June he said that he intended to remain chairman of the Inner War Council until the current visit of the King and Queen of Roumania was over. He also said that changes had to be made at the top of the military structure, but did not elaborate the point.

During June the work of the cabinet was taken up with the Roumanian visit. At the same time the Polish mark collapsed. In the course of the month its value fell from 52,000 to 104,000 to the dollar. Although the fall was halted by the end of the month, currency reserves were completely exhausted and the future looked bleak indeed. Social unrest expressed itself in strike actions as the economic decline worsened. The political atmosphere thickened. The right, numerically the most powerful force in Polish politics, though riven with splits, was inspired by Italy's example. Mussolini also impressed the Piłsudskiites.

On 2 July Piłsudski relinquished the chairmanship of the Inner War Council. Officially, he now retained only the chancellorship of the chapter of the order of the *virtuti militari*, Poland's highest order of military merit. This was not simply an honorary function. To Piłsudski it gave a realistic pretext to widen his personal contacts in the army. These could prove useful to him in the future.

The following day a banquet organized in honour of Piłsudski by a group of his associates was held in Warsaw's prestigious Hotel Bristol. In the course of the evening Piłsudski made a speech. He spoke of the rebirth of the nation and the attainment of its moral ripeness in the Polish State. He spoke of his own achievements and of the unanimity with which the Sejm offered him the leadership of the state. Then he sounded off against the *Endecja*:

> I was set on high, set higher than anyone in the past had ever been. So set I stood in the light. But there were shadows which ran around me, racing ahead and behind. These ever present shadows were many, and unavoidable, walking in step with me (whilst) mimicking and mocking me. Whether on the field of battle, or peaceful at work at the Belvedere or stroking a child – there was always one shadow that would not go away, that chased me and teased me. Spit-soiled, dreadful, bandy-legged gnome, expectorating its dirty soul, be-spitting me from all sides, unwilling to leave unscathed any of the sacred things which should have been spared – family, relationships, or people close to me, investigating my steps, making ape-like grimaces, turning every thought upside down; this terrible gnome dragged after me like an inseparable companion, dressed in flags of various types and colours – now foreign, now not, shouting slogans . . . dreaming up impossible stories; this gnome was my inseparable companion, in victory and in defeat.

There could be no doubt that the 'spit-soiled gnome' was the *Endecja* when Piłsudski continued with the following fragment, dedicated to Narutowicz, from the same speech:

> This gang, this band, which questioned my honour, was out for blood. Our President was murdered in what amounted to a street brawl, by these same people who had once showed similar base hatred towards the (country's) first (head of state) . . . they committed a crime. Murder is punished by law. Gentlemen, I am a soldier. A soldier is called upon to attend to difficult duties, often in contradiction with his conscience, with his thoughts, with dearly-held feelings. For a moment I believed that I should, as a soldier, have to defend those gentlemen . . . and my conscience wavered. Having wavered once, I decided that I could no longer be a soldier. I submitted my resignation from the army. These, gentlemen, are the causes and motives, behind my departure from the service of the State.

The next day the speech was reported in *Kurier Poranny* (The Morning Courier). It was the first time that Piłsudski had come out so violently and so publicly against the *Endecja*. In submitting his resignation when Witos came to power, earlier, he had made an obvious point. But up to the time of his speech it was not clear what Piłsudski intended to do. His silence in the days after the murder of Narutowicz seemed to suggest that he had personally withdrawn from the struggle for power. Indeed his five months as Chief of General Staff, during which time he undertook no obvious political activities, would appear to confirm this conclusion. But the speech at the Hotel Bristol revealed all. Piłsudski had to do political battle with the *Endecja* to break the coalition between Dmowski and Witos; the longer this lasted the less likely it was that Piłsudskiites would gain power. Smashing the coalition meant modification to the political formula hitherto held by Piłsudski. This had placed him above party politics and distanced him from party battles. Doing battle with the *Endecja* negated this formula, but only in a particular sense. Piłsudski did not come out as a worker of any party. He was not fighting the *Endecja* because it was right-wing, or because it represented this or that political programme. No. He took on a fight with (as he saw them) the degenerates of political life whose symbol was the *Endecja*. The battle was over moral purity, over the ethics of political life. And in this sense the formula of apoliticality, remaining over and above party politics, was adhered to.

This high ethical ground was a satisfactory battlefield for a number of reasons. First of all it released Piłsudski from the necessity of presenting his own personal political programme. He did not have to propose solutions to the complicated questions of the economy, the national minorities or foreign policy, to which neither he nor his advisers had the answers. But it was not only this. Each political problem defined its own limits of possible alliances. By transferring the fight to an ethical plane, Piłsudski increased the number of allies enormously.

The new approach to politics was really very accommodating. It allowed easy identification of the opponent. At that moment it was the *Endecja*, but it could equally be the parliamentary system itself, which, as the Piłsudskiites believed, inevitably led to the degradation of political life. Moreover, this plan of battle appealed to the emotions, to the noblest and highest feelings. In the contest for power by parliamentary methods this formula was unusable, but if it was a question of wanting to attain power by extra-parliamentary means . . .

CHAPTER SIX

The Recluse

Piłsudski had two ways of conducting the struggle for power from his homebase of Sulejówek, to which he had retreated, on the outskirts of Warsaw. Bearing in mind the instability of coalition politics in the Sejm he could try to undermine the parliamentary system through either a political or a military coup, which need not be mutually exclusive. Possibilities included Piłsudski's returning to public life at the head of the army after an outburst of mass discontent (as had occurred after the murder of Narutowicz) or a *coup* in anticipation of, or as counter to, similar action by the right wing. The justification in either case would be 'action to protect the Motherland'.

The political atmosphere thickened. The autumn of 1923 witnessed a sudden collapse of business confidence. Inflation, which had had a beneficial influence on the economy now rocketed away on a steep curve of hyper-inflation which threatened economic survival as the internal and external markets collapsed. In October panic broke out on the Stock Exchange. In the course of five days the official dollar exchange rate went from 350,000 to 500,000 zł. On the streets one dollar exchanged for 1,400,000 zł. Prices in the shops rose by between 10 and 20 per cent a day. (In an effort to stabilize the situation a new central bank, *Bank Polski*, was established in April 1924. This took control of the new unit of currency, the złoty, which replaced the Polish mark.)

At 9 on the morning of 13 October an explosion ripped through the arsenal in the Warsaw Citadel. Twenty-five were killed and around 40 seriously wounded. A government statement said that a coup had been attempted by 'criminal elements'. A wave of arrests followed. It was later confirmed that the explosion was a tragic accident, but, in the political climate of those weeks not many believed in accidents.

A note in Rataj's diary for 25 September sheds some light on the crisis:

> ... evening visit to Witos. I pointed out to him that the government had lost touch with the people and that relations between government and opposition had collapsed. This encouraged the spread of rumours that the government was contemplating a *coup d'état*. This only needlessly enlarged the opposition to it ... Witos tried to defend himself, but eventually admitted to the truth and promised to change methods. Thugutt had been to see him today and, in all seriousness asked, if he should attach any weight to rumours about a *coup*, declaring, on oath, that neither he, nor his

> party would support a *coup*. Witos further enlightened me that Polish fascists, among whom were some 'very important people' had also been to see him today. They told him that they (80,000!) were prepared to intervene against a left wing coup, but that they would only act in response to a call from cabinet . . .

This *vignette* exactly reflected the political climate of those weeks. Would it have been conceivable, in normal circumstances, that the head of an opposition group or club should come to the premier to ask if he was preparing a coup d'état and that the premier should entertain delegates of a secret organization and conduct talks with them? Let us also add that one of the fascist representatives who had talked to Witos was Jan Pękosławski. He was a founder member of an organization, which considered itself a 'political emergency service', called Polish Patriots at the Ready (*Pogotowie Patriotów Polskich* – PPP). The PPP was actively preparing a fascist *coup d'état*. Its military organization, numbering not 80,000 but not quite 800 persons, was led by Witold Gorczyński. It was he who had informed General Szeptycki of the aims of the organization. A later investigation also revealed that six generals and some dozens of officers belonged to the PPP. Though of course the details of its composition and aims were not known, the existence of this organization was a public secret. It was symptomatic of the prevailing situation that when Pękosławski and Gorczyński conducted talks with members of the cabinet far from being thrown out of doors, they were listened to with attention and not without sympathy.

The autumn of 1923 also witnessed considerable shifts within in the Polish revolutionary movement. Between 19 September and 9 October the Second Congress of the Communist Polish Workers' Party took place in Bolszewo, near Moscow. Forty delegates attended. Previous conferences, in February 1921 and May 1922 had marked important stages in the evolution of the party's programme. The realization that there would be no revolution in re-born Poland meant that the party was willing to contest the elections. Agrarian reform and a united front policy, seeking partnership primarily with the PPS, were also advocated. However, many within the party now felt that such initiatives were wrong. The Second Congress took place at a moment when it seemed that the revolutionary wave in Europe was about to break again. News came of a peoples' rising in Bulgaria and although it was quickly put down the actual fact of the outbreak gave weight to the belief that Europe, especially Germany, was on the threshold of revolution. Certainly events in Poland during the autumn of 1923 appeared to suggest that the capitalist system was on the brink of disaster. Hyperinflation and a chaotic economy hit painfully at working people. The government was not able to offer any convincing way out of this situation. It appeared that it had entirely lost control. Witos's statement to a delegation of civil servants to the effect that 'tomorrow will be worse than today' confirmed this view and spread quickly to further startle public opinion.

When, on 27 October, a major cabinet reshuffle (in favour of the right) was announced, (Wojciech Korfanty was nominated vice-premier, Roman Dmowski took foreign affairs, Andrzej Chłapowski labour and Władysław Grabski education) a section of that public opinion read into these moves preparation for a right-wing *coup d'état*. That the government would dismiss parliament and bring in dictatorship was seriously taken into consideration. Social tension mounted as strikes flared up around the country. One diarist noted: '22 October. Outbreak of strike action by railway engineers in Kraków. The miners strike continues . . . 25 October. Strike in Łódź. 26 October. Postal strike in Kraków . . .'.

The new cabinet decided to break the strike movement by force; it opted for power politics, for the politics of the iron fist. On 1 November the railways were placed under military authority and railwaymen were drafted into military service. Those refusing to obey the call up were to be treated as deserters.

Militarization can be seen as an effective method of defeating a strike, but only if the government is resolute enough to retain sufficient control to prevent the growth of workers' solidarity. It has to recognize that workers' organizations, in almost every case without regard to their political provenance, will do everything to force the removal of martial law. Their most effective weapon in this situation is the proclamation of a general strike. But the great risk, especially to the political standing of worker's parties, is that a general strike could turn into a fiasco. Politics is a game in which the players try never to show their cards. A general strike reveals attitudes and is a test of resolve. If it holds, the government has little option but to step down. But if the masses do not rise in its support, the government wins and consolidates its position. Thus workers' parties approach this form of battle with great circumspection. In this case, the PPS reply to government was to call for a general strike.

In cabinet, opinion divided over what to do next. Roman Dmowski, Wojciech Korfanty and Władysław Kiernik represented the hard line. Maciej Rataj, who was to play a very significant role in the events of the next few days, was an opponent of confrontation and an advocate of negotiations with the PPS. Wincenty Witos inclined towards the same.

Parties in opposition to government were also undecided on how to proceed. Communists, yet again convinced that the course of events would lead to revolution, tried to push the masses down this particular road. For their part, leaders of the PPS mistrusted the communists, feared a right-wing coup and suspected a take over by Piłsudskiites. Their other conviction, that Witos, leader of the *Piast* Peasant Party, was intent on a *coup* underlined their lack of faith in parliamentary democracy in Poland.

The general strike began on Monday 5 November. From the early hours of that morning alarming news from Kraków flowed into the Praesidium of the Council of Ministers. The strike in Kraków was universally supported and threatened total disruption. Crowds filled the streets. Spontaneous demonstrations and rallies were everywhere in evidence. Kiernik issued police orders to disperse the crowds and sanctioned the use of army in case of need. Clashes broke out. There were wounded on both sides. The cabinet met in continuous session with information arriving that Piłsudskiites were active in Kraków and that the local authorities appeared to be losing control of the situation in parts of the city. Early the next day the cabinet was told that police in Kraków had been issued with live ammunition and that a new and bloodier confrontation seemed inevitable. Demands for an immediate withdrawal of police and army from the streets of Kraków were ignored. It was also too late for meaningful negotiations. The crowd around the Trades' Unions headquarters in Kraków broke through the police cordon and was shot at. Several fell dead. The first sacrifices had been made.

To cries of 'Long live Piłsudski' and 'Down with Witos', two companies of the 16th infantry regiment were disarmed by a nearby crowd and workers commandeered the arms. A cavalry charge by *ulans* of the 8th regiment broke up in disarray as horses fell on pavements made slippery by water being poured over them. Workers at the market captured an armoured car. Rumours circulated that Piłsudski was on his way to Kraków and there were more cries in his support, cries too of 'long live the people's government'. A considerable section of the city was no longer in the control of police and army. An armed workers militia was in the process of being formed and there were dead and wounded on both sides.

The government in Warsaw was particularly worried by the fact that units of the army had allowed themselves to be disarmed and had fraternized with the workers. There was news too of similar occurrences, though on a smaller scale, in Tarnów and Borisław. But the reliability of intelligence reaching both government and opposition is a moot point. There was a very limited number of channels for this information all of which was mediated on its way to the centre by subjective opinion. Evidence of how the army felt was invariably biased since it was passed on by those who bore direct responsibility for the men. Ignorance of what was happening in sections of towns taken over by workers also affected judgements.

In sum, though the flow of information to the centre was vast it was insufficiently substantial to give the government an adequate picture of the dynamics of the crisis. And the question remained, what further measures should be taken to restore order? The government could continue with the politics of confrontation and attempt to break resistance without regard to the cost of life. Or it could seek political solutions by moving away from confrontation and towards compromise. The choice was reflected in the division of opinion within cabinet, as already mentioned; the room for manoeuvre was severely circumscribed.

The leadership of the PPS was no less concerned than the government by the turn of events. It feared losing political leadership of the masses in Kraków. The fear was well founded. An uncontrolled escalation of the conflict could break into a revolutionary wave. Events in Tarnów and Borysław were clearly heading in that direction. The PPS was against a proletarian revolution. In common with all parties of the Second International it hoped to introduce socialism by way of incremental reforms after gaining power through parliamentary elections. 'Revolution within the majesty of the law' as it was called, was a long way off. Nonetheless, preparations had to be made and these meant organizing, enlightening and leading the working class in the struggle for its fundamental rights. The socialist and communist programmes were thus diametrically opposed and, because both aspired to the leadership of the same social groups, conflict between the parties of the left was unavoidable. In order to counter the communist push for revolution, when it appeared to some observers that the communists could well find themselves at the head of the mass movement in Kraków, the leadership of the PPS was prepared to negotiate with the political parties of the propertied classes.

Piłsudski and his supporters were also perceived as a second danger by the leaders of the PPS. This threat stared them in the face. There was no doubt that the Piłsudski camp wished to see an escalation of the crisis to the point of the complete collapse of the state apparatus. Piłsudski himself maintained his silence. He may have been biding his time, waiting upon events before making his move.

One other uncertainty, for both PPS and government, was the attitude of the peasant party. At issue was whether or not a state of emergency would be declared. If so, was it to be interpreted as preparation for a *coup d'état* by the government or as preparation in anticipation of a right wing *coup*? The key to the question was tied up with the aims of

Witos. All else seemed of secondary importance. Eventually, Rataj was able to convince the PPS leadership that Witos did not intend a *coup d'état*. Their anxieties confirm just how brittle the system of parliamentary democracy really was.

In the meantime the situation in Kraków had suddenly changed. On the afternoon of 6 November an agreement, halting further military action, was signed between *Wojewoda* (Regional Governor) Galecki, the commander of the Kraków garrison, General Czikiel and the leadership of the PPS in Kraków. This agreement was accepted by the government which dispatched General Zeligowski and the vice-minister of internal affairs Karol Olpiński to Kraków where the workers were called upon to heed the decisions of the authorities. Calm returned to the city in which 3 officers, 11 servicemen and 18 workers had been killed and scores wounded on both sides.

Piłsudski was furious to learn of the deal struck in Kraków. He never forgave the socialist leadership for robbing him of an important opportunity to further exploit the crisis for his own political ends. We may be uncertain of whether he was preparing to take power by force or whether he was after something less at this stage, as, for example, the collapse of Witos's government. But one thing is clear and that is that the compromise between the PPS leadership and the government denied him the initiative in the political game then in play.

Thus, for the second time in a year, Piłsudski lost the chance of wielding political power. The scenario envisaged was the same in both cases: mass protest, incompetence within the government apparatus and the emergence of Piłsudski as the nation's saviour, the guardian of law and order. In the crisis after the death of Narutowicz this plan of action was halted at an early stage. Then, in November 1923, the Piłsudski camp had openly made attempts to take advantage of the outburst of social unrest and to stand at the head of the revolutionary masses. In each case failure could be blamed on the position taken by the PPS leadership. Piłsudski was denied the opportunity of personal engagement at a crucial moment in both crises. With regard to the revolt in Kraków it should also be said that Piłsudski was surprised by the turn of events. He did not foresee the situation being brought so quickly under control. His difficulty lay in finding the right time for his public appearance. Too early an entrance was ruled out by the unfolding scenario; he had to wait until the tinder of social protest was well and truly alight.

There was one other factor to be taken into consideration, the psychological impact on Piłsudski of the earlier crisis surrounding the death of Narutowicz. Much is made of this point in the Piłsudski literature, especially in explaining the Marshal's bouts of coarse behaviour and his growing hatred of society; of prevailing political culture. Undoubtedly the crisis which culminated in the death of Narutowicz shocked Piłsudski. It reinforced his views on the vagaries of political life in Poland. Earlier experience had developed a perception of deep division in Polish politics, but December 1922 showed him just how deep this really was. It showed him, too, the strength of the right. The incidence of organized protest was not the measure of this. Nor were the results of parliamentary elections bearing in mind a policy lacking in parliamentary traditions and the illiteracy which existed widely in independent Poland. Election results, as Piłsudski well understood, were an imprecise guide to the real strength of political parties; but the silent approbation of violence by the right, its enmity towards the murdered president seen in the pelting of his funeral cortege with lumps of muddied snow and their cult of murder both profoundly shocked Piłsudski and showed him their support.

Yet all was not lost. Such feelings were changeable and though change demanded time this could be made to work in Piłsudski's favour. The half-yearly changes of government offered him splendid opportunity against the right. Yet, could he count on mass support? The answer to this question in Kraków was an undoubted yes; but what of Warsaw? There is no way of answering these questions today.

As it turned out, November 1923 did not see Piłsudskiites managing to take advantage of the radicalization of the masses to gain power. They were left with only pointers for the future. The means had to be found of lifting the PPS blockade on their freedom of action. This could be achieved in two ways. Firstly, by strengthening the influence of Piłsudskiites in the leadership of the party. Secondly, by creating a situation in which the party leadership had no alternative but to support the activities of the Piłsudski camp. The first strategy did not hold great hope. The majority of PPS activists observed the activities of Piłsudskiites with fear and did not intend to allow the party to be drawn into their games. It was well understood that the aims of the party and those of the Piłsudski camp were quite different. The second possibility could be best achieved in the event of an attempted *coup* by the right. It was clear that the PPS would have to support Piłsudski against such a move. But at that moment the right had no opportunity to mount a *coup*. It had likewise lost its chance to make a bid for power in November 1923.

In only the sixth year of Poland's independence, the Second Republic was in political turmoil. Even the most seasoned and conscientious observers of those years found it difficult to keep abreast of events. Many unlikely schemes were proposed as, for example. the formation of a government under the chairmanship of Dmowski with the military portfolio in the hands of Piłsudski. Sosnkowski made efforts to flirt with the right and competed in such endeavours with Sikorski. Rataj wished for a cabinet based on the formation of an 'informal political association' comprising Moraczewski of the PPS, Kozicki of the ZLN, Dębski from *Piast* and Chaciński from the *Chadecja*. An additional problem was that the actual cadre of able politicians was rather small. This can be seen clearly in the composition of cabinets whose members were often drawn from outside parliament, a practice which became the norm.

After the fall of Witos's government in December 1923 Piłsudski's position weakened. His stand that he would not return to the army whilst the people responsible for the murder of Narutowicz remained in government lost its effect as social tensions lessened. The economic policy of the new premier, Władysław Grabski, brought improvements by curbing hyper-inflation. Political factors which had worked in favour of the 'recluse of Sulejówka' (as Piłsudski was now called) also began to diminish in strength and Piłsudski's stance in rejecting compromise no longer looked credible.

Though many in his camp despaired of the gulf between political intent and realization he turned to work in two directions. One was ostensibly apolitical. On 20 January 1924, he gave a lecture, also published as a pamphlet, on 'The Year 1863'. In February he published a study of 'Commanders-in-Chief'. It is interesting to compare the style of his writing with that of various of his political speeches of the time. 'The Year of 1863' is written in excellent Polish, in a style somewhat archaic and baroque, which may rather offend today's tastes, especially amongst Polish youth, but it is still strikingly impressive. In comparison, his political speeches were delivered in a primitive, barrack-room tongue. This distinction should not imply a split personality. He was fully aware of how he was expressing himself and was coarse on purpose. Piłsudski believed that the use of bad language was a successful form of political behaviour, especially as his opponents did not dare reply in kind. Nevertheless, his growing coarseness awakened the concern of even his closest collaborators.

His activity was directed, secondly, towards perpetuating and reinforcing the Piłsudski legend. A new departure, which became part of the cult of his personality, was the celebration of his saint's day (19 March) in 1924, his first since arriving at Sulejówek. The occasion was seen as a manifestation of public support for the Marshal. He was fêted at a banquet and at a concert in Warsaw and all day long crowds arrived by the train load to visit his home, singing and yelling his praises. These celebrations, repeated each year, were organized by the Legionnaires' Association. Their political purpose was quite clear. Not wishing to come into direct conflict with the government, Piłsudski remained at

Sulejówek. However, he still had to sustain a public following. Hence the personality cult.

This was also encouraged through his writing. Piłsudski's history of the Polish-Soviet war came out in the autumn of 1924 under the title 'The Year of 1920'. The book affirms the myth of Piłsudski as a victorious Commander-in-Chief. This was important to him though the success of the battle of Warsaw could not hide earlier failures. Piłsudski placed the responsibility for these on subordinates. In character assassination after character assassination Piłsudski blackened the reputations of his senior commanders in order to highlight his own superiority. The cry heard during the war of an 'Army without a leader' was made to mean that the army's Commander-in-Chief could be none other than Piłsudski. By furthering the myth of his military genius and by damaging the prestige of potential competitors Piłsudski hoped to ease his own return to head the army.

The name of Sikorski appears in his book only once and not in the best light. It left in the mind of the reader the conviction that Piłsudski had to correct Sikorski's mistakes. And although 'The Year of 1920' was written at a time when Piłsudski was still undecided on how to deal with Sikorski, relations between the two soon deteriorated. The ground had been well prepared. The tactic of casting blame on others freed Piłsudski from the need to account for his own shortcomings and gave him the political initiative over opponents, actual or potential, who had rather limited means of defence. To deny and overturn Piłsudski's judgement was well nigh impossible. Even the most well documented polemic in reply would leave in the mind of the reader the belief that Piłsudski had at least some cause in making the original charge.

Throughout the second half of 1924, Piłsudski maintained a low political profile by avoiding public appearances as much as possible. When he did speak in public his style was invariably measured and controlled. But in private meetings he talked a different language. This was echoed in the propaganda campaign conducted by the Piłsudski camp. It set out to destroy the reputations of Piłsudski's opponents and was immediately taken up by the press. The political climate became increasingly threatening.

Small traces of evidence exist of a conspiracy in favour of a military *coup* in mid 1924. This initiative did not come out of Sulejówek. Indeed the conspirators prevaricated over whether Piłsudski or Sikorski would lead the *coup*. At length they decided on neither and sought the support of legionnaires, led by General Orlicz-Dreszer and Colonel Wieniawa-Długoszowski, to create a base for future action. At about the same time a similar initiative was taken by the so-called Koc group. Loyal to Piłsudski it was led by Adam Koc and included Bogusław Miedziński,

Kazimierz Świtalski, Kazimierz Stamirowski, Józef Beck, Ignacy Matuszewski, Kazimierz Stamirowski and Henryk Floyar-Rajchman.

These nascent conspiracies arose out of the now widely held public
disillusionment with the existing parliamentary system and with the
constitution. Grabski's government which had, to its credit, improved
the economic situation failed miserably in other fields of policy. In the
east, ethnic tensions had led to a state of civil war. The reduction of
social welfare benefits caused widespread resentment. The outstanding
problem of agrarian reform remained unresolved. And the Sejm was
again riven by disagreements over the composition of the cabinet.

The widespread criticism of the constitution and its parliamentary
system suited the Piłsudskiites. Lacking interest in the reforms sought by
parties across the political spectrum they were impatient for action in
pursuit of power and made their feelings known to Piłsudski. Even his
closest circle was beginning to have doubts about his policy of waiting
on the sidelines. The end of a second year of residence at Sulejówek was
approaching. The benefits of the self-imposed stricture were rather
meagre and held no promise of future gain. Though the chances of
gaining power were not diminishing, they were not growing. Piłsudski
was nearly 58 and to entertain the possibility that he was simply too old
to regain the political initiative was excusable, the more so as in the
course of the preceding months he had taken no part in public affairs.
Sikorski was younger by almost 14 years and compared to Piłsudski
appeared more dynamic and those closest to the latter urged the 'recluse
of Sulejówek' to play his card. But their pleas remained unanswered.

The first half of 1925 brought a worsening of the economic situation.
Agricultural yields were disastrous. The numbers of unemployed again
started to grow and there were no jobs for school-leavers. The budget
deficit in the first quarter reached 43 million złotys, and in the second
quarter it grew by another 4 million. The deficit on the balance of trade
reached a staggering 400 million złotys. Matters were made worse
when, on the 15 June 1925, Germany stopped buying Polish coal. This
economic war coincided with a sudden deterioration in German-Polish
relations over the Silesian and Danzig questions. Germany posed a clear
threat to the existence of the Polish state.

The international situation had developed badly for Poland. The first
danger signal was the Dawes Plan of August 1924 which established
favourable terms for the payment of German reparations and gave
Germany considerable economic aid. The intention of making the
Weimar Republic a member of the League of Nations had also been
announced. France had failed in her pursuit of a hard line against
Germany and now warmed to compromise. In February 1925 Stresemann, the leading statesman in Weimar, proposed a pact of non-

aggression based on a guarantee of frontiers. This initiative, which had Britain's full support, allowed France an honourable way out of the *impasse* in Franco-German relations. This in turn, lessened the value to France of her alliance with Poland and French obligations towards Poland now became an encumbrance. The coincidence of the outbreak of German-Polish economic war with the new French policy line must have seemed obvious.

The worsening of Poland's economic and international position was beneficial to the Piłsudskiites. It gave credence to their propaganda message that Poland was lost without Piłsudski's leadership, a message that sounded increasingly attractive to some who had hitherto ignored the 'loner of Sulejówek'.

Sensing a change of fortune Piłsudskiites intensified their attacks on Grabski's government. At the very least they demanded the removal of Sikorski from the cabinet. Again the leadership of the PPS intervened to prevent a political crisis whose beneficiaries could only have been the right or the Piłsudskiites.

They in turn attacked the PPS for its support of Grabski's government by accusing the party of abandoning its class position. This was, in part, a reply to the PPS critique of the Piłsudski camp. In a series of articles published earlier in the spring, Mieczysław Niedziałkowski described Piłsudskiites as a radical group of the intelligentsia whose radicalism was weak in ideas and devoid of practical policies. At the same time he conceded that the help of the radicals should be welcomed by socialists in their struggle against the reactionaries. In his opinion, radicalism in Poland, as in the West, had to abandon the hope of power. This opinion was shared by Communist writers in Poland.

Public debate of this matter was displaced by widespread concern at the signing of the Locarno agreements in mid October. These were interpreted by a large portion of public opinion as a disaster for Poland. The diplomatic news weakened the position of the government. But worse was to come: in a sudden exchange rate crisis Grabski turned to the Bank of Poland for monetary intervention. The bank refused to act. The government had no option but to resign, creating a new political scene.

CHAPTER SEVEN

Coup d'État

Piłsudski made his move on 14 November 1925. He went to the Belvedere Palace to demand of President Wojciechowski that neither Sikorski nor Szeptycki should be entrusted with the armed forces portfolio in the new cabinet. This was more than a trial of strength: Piłsudski's intervention hit at the very heart of the constitutional system and set a dangerous precedent – he had assumed the authority to dictate terms to the President of the Republic. Wojciechowski's response was crucial. It went beyond Piłsudski's expectations. He formally acknowledged receipt of Piłsudski's demand, which had been presented in writing, and inquired further of him how best to fill the post. Piłsudski replied that he would discuss personalities after the candidature for Prime Minister had been announced.

The next day, the text of Piłsudski's demand as presented to Wojciechowski was published in the press and an important demonstration in support of Piłsudski took place at Sulejówek. On the pretext of belatedly celebrating the seventh anniversary of Piłsudski's return from Magdeburg, senior officers of the Warsaw garrison gathered at his villa. It was a large group including generals Skierski, Konarzewski, Krzemieński and Orlicz-Dreszer. The speech in Piłsudski's honour ended with the words: 'We cannot allow you to absent yourself from this present crisis as you would be deserting not only ourselves, your faithful soldiers but also Poland ... we bring you not only ceremonial compliments (and) our grateful hearts (but) also sabres experienced in victory'. This was clearly a declaration in favour of a military *coup d'état*. But no march on Warsaw followed.

Piłsudski's hesitation at this point has been the subject of much debate. The events, initiated by Piłsudski's visit to the Belvedere, which reached their climax in demonstrations in his support at Sulejówek, can be variously interpreted. Most memoirs argue that Piłsudski's aim was to force the President to eliminate Sikorski and Szepticki from government thus creating a precedent for allowing him to dictate the composition of future cabinets. On the other hand there are obvious grounds for believing he was contemplating a government take-over with the help of the military. Given Wojciechowski's compliant attitude, Piłsudski must have thought that there was a very good chance of a bloodless victory; the appearance of his military backers would have been sufficient to force Wojciechowski to submit. Yet Piłsudski backed away. Was it his characteristic fear of taking a decision, or were there other factors in play which have never emerged? That question must remain unanswered, but the hypothesis that Piłsudski had indeed planned to reach for power in the autumn of 1925 still seems very plausible.

After a great deal of manoeuvring and many failed attempts to form a government, including Wojciechowski's proposal to create a cabinet composed entirely of people outside parliament which was to be led by Władysław Raczkiewicz, Skrzyński formed a government on 20 November. It depended for support on what appeared at first sight to be a most unlikely coalition which included reactionary right-wing nationalists from the *Endecja* as well as radical socialists from the PPS. Yet, this coalition was not so startling to careful observers of political life. During the summertime vote on dramatic agricultural reforms the *Endecja* and the PPS came to certain agreements. There was therefore a logical consistency in the participation of the parties of the right and the left in Skrzyński's cabinet.

The decision by PPS leaders to join the coalition certainly provoked objections among a considerable number of party members and many *Endeks* were equally unenthusiastic. Witos and the peasant party were furious at not gaining the agriculture portfolio. Piłsudski and his camp, however, were delighted at the outcome. Sikorski and Szeptycki were eliminated from government and the coalition was so artificial that it would not be difficult to provoke a cabinet crisis at any favourable moment.

One portfolio, that of military affairs, remained vacant. On the 21st of November Wojciechowski invited Piłsudski to the Belvedere Palace to discuss the matter, but to avoid the impression that Piłsudski would dictate the appointment of cabinet members, he also invited Generals Majewski, Stanisław and Haller to seek their advice. 'Piłsudski,' noted Rataj,

> behaved provocatively, treating Wojciechowski as his servant. He took a note from his pocket and read from it a number of invectives against Sikorski, suggesting in abusive language that Sikorski would be best advised to leave Warsaw. ... He then recommended as good generals and as candidates (for the post of) Minister of Military Affairs Żeligowski, Tokarzewski, Skierski and Berbecki. Next, he pulled a second note from his pocket, read out a declaration hostile in attitude towards the government and announced that he would publish this because he owed as much to 'his' people. He then left, virtually without bidding so much as goodbye.

On 27 November, General Lucjan Żeligowski took over the Ministry of Military Affairs. He was, according to Sikorski, 'a kind and brave soldier, who had captured Wilno on the orders of Marshal Piłsudski . . . and remained an obedient tool in Piłsudski's hand . . .'.

Skrzyński's cabinet faced a very difficult economic situation. The productivity of Polish industry had markedly deteriorated and banks were in a critical situation over liquidity. The number of registered unemployed rose from 195,000 on 1 September to 311,000 on 1 December. At the same time prices were rising though wages remained static. A particularly big jump in prices, 16 per cent on average, took place in December. From the point of view of Piłsudskiites, the deteriorating economic situation and the difficulties faced by the government were welcome; growing social dissatisfaction could be exploited for political gain and Piłsudski lost no opportunity to do so. He had conversations with members of various parties. Władysław Glinka interestingly reports on Piłsudski's views: 'During talks at his residence in Sulejówek he said quite openly that agricultural reform, as proposed, could not be effected and that the 8 hour working day should be abolished. He advocated a reduction in social benefits, which he referred to as 'socialist achievements', to prevent the collapse of industrial and agricultural production. He promised conservatives the most important portfolios in the government he hoped to form'.

Yet, however close conservatives and Piłsudskiites had become, conservative support was of secondary importance in Piłsudski's mind. For the success of his plans, Piłsudski needed to gain the support of the left. He did not wish simply to come to power by means of a 'clean' military *coup d'état*. Power to him was only important for the realization of his one overriding aim, the reform of Poland's political structure. And this required mass support. In order to win the left over to his cause, the Piłsudski camp first set out to destroy their arch enemy on the right, the *Endecja*. In their propaganda they accused *Endeks* of plotting a *putsch* and presented themselves as advocates of far-reaching national reforms and as thorough-going democrats.

Piłsudski projected democratic sympathies not only in his speeches but also in his way of life. His demonstrative renunciation of a Marshal's salary after his retreat to Sulejówek, his fondness for the grey legionnaire's uniform which he wore constantly, his travels by second class carriage, his simple way of life – these were the elements he favoured in projecting himself to the national consciousness. 'Grandfather' as a description of Piłsudski emerged during the Sulejówek period. This emotionally charged image gave Piłsudski respectability at family level; the coarse and forbidding aspects of his personality gave way to a kindly paternal figure.

The political atmosphere in Poland during these months was highly charged with alleged threats of a fascist *coup*, a lack of faith in the parliamentary system and a widespread conviction that what was needed was a cathartic purge of the nation's moral and material life. Inspired by such convictions, the pro-Piłsudski press and followers set about uncovering corruption and theft. Public opinion was more and more shocked by each new revelation which suggested that Poland was being ruled by thieves – politicians who squandered the resources of the Republic. Yet another anti-parliamentary stereotype was seeded in the public mind. Throughout this period, Piłsudski led a very lively and complicated political existence. He talked with the right, made gestures towards the left and investigated the centre – all in preparation for taking power. But it is difficult to pin-point when the final decision was taken.

The method of procedure, however, was already clear. Piłsudski had firmly decided to gain power with the help of the army. This was a fundamental change in his planning since the events in Kraków of 1923, when mass demonstrations had exposed the government's weakness. Though risky, because the crowd could get out of control, that method had not presented any moral problems; it was to have been a *coup* in response to mass support. Now the format had changed. There would first be military demonstrations designed to rally mass support, even at the cost of giving the army the prime political role, which was precisely the point on which Piłsudski and his followers blamed their opponents and thus risked a civil war. Difficult moral choices had to be made. Piłsudski, however, refused in his own mind to admit the possibility of a military demonstration being transformed into armed conflict. He was convinced that the structure which he planned to destroy was so rotten that it would fall apart at the mere threat of attack. This explained why he had decided against making a move during the demonstrations in his support at Sulejówek. He believed that the system was not, at that time, sufficiently discredited in the eyes of the nation.

Acting within the new framework the Piłsudski camp made careful political preparations through a well-orchestrated propaganda campaign; military units which were to take part in political demonstrations had to be sure of public support. Only this could prevent bloodshed and at the same time provide moral justification for mutiny. There was also the key question as to the President's likely behaviour. Clearly, a *coup d'état* that had the President's blessing would ease matters considerably. That is why, during their political campaign, Piłsudski and his supporters carefully avoided attacking Wojciechowski. Judging by his behaviour during the crisis following the fall of Grabski's cabinet, they assumed that, in similar circumstances, he would cave in to pressure.

Among the political soundings, in preparation for the take-over of power, there were even attempts to influence the Communist movement. These were, at the time, rebuffed by the party leadership. In April 1926 a political intelligence report drafted by the Polish Communist Party (*Komunistyczna Partia Polski* – KPP) described Piłsudski as 'a megalomaniac and a pathological crank, yet one who gains more and more public support ... as the last illusion of the masses ...'. The communists believed that 'Poland was witnessing a moment of conflict between Piłsudski and the generals in opposition to him, between the mass of Piłsudskiites and fascism, between the democratic and radical lower middle class and the nobility and upper middle class'. This constituted recognition that, at very least, Piłsudski should not to be discounted politically and it confirmed his growing popularity. On 14 May, at the height of the crisis, the KPP declared:

'Workers you know that our intentions go further than those of the Piłsudskiites. But in this fight, the place of revolutionary workers is against the government ... and against fascism.' In other words, for Piłsudski. With the exception of Witos's *Piast* Peasant Party, such in fact was the view of the entire left; by the middle of May 1926 the Piłsudski camp was a national force to be reckoned with.

This was as much a result of the successful propaganda campaign as it was to do with a collapse in the public's faith in liberal democracy. The parliamentary system as it existed satisfied no one. It seemed unable to find solutions to the nation's problems especially as the economic situation seemed ever more hopeless.

Most, if not all, politicians were discredited in the eyes of the public. Piłsudski was the exception. In protest at the 'dishonour' at the heart of political life, he had chosen to stay in isolation at Sulejówek for nearly three years. Over this period he had accumulated considerable political capital. Despite all his setbacks, he had remained loyal to his country and wanted to work for its cause. Unlike Paderewski he had not turned his back on Poland. Piłsudski's public following believed that his opponents had done everything possible to destroy him and, in their selfishness, were willing to lead Poland to destruction. In such a hostile political environment many were willing to overlook Piłsudski's own shortcomings. Though we are not in a position to judge how many thought in this way, it is certain that such thoughts had, to some degree, infiltrated public consciousness though this did not, as yet, imply that most people believed in Piłsudski. It meant only that they had lost faith in his enemies.

On 19 April 1926, Zdziechowski introduced the government's economic programme to parliament. It was not acceptable to the PPS. The next day, two PPS ministers, Barlicki and Ziemięcki, resigned from the cabinet; the coalition within Skrzyński's cabinet had disintegrated.

Nevertheless, the President refused to accept Skrzyński's offer of resignation. He insisted that the budget had to be approved by the Sejm and, in the absence of an alternative grouping capable of forming a government, Skrzyński was told to soldier on. It was clear that his days in power were numbered and that the President had only postponed a cabinet crisis in the hope that a new working majority could be found.

On the same day that Wojciechowski rejected the resignation of the Skrzyński cabinet, a meeting between Wojciechowski, Skrzyński, Żeligowski and Piłsudski took place at the Belvedere Palace. The point at issue was the constitutional role and competence of the President as chief of the armed forces. After the meeting Piłsudski told the press that 'the talks were not in any way connected with the cabinet crisis'. This assurance was immediately taken to mean the contrary.

On 29 April *Nowy Kurier Polski* (New Polish Courier) published a long interview with Piłsudski. He talked about the parliamentary crises which Poland 'had experienced, more than any other country in Europe' and about the necessity to construct a 'strong government, independent of the Sejm (parliament)'. He declined to answer the direct question of whether he would take personal charge of such a government, but the fact that the subject had been raised publicly was significant.

Piłsudski's strategy was to prolong the cabinet crisis in order to justify a demonstration by an embittered army which reflected the mood of the people. He did all he could to torpedo the formation of a new cabinet. However, despite these efforts, a coalition of the right and centre was re-cobbled after prolonged and difficult negotiations. On Monday 10 May Witos went to the Belvedere Palace to seek the President's approval of the new government. Although it had the backing of the majority in parliament it did not find favour in the streets. Public opinion was hostile towards Witos; people remembered the coalition that had governed for three years and they had no pleasant memories to recall. Both left-wing and the Piłsudskiite press repeatedly stated that Witos' cabinet was going to introduce a special law by which they would organize a rigged election to gain power in a fascist *coup d'état*. Witos emphatically denied such charges, but to no avail.

Behind the scene of yet another cabinet crisis in the making, the military plot was hatched. Even before Skrzyński had first offered his cabinet's resignation on 18 April 1926, Żeligowski (still Minister of Military Affairs, replaced by General Malczewski on 11 May) was prompted by Wieniawa-Długoszowski to order a grouping of army units in the vicinity of Rembertów; war games under Marshal Piłsudski's personal command were to take place there on 10 May. The units selected for this exercise were all known for their loyalty to Piłsudski. Somewhat surprised by the Minister's order, the Chief of

Staff, General Kesler, in a letter to Żeligowski pointed to 'the fortuitous choice' of units.

On 10 May, when the news of the composition of Witos' cabinet became public, Piłsudski gave an interview to *Kurier Poranny*. It was, even for Piłsudski, unusually insulting towards Witos and his cabinet. Piłsudski directly accused Witos of 'corruption and the abuse, without precedence, of government power . . . for party and personal gains'. He blamed the new premier for demoralizing the armed forces and of threatening his (Piłsudski's) own life. He said further that 'such gentlemen as Mr Wincenty Witos and his colleagues abuse the honour of public duty and take advantage of the fact that they do not represent the electors to muddy the conscience of the army with their dirty deeds. But let not those gentlemen dare to think that the misappropriation of government funds for bribes and spying on political or personal enemies remains hidden from anyone'. He threatened the army's revenge and ended his interview by promising 'to do battle as before with the main evil of government: the foisting of an unfettered party political agenda upon Poland in pursuit only of financial and personal gains'. The interview did not attack the President. This was understandable. The President was to be the one who would help Piłsudski 'save Poland'.

The interview was published on 11 May. Government commissioners for the city of Warsaw decided to confiscate that day's issue of *Kurier Poranny*. The government was determined to hold out against Piłsudski. But the morning edition had already been distributed. The interview aroused strong public interest as did the news of the paper's confiscation.

That same day, the new Minister of Military Affairs, General Malczewski, revoked his predecessor's order requiring the concentration of army units in the Rembertów region. He instructed the immediate return of all units to their garrisons. The order coincided with the arrival in Rembertów of the 7th regiment Lancers from Mińsk Mazowiecki under the command of Lt Col Kazimierz Stamirowski. He refused to return to his home base. The government realized that this was the start of something serious.

Throughout the day, Piłsudski's followers demonstrated in Warsaw. The confiscated number of *Kurier Poranny* containing Piłsudski's interview was being openly sold on the streets. That night, 11–12 May, Stamirowski ordered Col Franciszek Sikorski (commandant of the 9th infantry division) and Col Krok-Paszkowski (commandant of the 22nd infantry regiment) to move immediately to Rembertów. At about 2.30 a.m. in Praga, a suburb of Warsaw linked to the capital by the Poniatowski bridge, Col Kazimierz Sawicki (commandant of the 36th infantry regiment) was awakened by the duty officer who entered his study accompanied by four senior officers. They were: Col A. Koc, Lt Col A. Minkowski, Lt Col Kwiatek and Maj Szczapa-Krzewski. Koc informed Sawicki that 'Marshal Piłsudski' had decided to 'clear up the mess in Poland'. That morning, 12 May, Piłsudski set off for Warsaw with an escort from the 7th regiment of Lancers from the Rembertów garrison.

In the city the morning papers carried news that Písudski's residence at Sulejówek had been attacked. This was quite untrue but gave Piłsudski and his troops a pretext for action. Moreover, it was not by chance that Piłsudski had, in his interview, accused the government of threats to his life. This was also untrue. But to an excited public these lies sounded convincing; those held morally responsible for Naruto-wicz's death could aim to murder Piłsudski. Sympathy went out to him; anyone who had been undecided now took Piłsudski's side. This marked shift in public opinion was of great importance in the events which were unfolding hour by hour.

The government was by now well aware that serious trouble was brewing. At 8 a.m. the President was briefed by his adjutant about the demonstrations in Piłsudski's support. An hour later the government commissioner for Warsaw, Tłuchowski, and the city's Commandant-General, Stefan Suszyński, further informed him of the tense situation in Warsaw. The President decided to leave for his residence at Spala, on the outskirts of Warsaw, which he reached at about 11 a.m. Shortly afterwards Witos telephoned to demand his immediate return to the capital.

Piłsudski was quite unaware of the fact that the President had vacated the Belvedere Palace. Consequently, when Piłsudski went there on the morning of 12 May, to inform Wojciechowski of his demands he found no one at home. Piłsudski turned round and went back to Rembertów at 11 a.m., about the time Witos made his call to the President at Sława. Only then did he order the occupation of the bridges across the Vistula to secure the passage of forces loyal to him at Rembertów, from the right bank of the river over to the city on its left bank.

There can be only one explanation of the fiasco. There was no detailed plan of action. The lack of an adequate system of communica-tion meant that Piłsudski had no idea of the President's movements. And just as extraordinary, neither Slawek nor Świtalski, Piłsudski's closest confidants, knew of his departure for Warsaw. That so much was left to chance by Piłsudski and his followers, in these decisive hours, is quite incredible. Any element of surprise was lost. The time which elapsed allowed the government to shore up its own defences.

The President returned from Spala at about 1.00 p.m. and went on immediately to join the cabinet meeting then in session. An hour later, at

2.00 p.m., a Government communiqué was published stating that 'criminal agitation, put about by conspirators and disturbers of the peace, was spreading in the ranks of the army. . . . A few military units, excited by false news and misled by forged orders have assembled at Rembertów and have refused obedience to the Government of the Republic'. In a separate statement the President reminded soldiers of their oath of loyalty to the government. Martial law was declared in Warsaw and in Warsaw province as well in the districts of Siedlek and Łuków regions in Lublin province.

The opposition parties, (the PPS, PSL *Wyzwolenie*, Peasant Party and Labour) announced that the only solution to the crisis was the immediate resignation of the Witos cabinet. This demand appealed to the masses. It also pleased Piłsudski. He had envisaged just such an outburst of popular feeling and indeed, as all sources agree, in those days of May the streets of Warsaw were all on the side of the rebels. This support not only facilitated Piłsudski's actions in a technical sense but, more importantly, made it easier to overcome difficult moral problems as different units of the same army stood one against the other. Some had to break their oath of loyalty to the government in order to be faithful to their Commander, others had to break that faith in order to abide by their oath. For many it was a tragic dilemma. Senior officers felt it most intensely. The commander of the 7th infantry regiment, Colonel Wieckowski, Piłsudski's man, committed suicide, believing that was the only way out of the dilemma. General Sosnkowski, who had been in prison with Piłsudski at Magdeburg, attempted to commit suicide for the same reason.

In the early hours of the afternoon of 12 May, the 1st Regiment of the Light Cavalry led by Major Strzelecki took control of the Poniatowski bridge. Machine guns were positioned in its supporting towers and a primitive barricade was hurriedly erected, made up mainly of coaches which had stopped on the bridge. At 5 p.m. Piłsudski stepped out of a car which made the journey from Praga. In the company of Dreszer, Stamirowski and Wieniawa he approached the President who was waiting for him at the bridge. Wojciechowski had initiated this meeting, which must have pleased Piłsudski.

He knew that the President had been against the appointment of Witos's cabinet and was right in believing that the President was only awaiting a pretext on which to get rid of such an unpopular government. Piłsudski's action was contrary to the constitution and to accepted political norms, but up until then there had been no bloodshed and events could be interpreted as the spontaneous reaction of a portion of the army embittered by political divisions. Neither Piłsudski nor his followers had so far attacked Wojciechowski, which meant that agreement between them seemed likely. Piłsudski undoubtedly counted on the bonds of an old friendship. But Wojciechowski had no intention of looking for agreement with a mutineer. He demanded that Piłsudski should subordinate himself to the legal government. The conversation lasted only a few minutes and wiped out all Piłsudski's hopes of taking power without the use of force. Now the military demonstration he had led would turn to battle. There was no other way forward.

Piłsudski had about 3500 soldiers at his disposal. He could also count on 800 members of the paramilitary organization *Strzelec*. These numbers gave him superiority over the government, which could muster about 1700 soldiers in Warsaw. Despite this imbalance a lightning victory could not be won. The battle for Warsaw lasted three days. Reinforcements arrived on both sides, giving Piłsudski 11,000 soldiers as against the government's 7000. In the bitter fighting 215 soldiers and 164 civilians lost their lives.

On the evening of 14 May, the President and government resigned. In accordance with the constitution the office of President was taken over by the Marshal of the Sejm who was Maciej Rataj. The following day he came to an agreement with Piłsudski and formed a government under the premiership of Kazimierz Bartel. Piłsudski was appointed Minister of Military Affairs.

Piłsudski had achieved his aim, albeit at a higher price than he had bargained for. He was completely in charge of the political situation. Yet he had no wish to flaunt this absolute power. He was quite willing to share it with Rataj and the parliament. This did not alter the fact that what was his to give was also his to take back. Piłsudski understood, perhaps instinctively, that absolute power did not need at all times to demonstrate its strength, but should only be invoked when required. The rejection of the constitution and the parliamentary system would be an unnecessarily ostentatious demonstration of strength, indeed a sign of weakness. To have overthrown the system would have gone against his own judgements in the years prior to the events of May. Piłsudski, despite pressure from his close associates, was repelled by the idea of a 'clean' *coup*; its consequence would inevitably have been open dictatorship.

The historical verdict on Piłsudski seems to acquit him of any aspiration towards dictatorship. The evidence for this conclusion lies in his sequence of actions in the years 1918–1922 and after May 1926. However, there can be a misunderstanding over the term dictatorship. In its narrow sense, this means the suppression of citizens' rights, the liquidation of representative bodies, government by terror. On that definition Piłsudski's apologists were right – he never reached for this type of dictatorship because he did not think it an effective or efficient exercise of power. But, more broadly, if dictatorship is simply defined as full powers of decision concentrated in the hands of an individual, then the views of Piłsudski's apologists are not justified by the facts. Both during his period of office as Head of State, as well as after May 1926, Piłsudski retained the decision-making powers in his own hands.

As previously discussed, Piłsudski's freedom of action as Head of State had been circumscribed. The group of legionnaires on whom he could depend fully for support was an insufficient base from which to launch his nation-building mission. This required the much broader support which only parliament could provide. This inevitably involved him in some compromise. But even so one should not exaggerate the limitations to his powers at that point. Every decision which he felt to be important, he took without consulting parliament or government. It was so with the Wilno and Kiev expeditions and also with the 'mutiny' of General Żeligowski. Piłsudski concentrated his energies on forming the army and on his eastern policy and in these affairs he had full power of decision. However, as events went against him, he had to share his power of decision with others until eventually he lost it all together.

When he reached for power the second time around, he was wiser and more experienced in affairs of state. Piłsudski had discovered how transient popularity really is and how changeable are the swings of public opinion. He was not tempted by the glory of status. That was a feature of high office meant for the small minded. Power to him meant the unassailable right to exercise his will in all matters which he deemed to be within his domain. He had attained such authority in May 1926. It remained for him to consolidate his position and to use his power to good effect.

He was determined to rebuild all civil institutions and to imbue them with a new sense of purpose. Parliamentary democracy, in its existing form, was according to Piłsudski, harmful to political life. This did not mean that the system had to be abandoned, rather that it should be changed. This required time, and Piłsudski believed that time was on his side; his complete authority and his aloofness from the vagaries of day-to-day politics allowed him to take the long view. The basic premise of his political philosophy, was that the state was superior to all other political organizations. He was against political parties because he believed that they had put themselves above the law in order to restrict the functioning of the state and had weakened it in their contest for ascendancy. His old enemy, the *Endecja*, were most guilty in this regard. To Piłsudski parliamentary politics had degraded government; it was never again to be dependent on clashing party political interests which had emasculated it.

Thus, the constitution of March 1921 required essential modification.

This was to come in time. He was content, at first, to abide by its rules, as with the procedures laid down in the case of the President's resignation. The fact that Rataj had managed the transfer of power to a new government constitutionally, was a distinct advantage to Piłsudski. It made the legitimization of the *coup d'état* in conditions of heightened social tension that much easier.

On 22 May Piłsudski spoke to calm the nation. He did not give any justification for the May events, but said that

> When brothers love each other, the bond between them is stronger than any other. When brothers quarrel and the bond breaks, their quarrel is also deeper than any other. This is the law of human life. We lived by that law during the days of battle in the capital. Into one earth sunk the blood of both, into earth as dear to one as to the other. . . . Let this warm blood, the blood of the most precious soldiers in Poland, sow new brotherhood in the earth beneath our feet, let it give forth a common truth. . . . Let God almighty have mercy upon our sins and forgive us and turn away His punishing hand, as we take up our posts strengthened and reborn . . .

This emotional speech was intended to bridge the chasm created within the army by the days of May. In attributing right to both sides and in seeking forgiveness equally for both, Piłsudski made clear that there would be no retribution against the losers. This was not magnanimity on his part but political common sense. As victor he could not take revenge which might have had unfortunate consequences. He understood that he had to do everything to reintegrate the army.

Piłsudski remained passive on all other matters of policy. He had no definite programme formulated and felt no need to advocate any precise political doctrine. He certainly had no intention of backing even the mildest of the PPS reforms. In social affairs Piłsudski wanted to maintain the *status quo*. His inexperience in the complex world of economics translated itself into silence. He also remained quiet on the vexed problem of the national minorities.

Piłsudski had earlier expressed his political credo: 'It is not a question of left or right . . . I am not of the left, (nor) for the left, I am for all my countrymen . . . People's government! I wonder whether a people's government . . . will give Poland what is needed. When I have an army, I shall have everything necessary'.

His attitude disorientated both his opponents and his allies. On 15 May, after the *coup*, a meeting of the PPS leadership formulated their party's demands: '1) An immediate dissolution of the Sejm and Senate. 2) Marshal Piłsudski to become President of the Republic. 3) A worker-peasant government to be formed without involvement of those parties which supported the corrupt Witos' government. 4) The policies of former governments towards the national minorities to be changed. 5)

Robbers of public funds who held public office, including Witos, to be punished immediately'. The tone of these demands was very firm, but without influence because Piłsudski had no intention of complying with them.

He was against the dissolution of the current parliament precisely because he wished to deny power to the left; an election at the time would undoubtedly have resulted in its victory. Piłsudski felt that having just defeated the *Endecja* he wanted to avoid a contest with the parties of the left who would inevitably have emerged as his next opponents after victory at the polls. Therefore there was no sense in strengthening their position. Besides, a parliament already disgraced in the eyes of the public was much more convenient to him. The demand to form a worker-peasant government was not convenient, especially as he now intended to attract the parties of the right into government, with the exception of the *Endecja*, whom he wished to isolate.

The right welcomed Piłsudski's approach and supported his wish to legitimize the *coup* by means other than elections. His approach gave them an opportunity to participate in the political game in and out of parliament. The right was under no illusions. They knew that elections would mean complete defeat. That is why the more cynical representatives of the right were ready to accept Piłsudski's demands for greater power for the executive and for the limitation, for a certain period of time, of parliament's supervisory functions. The former had already been advocated by the right, in rather different political circumstances, when victory seemed theirs. Now the demand was acceptable as a small price to pay in defeat. What the right had feared was annihilation by the Piłsudski camp, expecting the same treatment they would have meted out had they taken power. To their astonishment retribution was remarkably slight. Members of the dismissed cabinet were allowed to depart in safety. No political opponents were arrested. Although generals Malczewski, Rozwadowski, Zagorski and Jaźwiński were interned and sent to prison in Wilno, they were released as soon as the situation had stabilized. Four prisoners after three days of battle did not seem too serious.

Thus, the more Piłsudski distanced himself from the parliamentary left, the more the right and centre could look to the future with hope, especially as the new cabinet, led by Bartel, contained no one from the left. They could also take heart from Piłsudski's statement, in an interview to the press on 25 May. On this occasion he was at pains to deny dictatorship:

'. . . I maintain, that I managed to accomplish an unique historical deed, in achieving something resembling a *coup d'état* and immediately managing to legalize it. I effected a revolution, without revolutionary consequences.' That same day he said to a correspondent of *Le Matin*: 'Poland must be cautious, because she is young and poor. She must avoid risky experimentation. We are the balance between the policies of the left and those of the right . . .'.

Nobody at the time suspected Piłsudski of attempting to put into practice a radical right-wing programme; he was still seen as an advocate of the left and many held firmly to that illusion. Piłsudski was intent on distancing himself from his former allies, but by insisting that he was above politics, he hoped to manage this without causing a breach with them. As for the right, anyone who could read political texts might have thought that Piłsudski was endeavouring to seek its political neutralization. Yet those taken in by Piłsudski's posture of detachment could also have been led to the apparently absurd conclusion that he actually sought the political support of the right. And yet that is indeed what he wanted. Those who rejected this interpretation identified the right too exclusively with the *Endecja*.

It was certainly the case that the *Endeks* dominated the right and they therefore interpreted Piłsudski's gestures as aimed at them. Though understandably mistrustful of Piłsudski they did not reject his advances. The leaders of the *Endecja* must have noticed that Piłsudski's attitude towards them was much milder than before the *coup*. They were sufficiently experienced as politicians to understand that this was no coincidence. Piłsudski's renouncement of dictatorship meant that he intended to follow the rules of the parliamentary game. If that were so, sooner or later compromise was possible.

But the leaders of the *Endecja* were to pay dearly later for their failure to anticipate Piłsudski's plan to dethrone their party as the dominant representative of the right wing in parliament. He wanted to separate the right from the *Endecja* and to this end he turned to the conservatives.

The conservatives had at their disposal considerable financial means and well-organized political groups but only a small number of supporters. They did very badly in the elections of 1922, the only exception being the conservative Christian-National club led by Edward Dubanowicz and Stanisław Stroński, which found support in the Poznań region and in Lwów, returning 23 representatives to the Sejm and 10 to the Senate. It was the only conservative group with both influence in the villages and a close connection with the *Endecja*.

The main influence exerted by the conservatives was through their publications: *Czas*, *Słowo*, *Dzieńnik Poznański* as well as *Warszawianka* and *Dzień Polski*, titles which had a wide readership. Conservatives had influence amongst those whom we might accept as 'informed opinion'.

Conservatives were initially divided in their response to May's events. Some supported Piłsudski, others condemned him. But soon, the latter began to change their stance as they became convinced that he had no intention of implementing a left-wing programme. They watched his next moves very closely. The formation of the Bartel cabinet was his first step on the path to legalizing the May Coup. The next had to be the election of a new President. In a political sense this was most important and it was the victors' most difficult assignment. The disposition of strength in parliament was not favourable to Piłsudski.

On 21 May, Rataj announced a convention of the National Assembly on 31 May for the purpose of electing a President. Piłsudski could count on the votes of the parliamentary left but these would not have given him a majority. This could be achieved only by winning the votes of both the centre and the national minorities. The latter made up 20 per cent of the National Assembly, with 107 votes. But this was not a bloc vote; the national minorities owed allegiance to various political groups. Nevertheless, one thing was clear – the right wing could not count on their votes and nor could Piłsudski. But he could count on the support of Jewish groups, which had 47 votes at their disposal. Jewish representatives were ready to vote for Piłsudski not simply because they were against the *Endecja*, but because the course of events in May had revealed not the smallest hint of anti-semitism amongst Piłsudskiites. And in their operations in Jewish districts Piłsudski's units behaved with absolute correctness. This was a strong enough argument to secure the Jewish vote in favour of Piłsudski. He could also count on German votes. This second largest minority group disposed 22 votes in the National Assembly. Yet with even the most optimistic calculation this would not give him a majority. To realize this he had to gain a portion of the votes of the centre. Here the situation was complicated by the fact that all three parties of the centre (PSL *Piast*, *Chadecja*, and NPR) were part of the coalition represented in the government which had just been overthrown by the *coup*. But since the coalition lacked cohesion there was perhaps, still time to try to win part of the 'centre' vote; especially as the *coup* itself and events of the period directly after it exposed the weakness of the *Endecja*.

The proceedings of the National Assembly commenced at 10 a.m., on 31 May. A representative of the PPS proposed Piłsudski for President. Stanisław Głąbiński proposed Adolf Bniński. At this Senator Zubowicz called out 'He will lose Poland, as he lost his estate, playing cards'. The cry did not deter Dubanowicz from seconding Bniński. This had a very telling effect.

Bniński, the *voivod* (Provincial Commissioner) of Poznań was not amongst Poland's best known and popular politicians. His stand against the Bartel cabinet in the days preceding the National Assembly gained him the sympathy of Piłsudski's opponents. In this regard the endorsement of his candidature by the right was provocative; the election of Bniński would preclude any possibility of compromise with Piłsudski. But many on the right thought the risk worth taking; extremists believed that Bniński's election could plunge the country into civil war, which they believed was the only chance for the right to gain power. *Endeks* understood that Piłsudski was not going to resign from power and that an armed struggle, in a new contest for authority, was still a possibility. Should they manage to force through the victory of Bniński, such a clash would begin with the *Endecja* in a most favourable position: as defenders of legality. The leaders of the *Endecja* realized that this was their last chance. They counted on Piłsudski continuing in power long enough to lose popular support by being unable to solve the country's problems. This required time and that time could also be exploited by the Piłsudski camp to crush the *Endecja* out of existence. Such were their thoughts as the National Assembly came to its vote. The number of votes required for victory was 243. Bniński received 193, Piłsudski 292. He was elected as President of the Republic on the first ballot.

This was an enormous political success. The same National Assembly which had elected President Wojeichowski and which had been dismissed by the armed *coup*, now gave a vote of confidence to the instigator of that *coup*. Moreover it gave Piłsudski complete ascendancy over his main enemy, the *Endecja*, whose leadership, in advocating support of the contest in parliament now had to face the party critics of that policy. Then came an announcement that none had anticipated. Piłsudski refused to accept his nomination as President.

His motives were explained in a letter to Rataj: '. . . Alas, I am not in a position to accept . . . I could not muster sufficient confidence in myself for this work . . . which I have already attempted once done . . . the tragic murder of President Narutowicz whom I could not protect from his cruel destiny is too strong in my memory . . . I must reiterate, too, that I cannot exist in a job so circumscribed by the existing constitution . . .'

This snub to parliament and his criticism of the constitution were of importance in the future. For the present, he proposed the name of Ignacy Mościcki for the presidency. This too came as a complete surprise and to none more than to Piłsudski's nominee. Mościcki was an outstanding chemist, a professor of the Lwów Polytechnic and director of the state-run nitrates company at Chorzów. He did not take any part in political life and was generally unknown. He was a scholar and a good organizer, but these were insufficient qualifications for the highest post in the land. Yet he stood for the post.

The National Assembly met on the first day of June. A choice had to be made between Bniński, Mościcki (proposed by the Workers' Club) and Zygmunt Marck, proposed by the PPS. The required majority was 242 votes. Mościcki received 215 votes, Bniński 211 votes and Marck, 56. Rataj moved the assembly to a second vote. This time the socialists withdrew their candidate and transferred their votes in Mościcki's favour. He now received 281 votes and Bniński 200 and was nominated President.

He immediately asked Bartel to form a new government. After much backroom negotiation and consultation with Piłsudski, this was sworn in on 8 June. The second Bartel cabinet differed little from the first.

Throughout June the government worked on changes to the constitution. The debate on these lasted from 5–22 July and on 31 July the Senate carried a motion in favour of the amendments which were then overwhelmingly passed by the Sejm during August.

The Bill for Constitutional Change greatly enhanced the powers of the President. It gave him the right to dissolve the Sejm and the Senate and deprived parliament of any say in the matter. Until such time as a new parliament was elected the bill allowed the President, to reform existing legislation in favour of efficient government and gave him the authority to introduce legislation by decree. It introduced a fundamental change in the procedure for passing a vote of no confidence in the government. Such a motion could not now be voted on during the debate in which it was proposed. This gave the government a greater chance to put pressure on the Sejm against the motion. The bill also placed strictures on the length of time it took for parliament to approve the annual budget. A breach of the new regulations meant the automatic advance of the measures proposed by government to the next stage of the proceedings. This could result in a government project becoming law without a vote in the Sejm.

In less than three months since the last shots in the battle for Warsaw had been fired, Piłsudski had gained the legalization of his *coup*, the predisposition towards him of both a constitutionally formed cabinet and the new President, the latter now fully empowered to initiate constitutional reform. In contrast to other countries in which military *coups* had occurred these changes were carried out without the use of terror and in the full majesty of the law.

There were several reasons for this unique political phenomenon. The Sulejówek period was well utilized for the preparation of a *coup*, not in the sense of conspiracy but in the sense of an extensive propaganda campaign whose one and only aim was to promote popular conviction in favour of political regeneration. Piłsudski set great store in propaganda. His was a highly effective approach aimed at a politically

unsophisticated public, appealing not to the intellect but to emotion.
Therein lay its success. This could also be accounted for by the legend
which had grown up around Piłsudski: the archetypal great Pole, who,
as a sign of protest, sentenced himself to internal exile. This was
emotionally very powerful. Such influence freed Piłsudski from having
to define a programme. He himself became that programme and the
guarantor of national healing. Let us add to this another very important
and generally underestimated factor, the disappointment of hopes which
came with the attainment of Polish statehood. Castles in the air had
been bulldozed by a brutal reality which had proved that independence
did not heal social ills, nor eliminate injustice, nor create equal
opportunities for all. Some were led by their bitterness along a
revolutionary path. But the majority became more and more susceptible
to Piłsudski's propaganda. To them, Piłsudski, 'the recluse of Sulejówek'
became the only hope of progress. In Piłsudski's new found constituents,
an inert and politically unorganized mass, there was an enormous
reservoir of strength. They believed that he was the spokesman for their
interests. The stronger this conviction, the stronger the future disappointment would be. But at the time of the *coup* the support of the
masses gave Piłsudski a great advantage over his opponents. Surprised
by events, they did not understand what Piłsudski was aiming at. Those
who had always supported Piłsudski were equally disorientated.
Understanding the consequences of the events in May was, in many
political circles, a long and painful experience.

CHAPTER EIGHT

The New Order

The summer of 1926 was far from being a holiday period for the new team in government. They were soon overwhelmed by intrigue and personal politics as Piłsudskiites entered the corridors of power to take up key posts in the army and in the civil service. The re-organization which took place in the name of efficiency and economy had all the characteristics of a purge.

An example of the changes of personnel that were taking place could be found in connection with the administration of the national minorities. These minorities, which constituted one third of the total population of the Polish Republic, came under the remit of two Ministries: Internal Affairs and the Ministry for Religious Beliefs and Public Enlightenment. The portfolio for the first was taken by Antoni Sujkowski. He was the godfather of Wanda Piłsudska and his wife was a very close friend of Aleksandra Piłsudska, sufficient qualifications to hold a ministerial post. Directly after his appointment Kazimierz Bartel (the new premier) was reported to have said in anger, 'They have forced this idiot on me'.

Policy towards the minorities was considered in cabinet on 18 August. Młodzianowski opened the debate by asserting that no progress at all had been made with the problem of the national minorities in all the seven year existence of the Polish state; rather, indeed, it had grown more embittered and more complicated. He blamed this on the negligence of successive governments. His call for action was supported by August Zalewski, (Minister of Foreign Affairs) Witold Staniewicz (Minister for Agricultural Reforms) and Antoni Sujkowski (Minister of Religious Affairs and Public Enlightenment). In contrast Piłsudski emphasized successes and achievements in the assimilation of the minorities through the dissemination of Polish culture. He believed that the gravity of the problem of the nationalities could be over-estimated. From the tone of his speech it was evident that he was not in favour of the decisions made in haste by his co-workers. He wanted to prevent hasty action and was willing to contribute personally to further thinking on the matter, first seeking a detailed analysis of the problems.

A little over a month later, on 20 September, the Sejm had reconvened after the summer recess. A motion of no confidence was moved by the Christian Democrats against Sujkowski over the nationalities question. The minister had given his blessing to the idea of forming an Ukrainian

University in Lwów. This had provoked a sharp attack in the right-wing press. Mindful of Piłsudski's earlier federalist plans, which, in any case, were now no longer feasible, the right feared that Piłsudskiites were trying to further win over the national minorities to themselves.

The crisis gained sufficient momentum to cause the government's resignation. The President instructed Bartel to form a new government. He responded by fielding exactly the same team in exactly the same positions. Nothing in the constitution prevented him from doing so; the authors of article 58, which dealt with resignations, had not foreseen the possibility of a minister returning, in a new cabinet, to the same post from which the Sejm had demanded his resignation. Nevertheless Bartel's response was entirely against the spirit of the constitution. It was a challenge to the Sejm.

However, parliament avoided a new confrontation on this particular issue. A more immediate problem lay before it. The bill for a provisional budget, which had been passed by the Sejm, was amended in the Senate. Now, on 30 September, the Sejm was to vote on the amendments which had gone against the government. Earlier that day the cabinet met with Piłsudski at the Belvedere Palace. A decision was taken to dissolve parliament if the Sejm concurred with the Senate. No secret was made of this. Bartel went to see Maciej Rataj (Marshal of the Sejm) just before the meeting of the lower house of parliament to tell him that it was only a question of obtaining the President's signature on a document, which had already been drafted, authorizing the dissolution of parliament. The Sejm approved the Senate's amendments. Bartel went to Mościcki, but to his amazement he did not get the President's signature. He had, instead, to telephone Rataj to inform him that government had resigned and that the resignation had been accepted by Mościcki.

These extraordinary events throw light on Bartel's political standing. Formally, the first Prime Minister after the May *coup* occupied a powerful position. But in practice he was fully aware that it was neither he nor Mościcki, but Piłsudski, who decided policy. He nevertheless believed that he enjoyed Piłsudski's full confidence. In this he was wrong. Piłsudski needed Bartel to play a leading political role, but beyond a certain point he was dispensable; Bartel never did belong to Piłsudski's immediate circle, by whom all political decisions were taken. This group comprised: Aleksander Prystor, head of office to the Inspector-General, Józef Beck, head of office to the Minister for the Armed Forces, Kazimierz Świtalski, Director of the Political Department, Ministry of Military Affairs, Bogusław Miedziński, Walery Sławek, Ignacy Matuszewski, Bronisław Pieracki and, to some extent, Stanisław Car. Janusz Jędrejewicz was soon to join this group in which Bolesław Wieniawa-Długoszowski also held a favoured position.

These were the men who enjoyed Piłsudski's full confidence, who were entirely at his disposal and to whom he was, in time, to hand over more and more power. At first, they remained in the shadows, occupying positions of secondary importance within the government apparatus. But, because of their proximity to Piłsudski they wielded considerable influence. In dictatorial systems, real power is not always a function of formal authority; the governance of Poland was rapidly tending towards dictatorship.

During the night of 30 September–1 October, a group of about 10 military officers forced their way into the home of Zdziechowski, a member of parliament, and beat him up. His assailants told him that this was for interfering in the budget for the armed forces. The incident created a great sensation. An investigation was launched but was conducted in such a way as not to find the attackers. In the course of a conversation on 23 October, Rataj mentioned the case to Piłsudski. The latter replied that it was of no interest to him, adding, 'let Zdziechowski look for the guilty ones himself, I am not going to be the guardian of his fucking skin. I am not going to allow some scoundrel to put all officers under suspicion . . .'.

Thuggery towards political opponents was until this point in time a monopoly of the *Endecja*. Now, those who proclaimed the motto of moral change in politics, reached for the baton and knuckle-duster. Nothing was done to dissuade such attacks. In due course, the following politicians suffered similar outrage: Tadeusz Dołęga-Mostowic, Adolf Nowaczyński (who, as a result of a savage attack, lost his eye) and Jan Dąbski, chairman of the Polish delegation which had taken part in the peace negotiations at Riga and later Vice-Marshal of the Sejm. He was so heavily assaulted that he died after attempts to revive him in hospital had failed. In addition to this sad list, mention must also be made of General Włodzimierz Zagórski who was murdered in circumstances which remain unclear to this day.

Its true to say that in contrast to other European dictatorships at the time, these were sporadic incidents rather than systematically used methods of resolving political problems. Nevertheless this did not lessen the sinister overtones of such attacks. Man-handling political opponents degenerated further into the torture of Communist prisoners and the brutal treatment of national minorities. Terror first demoralized those responsible for its use. What appeared to be the easiest and most effective method of dealing with dissent left permanent scars on the social psyche; irrespective of who the 'unknown criminals' were, the political responsibility for their actions was borne by the government.

On 2 October 1926, a new cabinet was formed under Piłsudski's chairmanship. He also retained the portfolio of Minister for Military

Affairs. Kazimierz Bartel, the former premier, became Piłsudski's deputy and also Minister for Religious Affairs and Public Education. The nomination of Aleksander Meysztowicz as Minister of Justice, one of two conservatives (the other was Karol Niezabytowski) appointed to the cabinet caused something of a sensation; he was remembered for having participated in the celebrations of the unveiling, in 1904, of the statue of Catherine the Great in Wilno. Strange as the marriage between socialists and conservatives in government must have seemed, this was a challenge to the parliamentary left, indicating that Piłsudski was willing to ignore their wishes and to ride rough shod over their sensibilities. He also signalled a willingness to openly seek support from the right.

The composition of the new cabinet not only shocked the parliamentary left but also caused consternation amongst Piłsudskiites. And yet from the moment Piłsudski had taken power, his actions had a clear logic: to convince the propertied classes that they had nothing to fear from the new order in Polish politics.

The May *coup* had not been inspired by middle-class interests as was the case in many anti-parliamentary movements in Europe. Neither the squirearchy nor the capitalists had a hand in the decision to march on Warsaw. Indeed the battle was fought against the very system that had been accepted by these social classes. But the *coup* did not aim to destroy them. Rather, the mutineers' hopes were pinned on getting their support. This hope was based on the belief that the middle classes had, at the birth of the Second Republic, been coerced into accepting the parliamentary system by the threat of social upheaval and that when that threat had passed, parliamentary democracy had become inconvenient to them. Piłsudski well understood that power could be gained with the help of a few army regiments, but to hold onto it required a political base. This could be gained in one of two ways. Either through a social revolution, which meant rebuilding the class structure, or by becoming a spokesman of the existing system of social relations; in other words by becoming the spokesman of the propertied classes. These were the only two possibilities. Hence the significance of conservative appointments to government posts – the logical consequence of political developments since the May *coup*.

Piłsudski's next move was no less shocking to the left. On 25 October, in the company of the new right-wing minister Aleksander Meysztowicz and his adjutant Captain Remigiusz Grocholski, he paid a visit to the family residence of the Radziwiłł's in Nieśwież. The reason for the visit was to decorate the sarcophagus of Stanisław Radziwiłł (who, as Piłsudski's adjutant, had been killed in the battle for Kiev) with Poland's highest military award, the Golden Cross of the *Virtuti Militari*. Although it had been planned for some time and the list of guests invited to Nieśwież was co-ordinated at the Belvedere, this visit surprised many members of Piłsudski's camp.

The ceremony was followed by a formal lunch attended by about 45 guests. Speeches were delivered by Poland's senior aristocrats, Albrecht Radziwiłł, Janusz Radziwiłł and Eustachy Sapieha. Piłsudski proposed a toast, '. . . to the House of Radziwiłł which has, in the past, given us a number of men, who, in the service of their country, became famous either on the battle-fields or in the Senate . . . I drink today, not to the memory of the fallen hero because I believe that his memory will live among you, but . . . to the House of Radziwiłł, . . . may it long survive . . .'.

The visit to Nieśwież, had, it seems, a dual purpose. First of all Piłsudski wanted to speed up the process of integrating various conservative political groups. In discussions with their representatives, he sketched out a promising future and often emphasized the necessity of a strong conservative party. Contrary to rumour, he did not make any deal in Nieśwież, but undoubtedly used the occasion to create a basis for future political co-operation. What is important to realize is the extent to which Piłsudski was keen to stimulate internal changes within the conservative movement.

His second aim in meeting with heads of the landed aristocracy, was to emphasize his distance from the political left which had supported him in May. Their reaction to the Nieśwież visit was one of surprise and shock; the left believed that Piłsudski would continue to look to them for support after the May *coup*. *Robotnik* saw no political sense in the visit. In his article, Mieczysław Niedziałkowski hoped that it was 'a mere family gathering' which would go no further than that, since an alliance with the aristocracy would mean a break between Piłsudski and the interests of the peasant masses and the working class. However, neither the PSL-*Wyzwolenie* nor the *Piast* Peasant Party treated the visit as a sufficient reason to break with Piłsudski. It seems that the conduct of the parliamentary left was accurately observed by Rataj who wrote that 'all cooled down when they realized that Piłsudski's visit to Nieśwież was the first step on the way to encircling the National Democrats and cutting them off from the landed aristocracy. The hatred of the *Endecja*, inculcated and fanned over the years by Piłsudski, was so great on the left, that without much difficulty they were reconciled to the thought that Counts Radziwiłł, Sapieha, and Lubomirski are ideal political and social allies in the struggle with the National Democratic reaction'.

The left-wing parties in parliament had great difficulty in understanding what the post-May system was about politically; they still cherished strong illusions regarding Piłsudski himself but were most confused by his conduct of parliamentary politics. If, as they believed was the case, the Piłsudski camp was after the political defeat of the *Endecja*, which was also the aim of the parliamentary left, then co-operation between Piłsudski and the leaders of the left would follow. They could see that the support of conservatives could be helpful to the government in its struggle against the *Endecja*. They also knew that even with full government backing, conservatives had little chance of obtaining much support in parliamentary elections. Moreover, since parliament was approaching another election, this would force the government to co-operate with the left. It therefore followed that the left should not burn its bridges and that it was necessary, in the words of the resolution passed by the main council of the PPS on 18 October 1926, 'to maintain an objective attitude towards the government'. From the point of view of political mathematics this was sound reasoning, but there is more to politics than mathematical calculations.

The leaders of the parliamentary left were wrong not only in their political prognosis but also in their attempt to make sense of Piłsudski's moves. One of these, running in parallel to his visit to Nieśwież, concerned the opening of a new session of the Sejm. On 2 October 1926, the day on which the new cabinet was formed , Piłsudski and Bartel paid a visit to Marshal Rataj. 'The meeting', noted Rataj, 'passed off quietly and . . . in a friendly atmosphere, though it began with a clash'. Piłsudski's opening remarks indicated, that in contrast to Bartel, he was not going to 'play games' with 'gentlemen of the Sejm' and would not allow any 'tricks' from them. To this Rataj replied that he was ready for most loyal co-operation with the government but that he would equally well defend the privileges of the Sejm.

On 23 October Piłsudski again visited Rataj to inform him that the budget estimate would be presented to the Sejm on time, and that parliament would be recalled for 29 October. When Rataj asked for the President's decree with regard to this he was told that he would receive it on 29 October. To avoid conflict Rataj notified MPs in writing that the Prime Minister had informed him that a decree recalling parliament would be announced on 29 October and that the Sejm would meet the next day. He assured them that his action was in accordance with the constitution.

On the eve before the announcement of the decree recalling the Sejm, Piłsudski once again visited Rataj. He told him that, as Prime Minister, he would read out the President's order and MPs would have to hear it out in standing position. In reply Rataj said that this demand was not entirely acceptable. The Sejm would hear out the President in standing position but it was a different matter to hear out the President's proclamation read by the Prime Minister in that position. Rataj said that he planned to consult the political clubs for their opinion and added that the greatest opposition to the demand would come from the left wing rather than the right. The next day the pro-Piłsudski *Głos Prawdy* (The Voice of Truth) published Rataj's opinion about the left, but that was not the only disloyalty shown to Rataj by Piłsudski during this affair. On a later visit to Rataj, Piłsudski stated that the President's decree would be presented to Rataj on 30 October at 5 p.m. that Rataj would read it and that MPs should hear it out standing up. On 30 October a group of party representatives met as the Convention of Seniors and rejected the demand that the Sejm should hear out the President's decree standing. Rataj informed Piłsudski of this view and went on to see Mościcki, to whom he gave an account of the entire matter, emphasizing that if the President were to appear in the Sejm, the problem of standing up would not exist.

After his return, Rataj started to write a letter to Piłsudski informing him of the attitude of the Seniors when Bartel and Meysztowicz called on him as Piłsudski's envoys. They informed him that the opening session of the Sejm would be later than the agreed time of 5 p.m. Then, just before the appointed hour, the head of the President's chancery, Stanisław Car, handed Rataj a memorandum from Mościcki in which he was asked to come to an agreement with Piłsudski over details concerning the opening of the Sejm session. He was also handed a copy of a memorandum sent to Piłsudski in which Mościcki stated that he was inclined 'to the proposition of the Sejm Marshal' and would personally perform the opening of Parliament ceremony. Mościcki also recorded his wish to cancel his instruction, of 29 October, about the Sejm's opening. Rataj was even more surprised to learn from Stanisław Car, whose official function as head of Chancellery was to interpret the constitution, that according to its 25th article, whilst the Sejm had to be recalled by the end of October, this did not imply that its session had to open by that date. As the future would show, this interpretation was very dangerous for the Sejm because it allowed the government to impede parliamentary activity.

Rataj proved to be a very weak opponent in this war of nerves and had not detected that danger. Unwilling to cause a breach with the President and government over this interpretation of the constitution he decided to convince the Convention of Seniors that the session of the Sejm called for on 31 October should be opened on 2 or 3 November. They accepted 3 November. This was the first important success for Piłsudski in his contest with parliament. The Marshal of the Sejm and the Convention of Seniors had not only accepted that the recall of the Sejm need not necessarily imply its opening, but they themselves approached the President with the initiative to change the time of its opening. The Sejm could not have made Piłsudski a better gift. But Piłsudski was not satisfied with it. Late that same fateful day of 30 October, Bartel brought a letter from Piłsudski to Rataj. It was so insulting that Rataj refused to accept it and said that, if he were to accept it, he would be obliged to read it to the Sejm. Confused, Bartel took the letter back and shortly afterwards informed Rataj by telephone that he could consider the letter non-existent and that Rataj was to organize the ceremony of the opening of Parliament. Piłsudski himself would take care of arrangements regarding the journey of the President to the Sejm.

Next day, on 31 October, at midday, Rataj consulted his deputy, Ignacy Daszyński and addressed a letter to Piłsudski in which he proposed the opening of the session for 3 November and suggested that the ceremonial arrangements be taken care of by the Head of Protocol. That evening Aleksander Prystor brought him Piłsudski's reply.

Rataj was dismayed by what Piłsudski wrote. Making public the proposal to open parliament on 3 November would interfere with his existing preparations to open the session that day and would cause a complicated legal situation regarding the constitutional rules concerning the recall of the Sejm and the start of its new session. Rataj's proposal raised issues too important even for cabinet to discuss, so 'after receiving your letter, Sir, I at once informed the President . . . that there was no need for him to make preparations for the ceremony of the opening of the Sejm today'.

Rataj was right to be surprised and confused but, as yet, he did not understand that he had fallen into a cunningly set trap. Piłsudski had not only managed to suggest that the initiative to separate the recall of parliament from its opening session had come from representatives of the Sejm but that such re-arrangement had not crossed his mind. His letter made Rataj guilty that parliament was not going to be opened on 31 October; if there was an infringement of the law, then responsibility for it fell on the Sejm and on Rataj personally. His first mistake, which gave rise to others, was to proceed with arrangements for the convening of parliament without proper authorization, which could only have come as a direct order from the President. Neither should he have engaged in the ridiculous dispute over whether MPs were to sit or stand during the reading of the President's decree, nor consented to Mościcki's acceptance of Piłsudski's proposals concerning the ceremony. The Marshal of the Sejm was not obliged to execute the President's recommendations as set out in Mościcki's letter to him. By agreeing to them, Rataj entangled himself into taking joint responsibility for the time limits concerning the start of the Sejm session and ended up by having to take sole responsibility for them. He did not appreciate the extent of the deviousness of Piłsudski's camp, believing throughout that, at the very least, he could depend on their loyalty.

Piłsudski had achieved the political aim of ridiculing parliament. The whole affair, from the question of whether MPs should sit or stand to the question of when parliament should meet was conducted in public to lessen the dignity of Parliament. Eventually the ceremony marking the recall of parliament took place on 30 October. All the chairs were removed from the assembly hall as an added insult to the Sejm. The majority of MPs boycotted the ceremony.

In the months following the May *coup*, parliament lived with the illusion that there was a possibility of co-existence with the post-May government. It had accepted dictatorship and tried to work with it. But this was not possible. Piłsudski was determined to undermine the parliamentary system. He had, with Rataj's unwitting assistance ridiculed parliamentary protocol. The constitution itself had become negotiable. Next, the pro-government press conducted a propaganda campaign against the Sejm, accusing MPs of selfishness, corruption, stupidity and demagoguery. They were called to account for their 'high personal allowances' and condemned for looking to their own personal interests and those of their party, rather than seeking to uphold the national interest. In painting this group portrait darker tones were used unstintingly.

It is difficult to investigate the effectiveness of this propaganda with its appeal to mass emotion and ready-made scapegoat to account for past failures. Success, on the other hand, was credited to the new government. In this task, the propaganda campaign was aided by a clear improvement in the country's economic situation in the period following the events of May. Unemployment decreased and, for the first time in the history of the Second Republic, a surplus on current account was declared in 1926. This was in no sense an achievement of the post-May *clique*. Changes advantageous to Poland, in the international economy had begun before the *coup*; the long miners' strike in Britain opened up the European market for Polish coal. But the average reader of the popular press associated the improvement in the economy with government policy and his confidence in the government grew.

The lack of a concrete political programme was another characteristic of the post-May government which went in its favour. In his radio broadcast in November 1926, marking the eighth anniversary of Polish independence, Piłsudski failed to mention any aspect of future policy. Instead he told the fairy tale of the frog which changed into a beautiful maiden and of the legions which had been transformed into the Polish army.

Reticence on matters of policy seemed to go down well with the

general public. Here was a government which did not delude the people
with empty promises. It got on simply and honestly with the task of
government. Great emphasis was placed on public image and the cult of
Piłsudski was being carefully nurtured. His saint's day on 19 March
became an unofficial public holiday. Marches and military tattoos were
organized. Representatives from schools, offices and factories signed
their names in special commemorative books displayed for the occasion
at the official residences of respectively the district commissioner and
regional commissioner. Everything was performed with elaborate style
and ceremony. A certain contradiction existed between the splendour of
those celebrations and the modest exterior of the man himself. Piłsudski
lived a life of self abnegation. He was not attracted by the high life. He
shunned the delights of the table; he was no *gourmand* and hardly ever
touched alcohol. Nor did he care about his appearance. To him these
things were of minimal importance. Increasingly, he kept away from
people and preferred solitude. He had never enjoyed good health and
was now ailing more often. His way of life worsened his condition: he
was a heavy smoker, drank very strong tea and went to bed very late,
often retiring at dawn. Piłsudski was getting on in years. In 1927 he had
attained the age of 60.

During these months since the *coup* the governing camp had clearly
emerged as the group which held Piłsudski's trust. Other allegiances
were no longer relevant. For example, one cannot simply assume that
members of the parliamentary left, who had supported the May *coup*,
were members of Piłsudski's camp. They had been convinced that
Piłsudski would, at least in part, realize their political programme. But
this proved to be an illusion. Differences between Piłsudski and the
parliamentary left grew daily more visible, making a split inevitable.
Only its delay needs explanation. This was due firstly, to Piłsudski's
disorienting tactic of not formulating a political programme, which
curbed the process of polarization. Secondly, the parties of the left, PPS,
PSL-Liberation (*Wyzwolenie*) and the Peasant Party, had many members
who were declared Piłsudski men and to whom any instruction from the
Belvedere remained law. Such loyalty was deeply rooted amongst
activists in the socialist movement. To them, Piłsudski remained the
highest authority and they were always ready to submit to his will;
working within the various groups of parliamentary left they provided
essential support to the Piłsudski camp.

The largest contingent of this camp consisted of former legionnaires
and members of the POW. The most important group was composed of
those who had served under Piłsudski in the First Brigade. Fate had
furnished them with various destinies, but the majority remained
faithful to the 'Commander'. After the May *coup* power was concen-

trated in their hands and their influence was to grow with time. Their strength lay in Piłsudski's trust.

A spirit of radicalism and democracy pervaded the political intentions of this circle. The May *coup* was seen as the beginning of the restoration of the Republic. This restoration was variously interpreted but all wished to rid Poland of social injustice. They trusted that poverty and unjust wealth would disappear. They yearned for the realization of the castles in the air which they had dreamt of in the trenches. They totally disregarded the political role of the parties and of parliament, believing that the selfishness of politicians had brought Poland to the edge of the abyss. Finally, they believed that as they had gained Poland's independence, it was their duty to govern and their destiny to do so because of their moral purity.

In a political environment characterized by sharp ideological divergences and splits, this group was held together by the cult of their leader. It was a bond that only his death could loosen. Those individuals who lost faith in the leader and broke away, were the exceptions who proved the rule. To the outside world the cult of the leader gave the group a certain uniformity. Internally, differences could lead to intense struggles in the attempt to win the confidence of their leader, gain power and influence decisions. These struggles were not simply about personal ambition. There was also fierce competition on matters of policy; success came to those who correctly anticipated their leader's wishes and who gave shape to his political ideas.

One other feature of the post-May camp which was most important in terms of its development was the inflow of neophytes and careerists. They were spitefully referred to as the 'Fourth Brigade', the Legions having only had three brigades. This inflow was an unavoidable occurrence. It was also, from the governing group's point of view, necessary. The victors of May had had the fleeting support of the Warsaw crowd, but such was not the case in all parts of Poland. Overall, theirs was a very narrow base of public support.

Excluding the membership of the parliamentary left, the Belvedere camp numbered 20–30,000 people at most; enough to gain power, but not enough to exercise it. They were able to fill the posts wielding political control of the government's administrative apparatus, but there were too few of them to control the whole administration. New people had to be found at all grades. Piłsudskiites did not possess the professional experience required for the civil service. However, control of the army was, from their point of view, easier. This was because in the military Piłsudski's authority reigned supreme and because the principles of discipline and of loyalty towards the state still prevailed.

The months after May witnessed the unusual situation of a dictatorship functioning whilst retaining the structure of parliamentary democracy. Parliament accepted the existence of the dictatorship and tried to operate within its parameters. The dictator accepted the existence of Parliament, the opposition parties and their press and thus created the illusion that such a system was the aim of the *coup*.

Parliament was nearing the end of its term and the governing camp had, of necessity, to face the question of elections. During the summer of 1927 Piłsudski decided not to change the electoral law; in other words, the elections would be held according to the same rules as in 1922. This meant, in practice, the acceptance of the party system. The Belvedere camp had, in contesting the election, to swallow its fundamental ideological objection to party politics. Sławek and Świtalski, to whom Piłsudski entrusted the electoral task, were faced with the very difficult problem of reconciling the post-May camp to the necessity of gaining a parliamentary majority which would enable change to the Constitution. They decided to give the election the character of a plebiscite, dividing voters between those who would vote for Piłsudski and those who would vote for the system prior to 1926. This avoided the necessity of forming a political party of the post-May camp and, above all, avoided the necessity of formulating a political programme. This approach pandered to the persuasions of the Piłsudski camp.

Piłsudski's intention was that the electoral bloc which would return his camp to power should not be formed by agreement of the political parties, but by all those who supported the government, whatever their political or social persuasion. This approach replaced a political programme by what were referred to as the 'interests of the state'. Piłsudski believed he would thus get conservatives, socialists, peasants and the national minorities to co-operate and also that he would gain the support of representatives of all social classes; a well governed state would harmoniously express the interests of everyone and lead to the political consensus needed to resolve unavoidable clashes of interest without allowing such conflicts to endanger the cohesion of the state. This was a conception of solidarity which arose from an assumption that the state was the highest form of social organization representing the common good rather than the separate interests of classes. Piłsudskiites believed that political parties, in their existing form, were by definition unable to renounce particular interests and were therefore unable to address the common good. Yet it was felt that an official ban on party activity would do more harm than good because the nation was not, as yet, able to understand the rationale for such a ban.

How was the governing bloc to prepare its list of candidates and under what slogan should they go to the polls? Answers to these questions were arrived at gradually. On 19 January 1928 a 'Non-Party

Bloc of Cooperation with the Government of Marshal Józef Piłsudski', was announced. The last words were dropped by the time the 'Non-Party Bloc of Cooperation with the Government' (*Bezpartyjny Blok Współpracy z Rządem–BBWR*) took shape through the establishment of local committees under the personal direction of the district and regional commissioners. With the help of the state apparatus a homogenous organizational structure was created during January and February of 1928. In order to encourage the membership of well-known local figures on these committees, formality was kept to a minimum; the only requirement was a declaration of loyalty towards Józef Piłsudski. People of various and very often ideologically and politically opposed points of view sat on the committees. Attempts were also made to ensure a socially representative membership; one would find sitting on the committee peasants, craftsmen, landed gentry, business men, doctors and lawyers, not to mention teachers, who, as state employees were ordered to join. Workers were the most difficult to recruit; the post-May camp had very little influence in this class.

The BBWR was linked to all the political organizations of the post-May camp. It had at its disposal a range of means to exert pressure and influence decisions. It could invoke the help of the tax inspectorate, arrange the official transfer of inconvenient civil servants and dispense bribes. It could also call on police repression, as against the communists. Finally, Piłsudski transferred 8 million złs from the surplus on current account to the BBWR as a fighting fund. This was an illegal act.

All political parties prepared themselves for the third parliamentary elections to take place in the 10 years of independent Poland's existence. The first election for Parliament had taken place in chaotic circumstances, before Polish borders had actually been settled. The next elections in 1922, the first in the history of the Second Republic, were held according to the classic rules of parliamentary democracy. They revealed the nation's political fissures and a relatively undeveloped political culture, understandable in terms of the history of the partitions.

The elections of March 1928 were held in different circumstances again. Parliamentary democracy was negated by the May *coup*. Its spine was broken and it was left to vegetate. The rest of its skeleton was left relatively unchanged. One dissimilarity to previous elections was that in 1928, for the first time, the government itself was represented as a contestant. That changed the electoral campaign in a fundamental way. The government chose to contest the election as a plebiscite. A vote for the BBWR was a vote for Piłsudski. Voting for any other list was a vote against Piłsudski. This was a very convenient formula. Not only because it excused the government from the need to define its political programme, but because it placed no restriction on its political *clientele*.

Thus, in any one constituency, representatives of very different and often antagonistic groups could appear on the BBWR list. But at the same time this system concealed a serious danger. An electoral defeat after a propaganda campaign calling for a plebiscite would be severely damaging. It would mean a lack of public support for the legacy of the May *coup*.

Sławek and Świtalski, in charge of the campaign, tried, firstly, to present the BBWR not as a classic electoral alliance of parties supporting government, but as a broad platform of political activists from many different socio-economic backgrounds. This was a step towards the liquidation of the party structure. In practice the policy failed to retain the purity of its line; the BBWR soon took on all the features of a political party. Secondly, attempts were made to weaken the opposition by preventing the formation of rival electoral blocs. Piłsudskiites correctly calculated that splitting the vote gave the BBWR a better chance at the polls; such fragmentation would not only weaken their rivals but would also disorientate the electorate. Thirdly, the BBWR had at its disposal the full use of the government's administrative apparatus. This gave it a massive coercive and financial advantage.

Different methods of exerting influence were applied, according to region. In the east of the country, inhabited by a non-Polish majority, the administration exerted pressure uninhibitedly. In central Poland they had to reckon with public opinion and tried to avoid gross breaches of the law. In the western regions, formerly under Prussian occupation, administrative action was even more circumspect.

Despite this degeneration in political ethics, the decision taken by various dictatorships of contemporary Europe to turn the elections into a complete farce was not taken in Poland. Opposition parties were allowed to conduct electoral campaigns; they could, within certain restrictions which did not amount to much in practice, publish their own literature. Yet, within this seemingly unhandicapped contest of strength, the governing camp had a clear advantage. In some measure it dictated the rules of the game; but opponents were not deprived of chances. It is difficult to say whether this situation arose from the conviction that it was possible to achieve success without drastic breaches of the law, or whether perhaps Piłsudski set little store by electoral success.

The electoral campaign marks a clear turning point in the history of the post-May camp. A process of transformation began almost immediately after the *coup*. The new regime which came to be known as the *Sanacja*, a term which denotes a proposed change in political morals, is used in contemporary political language to describe the May victors. We have attempted not to use the term so far, leaving it for the period after 1928. The period between May 1926 and the elections of 1928 was a transition stage in which the Belvedere camp was transformed into the *Sanacja* camp. Settling the problem of terminal dates or points of origin in the study of social processes is a matter for discussion. It seems, however that, with reference to the ruling camp, there is no doubt that 1928 was a year of qualitative change.

CHAPTER NINE

Man of Destiny

The first parliamentary elections since the May coup took place in March 1928. The poll was very high with a turn out of 11,728,360 or 78.3 per cent of the electorate. The BBWR returned 122 MPs and became the strongest party in the Sejm. This figure did not, however, constitute a majority. Indeed, seen as an expression of public support for the post-May government, the election was in no way a success. Despite its enormous advantage in having the support of the administrative apparatus, the BBWR gained barely 25 per cent of the votes. If the elections had actually been a plebiscite, then Piłsudski would have lost. If, on the other hand, the elections measured political rivalry within the parliamentary system, then Piłsudski, in comparison with previous Sejm, had considerably strengthened his position.

Put differently, the election had greatly reduced the strength of his enemies to the centre and right of the political spectrum. After the previous election this bloc could count on 57.9 per cent of the votes in the Sejm. Now the figure was 20.5 per cent: The *Endecja* came down from 28 per cent to 8.4 per cent and the centre from 29.9 per cent to 12.1 per cent. The defeat of the *Endecja* was most severe. Having had 100 MPs they were now down to 37, smaller not only than the BBWR, but also the PPS and PSL-*Wyzwolenie*. Their position was not much different in the Senate. In the elections to the upper house, the BBWR returned 46 senators, the PPS 10, *Endecja* 9, *Wyzwolenie* 7, *Chadecja* 6, NPR, *Piast* and Peasant Party (PSL) 3 each and the parties of the national minorities 24 in sum.

The Senate was of secondary significance. In so far as a political contest was still possible, the decisive political forum was the Sejm. Indeed by deciding to hold an election, the *Sanacja* signalled its intention to accept Sejm's existence (with all the consequences which followed). And although it was realized that basic political decisions would be made not in Sejm, but in the Belvedere Palace the *Sanacja* were still preoccupied with the analysis of the Sejm's political make-up.

Pro-government parties had at their disposal 130 votes, short of an overall majority by 93. In practice, the prevalence of political splits in parliament meant that an absolute majority was not needed to govern; as a rule some parties remained neutral towards the cabinet and this allowed it to govern. Also, within the parliamentary left, especially the PPS and PSL-*Wyzwolenie*, there still existed an influential group of

Piłsudskiites amongst whom hopes were reborn of the possibility of agreement with the *Sanacja*, especially as it was known that internal differences existed in the BBWR.

What remained in doubt was whether a common political programme could be agreed. Another unknown was whether the BBWR constituted a bloc only for electoral purposes. If so it might split into a number of groups in the Sejm. This eventuality made the chances for agreement between the *Sanacja* and the parliamentary left look more realistic. After all, alliance with activists of the parliamentary left would enable the *Sanacja* to achieve its aim of destroying the *Endecja*; in that regard the interests of the parliamentary left and those of the *Sanacja* were convergent. However, in place of the *Endecja*, a group representing the gentry and the interests of industry and commerce had entered the Sejm through the BBWR. From the point of view of the left this was a negative outcome of the struggle against the *Endecja*. But in spite of everything, this group seemed to be less dangerous than the *Endecja*, mainly because its place in the Sejm depended on its support for the government, without which it would never have been elected. The parliamentary left reasoned that this dependence of the representatives of the gentry and of industry on the government made it possible for the left to influence this group's policies by partnership with government. A government headed by Piłsudski.

Piłsudski, however, did not intend to seek partners for a political coalition. In his plans, the Sejm was to fulfil an extremely limited role. It was to restrict its activities to approving the budget and to constitutional reform. The latter task was not to be hurried. Firstly, because the BBWR controlled insufficient votes to carry out changes to the constitution and secondly, Piłsudski did not have a clear conception of the shape of the new constitution.

The ceremonial opening of parliament took place on 27 March. Besides the formalities of oath taking, MPs had gathered to nominate the Marshal of the Sejm. It was known that Piłsudski's candidate was Bartel. His support came not only from the BBWR. He was thought of as an advocate of the normalization of relations between government and parliament and enjoyed the reputation of being a liberal politician with good relations with a number of Sejm leaders. In the opinion of many MPs the selection of Bartel would guarantee that the government would co-operate with the Sejm and that a *modus vivendi* would be worked out. Finally, as a member of the largest party in the Sejm, Bartel seemed the logical choice for the office of Marshal. So he had a good chance of victory though his choice required some negotiation between the BBWR and other political groups.

Piłsudskiites firmly believed that the BBWR should not have to negotiate with anybody else, that 'the Commander's' will was sufficient to swing the decision in Bartel's favour. It seems however that they wrongly assessed the configuration of power in the Sejm. It was obvious, that neither the *Endecja* nor the parties of the national minorities could put up successful candidates. Of the parliamentary left only the PPS decided to put one forward. He was Ignacy Daszyński. No one stood from the centre.

Daszyński did not seem to be a dangerous competitor and his endorsement by the PPS was interpreted as a means of allowing socialist MPs to avoid having to vote for Bartel in the first round. It was assumed that they would do so in the second. It was also assumed that Bartel would get the votes of PSL-*Wyzwolenie*, the Peasant Party, at least part of the *Endecja* vote, the *Piast's*, the NPR and the national minorities. This would be more than enough to secure his election.

The mistake in these assumptions lay in ignoring the change of mood within the *Wyzwolenie* and Peasant parties. Both had become disillusioned by the Piłsudski camp and protested against the methods used by the government during the election. Moreover the elections had given the Sejm new heart. This was not like the previous Sejm, which had felt discredited, defeated and demoralized at the end of its parliamentary life.

In the first ballot 434 MPs participated. They cast 385 valid votes and so the required majority was 193 votes. Daszyński got 167 votes and Bartel 136. In the second ballot 433 MPs took part. Spoilt papers numbered 36, so the required majority was 199 votes. Daszyński received 206 votes and Bartel 141. The result indicated that despite significant political fragmentation of the Sejm, the BBWR camp found itself practically isolated. It also demonstrated the political attractiveness of the PPS. They, together with *Wyzwolenie* and the Peasant Union had a total 129 MPs.

Daszyński, in the first ballot received 38 votes and in the second as much as 77 votes above this figure. Assuming that all PPS MPs voted for Daszyński, these figures indicate that the candidate of the PPS received 143 votes from other clubs. Thus a very dangerous balance of power emerged for the BBWR. In a sense the BBWR found themselves in a situation similar to that of the *Endecja* in the previous Sejm, the largest party but deprived of the possibility of playing an independent political role. There was only one difference and it was decisive. To gain power, the *Endecja* had to seek for a coalition. The *Sanacja* had power and it was independent of the disposition of political forces in parliament.

When Daszyński's election was announced, the BBWR and members of the government left the hall of the Sejm ostentatiously, expecting that the Sejm would be dissolved. But Piłsudski did not take that step. The result of the ballots disclosed the weakness in political support for the *Sanacja* and forced him to take cautious action. He considered retention of the parliamentary system to be a necessary pretence even though its powers were to be severely restricted.

Given the disposition of strength in parliament its dissolution would have been difficult to explain to the public and would have necessitated calling a new election where it was unknown whether or not the results would be advantageous for the governing camp. The risk was not worth taking. For its part, the parliamentary left had no wish to intensify conflict with Piłsudski. It was afraid that such action would not be understandable to its political *clientele*.

Hence the offers of co-operation between the Sejm and the government which were included in Daszyński's inaugural speech. Piłsudski's response was to instruct the BBWR to join in with the work of the Sejm.

Not long after, during the night of 17–18 of April, Piłsudski suffered an apoplectic attack. In the official bulletin published on 20 April it was stated that he had been admitted to Ujazdowski Hospital for a few days because of a pain in the hand. On 25 April the public were informed that, after treatment, the pain had ceased and that the patient had returned home. Two days later he was at his desk but on 2 May it was announced that on the doctor's advice, he would not take an active part in the government's work until 6 May. On 7 May he returned to work. One week later the public were told that doctors advised him to rest during his convalescence. Piłsudski was 61 years of age. The apoplectic attack, a result of sclerosis, partly paralysed the right side of his body. The paralysis receded but he did not regain full use of his right hand. Piłsudski was, according to various reports, a very difficult patient. He disobeyed doctors' orders and often refused to take medicines. Though the diagnosis of his condition was kept strictly confidential, his behaviour undoubtedly accounts for the ever changing medical bulletins.

Parliament continued to work throughout Piłsudski's illness and its first session ended with the passing of the finance bill on 15 June, by a large majority of 159. The main opposition came from the PPS some of whose members ostentatiously abstained from voting. Their behaviour did not go unnoticed by Piłsudski. Nevertheless, the Sejm and Senate showed maximum goodwill towards the government in the debate over the budget, passing the bill five weeks before it was actually due for final approval.

It seemed that compromise provided a real possibility of co-existence with the government. This illusion disappeared fast. On 25 June, a few days after the formal ending of the parliamentary year, a meeting of the government took place in the presence of the President. Sławek recalled,

'After greeting the President we took our places at the (conference) table, the Commander asked to speak, . . . he then announced his resignation as Prime Minister. . . . In all honesty, none of us . . . was aware of the Marshal's decision to resign . . .'. Beside the question of his state of health, Piłsudski explained that because Presidential powers were so limited, all the burden of government fell on his shoulders as premier. He complained bitterly over relations with the Sejm and stated that he could no longer endure their behaviour. He said that he was pleased to have been ill during the passing of the budget, otherwise 'bones would have been broken'. Turning on his ministers he barked: 'There *had* to be a *chef de cabinet* who could shit more easily. I have nothing more to say . . . Mr President can see that I am being driven to madness but I am forbidden to rant and rave'.

This outburst was very odd, not only in content but also in the way it was expressed. These broken sentences suggest extreme mental tension or even signs of an unbalanced mind. Piłsudski spoke to a small audience of people in high office who were wholly dependent on him and who had obediently executed his orders. He did not spare them the contempt which he felt towards them and he demonstrated this, too, in a surprise decision as well as in the way that he spoke to them. They were made aware that they were pawns to be moved by him across the chess board.

It is difficult to say precisely when he began to alienate the people within his circle – men of high calibre who worked with him on the basis of partnership rather than in complete subordination. Dominant among this group were officers who had served in the First Brigade, described by their critics as the 'legionary mafia'. There was a lot of truth in this tag. Strong ties and group solidarity developed through common interests, a shared past and similar age group. Ideologically, they formed a rich mosaic, ranging from the radical to the reactionary to the indifferent. But above all else they were completely submissive to the Commander. It was a matter of secondary importance how much of this was the result of personal fascination and how much the result of cool political calculation. The complex workings of their minds were so closely knit together that no scalpel could prise them apart. They fell victim to the cult of the Marshal, the legend which they built around Piłsudski.

He too had changed since the time of the Legions. Always a very strong egotistical personality wielding great influence over his circle, he had always had the ability to win others over to his way of thinking. Now though, he saw himself as a man of destiny. When did he actually begin to believe in his own greatness? In November 1918, when at breathtaking speed his lot changed from being a prisoner at Magdeburg into becoming his country's leader? Or was it later, during the Kiev expedition, when he emerged as the victorious Commander-in-Chief? These episodes were relevant in his struggle for ascendancy but, even more importantly, were the bedrock of some of his innermost convictions. He believed that he was able to shape the course of history, that Poland's destiny was dependent on his will and that, like other greats from the past, he should dominate over all others. Therefore he had no need for advisers or for intellectual partners, only for people to carry out his will in an efficient and trustworthy way. These were the most important criteria. Orders and instructions were all that mattered in directing his selected team. They accepted this unquestioningly, because, independently of how far they were fascinated by him, the leader was indispensable to them; without him they were not important, or, at least, they meant very little.

The personal struggle, which went on at different times and with different intensity within the Piłsudski camp, was always a struggle for the confidence of the Commander. It was never a struggle against him; his position in the camp was never at risk. His ascendancy was secure and his power absolute. Yet Piłsudski was not a typical dictator. In a dictatorship relations between the dictator and his political team are shaped differently. Most often they are based on fear of permanently falling out of favour which might end in physical destruction and would certainly end in political destruction. The dictator holds total power in his hands and watches, through an extensive control system, to see if his policies are being realized. By comparison, Piłsudski was interested in only a select few issues; in the remaining matters he left a free hand to his team. But it was he who dictated his camp's political line and he alone who decided its future, as, for example, when the cabinet found out about his resignation and therefore about its own dissolution only at the moment he announced it. That way he both prevented all discussion and determined the place of others in the hierarchy.

The government's resignation was announced on 27 June. Kazimierz Bartel, once again, became Prime Minister. Three days after the formation of the new cabinet, Piłsudski granted an interview to the editor of *Głos Prawdy* (Voice of Truth), Wojciech Stpiczyński. Piłsudski denied that the reason for his resignation was his state of health and focused on the problem of the constitutional prerogatives of the Prime Minister and President and the lack of co-operation with Sejm. He looked back in anger, describing the Constituent Assembly as 'a Sejm of harlots' and expressed regret at not having 'dispersed it and crushed it, as it deserved, with a victor's foot'. Such action would have avoided the events of May. What most irritated Piłsudski was parliamentary privilege: 'Every MP has the right to scream, to yell, to hurl insults, to make slanderous statements . . . to behave like a swine and a scoundrel, yet those who work so hard for a mere pittance, as in the case of ministers, have to affect enormous respect for this assembly'. In his opinion it was a 'Sejm of corruption' and he, again, described MPs as 'public whores' who had no conception of the proper way to conduct the affairs of state. Consequently he had little choice but to resign in order to free himself for the task of seeking to reform constitutional law.

Contrary to expectations, Piłsudski refrained from direct action against the Sejm. Nevertheless, this most important interview clearly described his attitude towards parliamentarianism and announced his determination to subordinate the Sejm to his authority. It had seemed that Piłsudski had reconciled himself to the defeat his camp had suffered at the selection of the Marshal of the Sejm and that co-operation with Daszyński had taken a constructive turn over the efficient passing of the budget by parliament; in other words, that the co-existence of dictatorial power with the democratic representation of the nation was possible. Piłsudski's interview brutally shattered these illusions and by making offensive remarks about MPs he aimed to discredit the Sejm in the eyes of the public.

It did not seem to bother him that in his attack on MPs he also discredited parliamentarians of the BBWR. He thought little of their sensibilities. His attack on the new Sejm was directed at the parliamentary left because it had emerged as a power in the Sejm. The attack was all the harsher because it was made at a moment when there was no conflict between the government and the Sejm yet it erased all hope of finding a *modus vivendi*. But Piłsudski's tactics relied on confusing his opponents.

He did so again on 12 August, 1928, at the annual congress of the Legions which took place in Wilno. In his opening speech, Piłsudski was expected to address a subject of topical interest. However such expectations were disappointed. Piłsudski began by saying that since he was speaking in Wilno, he would refrain from making statements that would provoke 'dissonance or bitterness'. He stayed true to his word and did not stray beyond a sentimental and egocentric recollection of military history. Politics may be said to be the art of interpreting information. In his Wilno speech, Piłsudski supplied his opponents with no material for interpretation but rather obliged them to guess at his intentions. A week later he left for a six-week holiday in Roumania, leaving unresolved the question, 'What next?'.

Meanwhile, the first signs of an agreement between the parties of the parliamentary left, PPS, PSL-*Wyzwolenie* and Peasant Party emerged during celebrations of the tenth anniversary of Polish independence. Official celebrations took place on 11 November, coinciding with the anniversary of the armistice. Piłsudski officiated at the military parade in Warsaw and for the first time reviewed his troops not on horseback, but in a carriage. The left had published a joint appeal inviting support in favour of celebrating independence on 7 November, the day on which the Lublin government was formed. The alternative dates for marking independence each had, of course, its own political significance associating the rebirth of Poland with different ideological standpoints. The left's appeal ignored Piłsudski's role and that of the army, emphasizing instead that 'the nation owed its independence to the efforts of the working class'.

Historical anniversaries often fulfil an ideological and political role defined more by the past than by the present. This was certainly true of the 1928 independence celebrations; both the choice of date and the event itself reflected the political ends of those initiating the celebrations. During Lublin's celebrations, Ignacy Daszyński, the city's local government leader and the man elected Marshal of the Sejm against Piłsudski's will said: '. . . the instinct of self preservation and political sense pointed to the Democratic Republic as Poland's only way into the future'. The message was clear. It was elaborated on by Stanisław Thugutt, former Minister of Home Affairs and one of the leaders of PSL-*Wyzwolenie*, who published an article in *Robotnik* entitled 'Lublin Lessons'. In his view the power of the Lublin government, of a united left, accounted for Poland's independence. None of his readers doubted that his text concerned the present. Celebrating the first days of independence, it carried the message that all parties concerned with the defence of democracy should unite under the umbrella of the parliamentary left. Co-operation between these parties continued with the formation, on 14 November, of a joint committee for 'the defence of the Republic and of Democracy'. This development had been prompted by he debate in the Sejm on constitutional reform begun in October in tandem with the debate on the new budget. It signified a consolidation of the left wing opposition to the *Sanacja*.

The newly founded democratic front was weak because rather than developing out of shared convictions it had come about as a response to the régime and was therefore subject to change, or even the hint of change, in government policy. Piłsudski understood this well and it seems clear that he deliberately promoted ambiguity in matters of policy. At one time the BBWR would terrorize parliamentarians by the brutality of its methods and at another Bartel would publicly distance himself from such methods, deceiving the left into believing in the possibility of co-existence between itself and the *Sanacja*. Such duality reflected the power struggle between the group of colonels in control of the BBWR and the liberal wing of the *Sanacja* whose spokesman was

Bartel. Piłsudski himself had, publically, kept silent on political matters ever since his interview with *Głos Prawdy*, but encouraged the struggle within his camp; it was advantageous to him because it confused his opponents. He could ignore the disposition of power within his own camp because his word was final and his decisions, irreversible. That he often avoided making decisions, only further encouraged the struggle within the *Sanacja*. Also, in a body as socially and politically heterogeneous as this, internal conflicts were inevitable. But they would have had little influence on Piłsudski's decisions. In contrast to a parliamentary system where political decisions are the result of various influences at many levels, the *Sanacja* system limited the number of participants in the decision-making process; not only were the most important decisions taken by Piłsudski but he increasingly narrowed the circle of people who had access to him. They themselves narrowed it even further.

The relative power of individuals within the hierarchy of the élite was determined, not by office, but by the possibility of personal contact with Piłsudski. Sławek and Prystor, who always had instant access to Piłsudski, occupied positions within that hierarchy which were, without any doubt, more powerful than those of members of the cabinet apart from Bartel and Mościcki. They always had access to Piłsudski, though only as a matter of courtesy. In reality, Mościcki's role in political decision-making was negligible and Bartel's little greater. Lower down in the hierarchy came those whom 'the Commander' chose to summon and the frequency with which they were summoned defined their position on the lower rungs of the hierarchy. Lower still were those who met Piłsudski because of their particular role in government or army though they were never actually summoned to his presence. Sometimes they had a chance to exchange a few words with him, but most often were just passive observers. The hierarchy was further complicated, because each member, at every grade, had his own, often very wide, network of contacts. These were part of the system of authority, by which is meant involvement in the decision-making process. For example, those closest to Sławek and Prystor had greater authority than holders of high office.

With the passage of time, Piłsudski gradually transferred more power to his co-workers, narrowing his own interests to foreign policy and the armed forces. The structure of the governing élite began to crystalize; the division between formal power and real power was obliterated as the executors of real power took over the highest position in the country's apparatus. In principle the division between real and formal power was retained to 1930, a duality which naturally caused conflicts, as members of the cabinet could not always accept that they had very little influence on cabinet policy, even on policy within their own sphere of activity.

Functioning within this framework was not easy. Piłsudski made a habit of concealing his plans, even from his closest and most trusted co-workers. There was always the possibility that their own initiatives would be thwarted. In practice the possibility of obtaining Piłsudski's opinion on basic questions of policy did not exist. As a case in point, Piłsudski remained silent throughout the debate on constitutional reform until its final stages when his judgement overturned much of the work undertaken by Sławek and Świtalski. That was only one example and one could add many similar. Piłsudski was very often susceptible to changes in mood and those who went to see him could never be sure of the course, content nor outcome of their conversation. Sometimes he imparted instructions in clear, simple soldierly fashion. At other times his language was Aesopian and full of ambiguous metaphor. A dis-cussion with Piłsudski never amounted to an exchange of views. At times he remained silent, having already reached a decision. At others he listened to the opinion of others and then formulated his own. But a discussion in which points of view clashed and thus offered the possibility of a change of opinion; in which each participant had the opportunity of convincing the other – was an unthinkable form of communication. Piłsudski was always arbiter, never participant.

The way Piłsudski conducted affairs of state was epitomized in his handling of the budgetary crisis which now came to dominate political life in Poland. The finance bill passed by the Sejm on 22 March 1927, had authorized the government to spend almost 2 billion złotys in the financial year 1927–1928. Government expenditure exceeded this amount by almost 560 million złotys. It would not have been abnormal for the government to ask the Sejm to approve the additional credit. However, up until the Christmas recess, the government did not do so, despite the fact that the omission would undoubtedly create major difficulties. But Piłsudski had no intention of explaining himself before the Sejm. In the middle of December he demanded that Gabriel Czechowicz, the Finance Minister, provide an increase in the dis-cretionary fund from 200,000 złotys to 8 million złotys. These monies were advanced and were spent on the election campaign of the BBWR. On 12 February 1929, PPS, PSL-*Wyzwolenie* and the Peasant Party proposed a motion of censure in the Sejm against Czechowicz. The debate ran for two weeks and when it came to the vote, a large majority (220 votes for, 132 against with 6 abstentions) voted against the government and demanded that Czechowicz should come before a state tribunal to account for his action. The voting showed the isolation of BBWR in the Sejm.

The trial before the State Tribunal began on 26 June 1929 and lasted three days at the end of which the tribunal declined to pass a verdict, returning the case to the Sejm. This decision was a success for the opposition in regaining the initiative for itself and for parliament. Moreover, although the tribunal had declined to pass judgement on Czechowicz, this did not mean that he was found not guilty, a verdict on which the *Sanacja* had counted. It would have provided the *Sanacja* with excellent propaganda; they had lost this opportunity to discredit parliament.

Piłsudski was determined to save the government from further embarrassment in the Sejm. On 28 November 1929, in a meeting with Sławek and Świtalski, he told them that he had made up his mind that the current session of the Sejm was to be its last. He had decided that parliament was to be challenged after a lengthy crisis in which 'the Commander would . . . intervene personally in March'. On 12 March 1930, Bartel, considered a liberal within the *Sanacja* for his willingness hitherto to work with the Sejm, made an unexpected and vicious attack on parliament. He told the Sejm that it 'had outlived its usefulness' and that it was 'unable to meet the requirements of a modern state'. This was to have far-reaching consequences.

The reply from members of parliament came in a vote of no confidence in the Minister for Labour and Social Welfare Aleksander Prystor, who had incurred the wrath of the PPS in trying to remove members of the party from membership of committees administering funds for sickness benefit (*Kas Chorych*). Under conditions then prevailing in the Sejm the PPS would merely have registered one more protest. Bartel's speech altered the situation; the PPS motion of no confidence gained the support of most parties of the centre and left as well as that of the *Endecja* (only the *Piast* Party abstained) and the government was forced to resign.

The crisis which Piłsudski sought had now arrived. Parliament and its members could be accused of lacking a proper sense of responsibility as the budget had yet to be agreed. It was, moreover, an opportune moment to distract public attention from the Czechowicz affair.

Corrupt practices at the heart of Polish political life now shifted backstage to give centre stage to a farce concerning the appointment of a new Prime Minister. President Mościcki, having failed to interest Piłsudski in the job, nominated Julian Szymański. This elderly but presentable and charming man was a strange choice because he lacked political experience. Szymański accepted and sought Piłsudski's views over policy. Piłsudski advised him to exclude members of the Sejm from the business of government, even from discussion of the budget, a matter which came to public attention. Utilizing proven methods of delaying parliamentary sittings, Piłsudski furthermore said that it was not necessary to recall the now defunct parliament for at least six months. This greatly angered the opposition. No party or grouping outside the BBWR would accept Piłsudski's perception of the Sejm as a mere facade behind which the *Sanacja* was to govern the country. Poland was witnessing the completion of the process, initiated by Piłsudski in May 1926, by which the Sejm was to be rendered politically impotent. It appeared that a clash between Government and Opposition was imminent. At its centre stood the Sejm.

The entire Opposition feared loss of the initiative in this crisis. Their future depended on its outcome. upon whose outcome depended their future. They could not allow their contest with the *Sanacja* to go outside the Sejm. All members of parliament had a vested interest in its survival at a time when most feared losing control of the course of national events. Such fears were not exaggerated as the Polish economy withered in the first chill winds of the Great Depression.

In the absence of government policy to deal with the rapidly deteriorating economic situation, the parties of the centre and left decided to act in concert. On 20 June 1930, a joint meeting of their respective parliamentary clubs took place. 142 MPs and Senators participated. They elected a Provisional Executive Committee of Centre-Left (*Centrolew*) and passed a resolution blaming the government for the catastrophe which had befallen the masses in villages and towns. It regretted the state's interference in the work of the Sejm and Senate and called for the resignation of the 'dictatorial government of Józef Piłsudski' and for 'the establishment of constitutional government, based on the people's confidence'.

On 29 June, a 'Congress for the Defence of the Law and Freedom of the People' took place in the hall of the Old Theatre in Kraków. It was attended by about 1500 opposition party delegates and chaired by Michał Róg of the PSL-*Wyzwolenie* and Vice-Marshal of the Sejm. At the end of the day a mass demonstration took place at the Kleparski Market. The numbers involved have been variously estimated. Witos stated that there were about 250,000 but 30,000 is nearer the truth. Even so, theirs was a significant expression of discontent.

On 30 August the President dissolved parliament and announced elections for November. In reply the *Centrolew* decided, on 9 September, to form an electoral bloc. That night the police arrested the following former MPs of the opposition: Norbert Barlicki, Adam Ciołkosz, Stanisław Dubois, Herman Lieberman, Mieczysław Mastek and Adam Pragier of the PPS; Władysław Kiernik and Wicenty Witos of the PSL *Piast*; Kazimierz Bagiński and Józef Putka of the PSL-*Wyzwolenie*; Karol Popiel of the NPR; Aleksander Dębski and Jan

Kwiatkowski of the National Party; Adolf Sawicki of the Peasant Party; also five former Ukrainian MPs: Włodzimierz Celewicz, Osip Kohut, Jan Leszczyński, Dimitry Palijew and Aleksander Wisłocki. Wojciech Korfanty was arrested on 26 September after the dissolution of the Silesian Sejm.

The arrests were made, without a court writ, on the orders of Minister Składkowski. The violation of the legal process was furthered in sending those arrested to the military prison at Brześzc-on-Bug. Held in isolation, they were persecuted, humiliated, tortured and abused. News of their fate reached the outside world a fortnight after the arrests.

The Brześzc arrests were not undertaken in a moment of anger. Such action had been considered and prepared for quite some time, as a signal of political change. Piłsudski had decided to disperse Parliament half way through its term because, in his opinion, further tolerance of the opposition only led further down a blind alley. Also, the governing camp was too weak to risk a clash with the opposition outside parliament. Mounting social tensions caused by the economic and political crisis, sharpening nationalist conflicts in the eastern border-lands, increasing divergences within the governing camp and greater solidarity within the opposition, meant that the prevailing political situation no longer made sense.

Piłsudski did not choose to reject the democratic camouflage of his dictatorship. He understood that it was easier and more efficient to govern by maintaining the appearance of existing democratic institutions. That is why, despite expectations in some circles to the contrary, the *Sanacja* camp decided to call parliamentary elections according to existing electoral procedures. But this election had, at any price, to be won by the *Sanacja*.

Victory was possible only by paralysing the opposition. The Brześzc arrests were the beginning of a large wave of arrests during the election campaign. They deprived about 5000 people of their freedom, including 84 former MPs and Senators. Out of 1600 supporters of the *Centrolew* 1000 were PPS activists. In such a climate the 'Brześzc elections' of November 1930 took place. Brześzc stands in the history of the *Sanacja* and in the history of the Second Republic as a turning point almost as important as the May *coup*.

CHAPTER TEN

The Last Years

Parliamentary elections, the last before Piłsudski's death in 1935, took place in November 1930. They were held in an atmosphere of political terror. Brute force was used by the state to sway the vote in favour of the regime. The BBWR gained 55.6 per cent of the vote which gave it a majority of 247 MPs in the Sejm. The *Sanacja* had an even greater majority in the Senate and had thus gained political control of both chambers of parliament; the opposition could no longer overthrow the government nor reject its proposals. There was, however, one very important exception; the government's majority was insufficient in matters of constitutional reform which required a majority of at least two-thirds of the vote.

Kazimierz Świtalski, one of Piłsudski's most trusted co-workers was nominated Marshal of the Sejm and Władysław Raczkiewicz became the Marshal of the Senate. Piłsudski himself briefly held the office of premier. On 4 December he resigned in favour of Walery Sławek but retained the military affairs portfolio. Having overseen the composition of the new government, Piłsudski left for a three-month holiday in Madeira. After his return, he summoned Mościcki, Sławek, Prystor, Świtalski and Beck to the Belvedere Palace. He told them that he cast too great a shadow on political life in Poland and that he would gradually step aside from various spheres of activity, concentrating his attention on military affairs and on foreign policy. When Sławek asked him whether the present system in which Piłsudski was consulted on all important questions would remain, he replied in the affirmative. However, in practice, he was to leave more and more matters to those he most trusted. The deterioration in his health meant that he had to cut down on his activities. Piłsudski increasingly led the life of a recluse at the Belvedere and at his flat in the nearby building of the General Inspectorate of Military Affairs. It became increasingly difficult to get in to see Piłsudski through the wall of adjutants protecting his privacy.

His worsening state of physical health also affected his mental health; always mistrustful of his co-workers, Piłsudski became pathological in his suspicion of them. As an example one might cite the case of Aleksander Prystor. He belonged to Piłsudski's close circle and was a family friend. However, in May 1933, when Prystor was Prime Minister, Piłsudski summoned Sławek and Świtalski and to their complete surprise told them that if Prystor remained as Prime Minister, he, Piłsudski, would look upon Prystor with 'unfavourable neutrality'. Naturally, Prystor immediately handed in his resignation, but nobody ever found out the reason for Piłsudski's stand.

Piłsudski was, in his last years, to have bouts of uncontrollable aggression. His loss of self-control became one of the most guarded secrets of the *Sanacja* élite. His periods of deep depression were interlaced with periods of great mental clarity when he astounded his co-workers with the degree of his political competence, particularly in the field of foreign affairs.

The year of 1930 had witnessed a profound change in the international situation. The great crisis, precipitated by the crash on Wall Street, not only shook the economic foundations of Europe but also changed its political order.

Hitler came to power on 30 January 1933. At first, the direction of German policy was uncertain; on 12 February a correspondent of the *Sunday Express* interviewed Hitler; the new German Chancellor was sharply critical of the configuration of the Polish-German border. However, the next day the official Wolf Agency published a denial of the report which clouded the issue again. A few days earlier when the diplomatic corps was introduced to Hitler, he had had a lengthy conversation with Ambassador Wysocki, to whom he declared that Germany needed peace more than Poland; the signals coming through to Warsaw from Berlin were ambiguous.

In reply to a question in the Sejm about Hitler's anti-Polish interview, Beck, the new Polish Foreign Minister, stated that the Polish attitude towards Germany would 'match precisely' Germany's attitude towards Poland and depend more on Berlin than on Warsaw. This clear message was, however, soon followed by a different signal. On 6 March, a day after the elections in the Reich, the Polish base at Westerplatte was strengthened by a battalion of marines. This was an infringement of international agreement and, after pressure from the League of Nations, the battalion had to be withdrawn. Nevertheless this Polish demonstration had a clear political purpose. It was a warning to Hitler that Poland was not prepared to make any concessions over Danzig and a warning to the western powers that Poland would not agree to the revision of its frontiers.

At about this time rumours began to appear that Poland was considering the possibility of a preventive war against Germany. A great deal has been written about this but supporters of the view that Piłsudski considered a preventive war still cannot supply documentary evidence of it. On the contrary, as historians have gained access to the archives, it has become evident that theories of suppositions regarding a Polish initiative are unconfirmed by these sources. Despite this, arguments in support of the case still exist. And although the possibility was only slight, rumours of preventive war alarmed Berlin at the time and it was felt that they should not be ignored, especially as Polish military superiority over Germany was at that time enormous; the Polish army consisted of 226,000 soldiers whilst that of Germany was restricted by the Treaty of Versailles to 100,000 soldiers.

This disparity in strength and the rumours about the possibility of preventive war supplied Hitler with arguments with which to press his case for rearmament. His ultimate aims went much farther than those of Weimar politicians. He sought more than the revision of the Versailles Treaty and a return to Germany of its pre-1914 territory. Hitler sought German domination of Europe. He needed time to prepare Germany for this role. Thus the normalization of relations with Poland became an important matter, especially in the light of the Polish-Soviet non-aggression treaty of 1932.

Hitler realized that it was up to him to take the first step. He spoke with the Polish Ambassador on 2 May 1933 in the presence of von Neurath, the German Foreign Minister and gave Wysocki a lengthy assurance of Germany's peaceful intentions, also stating that as a nationalist he could not question Poland's right to existence. Wysocki sought specific assurance over Polish rights in Danzig but here Hitler was evasive. The communiqué issued next day stated that the discussion ranged over political problems concerning Polish-German relations and that the 'Chancellor expressed the wish that the two countries should jointly and dispassionately investigate common interests'. Warsaw treated Hitler's invitation cautiously, but attached great importance to it, deciding on a policy of *détente* towards Germany. This found expression in the words of Beck to von Moltke, the German Ambassador, on 19 May, referring to the city council elections, which were to take place on 28 May and which the Nazis were clearly going to win, he saw these were 'an internal matter for Danzig'.

In the second half of September, Beck held discussions in Geneva with von Neurath and with Goebbels. In each case the initiative came from Germany and represented a step towards normalization of relations. The importance which Poland attached to relations with Germany was demonstrated by the replacement of Wysocki in Berlin by Józef Lipski in early October.

On 14 October Hitler declared that Germany was to withdraw from the League of Nations and the Geneva conference on disarmament. He also dissolved the Reichstag and announced an election for 12 November.

Hitler's speeches during the election campaign were not only free of any anti-Polish references, but even pointed to the necessity for agreement and peaceful relations between the two countries. On 5 November, Piłsudski held a meeting with Beck and Lipski. After hearing Lipski's opinion of the positive mood in Berlin Piłsudski turned to Beck and said: 'Well, let's give it a try'. Lipski was instructed to seek a meeting with Hitler. This took place on 15 November.

Lipski began by saying that a National Socialist government coming to power in Germany caused great consternation in international opinion and foreshadowed the possibility of serious political conflicts. In these circumstances it was necessary to make some provision for strengthening Polish national security. Nevertheless, the Marshal, (Piłsudski) who was never influenced by the 'atmosphere of alarm created by the media', put his trust in the Chancellor and his policies. He further stated that Polish-German relations were improved, thanks to the Chancellor's personal intervention, which vindicated Piłsudski's faith in him. *Vis-à-vis* the current international situation, 'the Marshal believed that Poland's security depended . . . firstly on direct relations with . . . another country', in this case Germany and secondly on wide participation by the nations in the League of Nations. This second form of security was described by the Marshal as 'an absolute guarantee', arising from the fact that member countries of the League of Nations 'are governed by the articles of the League', such as procedures to follow in case of conflict. The decision of the German government to leave the League of Nations deprived Poland of this second element of security, a decision which had 'strongly affected international opinion and had promoted a mood of anxiety'. In such circumstances, the Marshal's, responsibility for the security of his country, 'forced him to consider the situation very carefully'. He did not want to 'strain relations between the two countries by issuing orders to further strengthen Polish security before asking . . . the Chancellor to consider the possibility of compensating for the loss of that (second) element of security in terms of closer Polish-German relations'.

Hitler made lengthy declarations of goodwill towards Poland. He portrayed aggressive goals as alien to him and wars as achieving nothing but devastation. He saw Communism as the threat. He suggested that Polish-German relations should take the form of a treaty.

On 27 November Piłsudski listened to von Moltke outline a proposal for a non-aggression treaty. Negotiations lasted nearly two months, prolonged by the Polish side trying to gain the maximum benefit from Hitler's anxiety for a normalization of relations with Poland. Finally, on 26 January 1934, Lipski and von Neurath signed the pact, pledging direct negotiations in matters of mutual interest and renouncing the use of force between them for 10 years. A communiqué issued after the signing ceremony spoke of the pact's benefit to other European countries and assured them that the pact contained no additional secret agreements.

The question arises, of how either side benefited from the treaty? For Hitler the answer was quite straightforward. He had ended the isolation of the Third Reich, weakened the Polish-French Treaty and Versailles system, liquidated the Polish threat and gained time for solving internal problems including rearmament. The price which he paid for all this was not a high one. It was actually nothing. He knew that at an appropriate time, he would break the treaty, unless he could first manage to draw Poland into war with the USSR.

For his part, Piłsudski believed that the Nazi victory in Germany meant the end of the historic process of German unification and the rejection of the existing hegemony of Prussia. He attached significance to the fact that Hitler was not Prussian and that there were no Prussians in his inner circle. Agreement with Germany eliminated the danger to Poland of a return to the politics of Rapallo, when the Soviet Union and Germany were partners, and gave Poland greater freedom of manoeuvre in the field of foreign policy. The fundamental benefit of the pact was the apparent elimination of the Danzig problem.

Soon after the January declaration came two more important agreements. On 27 February the so-called 'press agreement' was signed. This meant that Germany would relinquish revisionist propaganda with reference to the Versailles treaty. Then, on 7 March, the Polish-German economic protocol ended the customs war which had lasted since 1925. These were measurable benefits.

On 7 March 1934 a meeting was convened at the Belvedere Palace to which Ignacy Mościcki, Kazimierz Bartel, Aleksander Prystor, Janusz Jędrzejewicz, Walery Sławek, Kazimierz Świtalski and Józef Beck were invited. It was a so-called 'tenants meeting': nearly all were post-May prime ministers who had resided at one time or another at the official Prime Minister's residence. Piłsudski believed that in the post-May system, a change of cabinet should not mean a change of politics and that there should exist a group of people who would take turn about as prime minister without differing in matters of policy. Piłsudski addressed his audience on foreign policy, especially on the need to maintain a balance between Polish-German and Polish-Soviet relations. Poland now had a non-aggression pact with both her neighbours but he warned that peaceful relations with them would not last for ever and that good relations with Germany 'might last another four years'.

Piłsudski was not so wrong in his view of Polish-German relations but he did not understand the malevolence of the Nazis and deluded himself that the non-Prussian composition of Hitler's *clique* was significant. He did not trust in the League of Nations and its collective security, fearing, and not without reason, that the western powers would always be inclined to favour Germany at the expense of Poland.

Piłsudski's other main interest was in military affairs where his influence was rather negative. As a consequence of his experience in the war of 1920, he attached great importance to the cavalry and thereby underestimated the utility of modern arms such as armoured brigades and air force. This was attributable to a conservative way of thinking. He failed to notice and did not understand the transformations which had taken place in the war game. He epitomized the leader who, in winning one war, badly prepares his army for the next. Piłsudski devoted too much time to the politics of promotions. He took an interest in promotions at even the lowest ranks. This took up a lot of time and was, in most cases, a needless distraction. But one has to admit that his care of the officer corps gave good results. Events proved that whilst the Polish army yielded to the German army technically, it was equal to it in regard to the quality of its soldiers.

During his last years, Piłsudski devoted very little time to internal policy. He decided on the personnel of cabinets but interfered little with the work of ministers. He recognized a sharpening of the political conflict after Brześc and yet allowed the continued existence of legal opposition parties and of their press. The latter was certainly harassed by confiscations and repressions, but contrary to trends in many contemporary dictatorships in Europe, that press continued to exist. Political opponents could find themselves at the mercy of a very strict régime at the internment camp which he founded at Bereza Kartuska in 1934. However, despite all, his was a dictatorship incomparably milder than in other countries.

The *Sanacja* was hampered in its attempts to reform the constitution by the lack of a two-thirds majority in the Sejm. However, in 1933, the BBWR presented its proposals for constitutional reform to the constitutional committee of the Sejm. On 26 January 1934, the Constitutional Committee introduced these at a plenary session of the Sejm. Opposition MPs left the hall ostentatiously refusing to discuss the proposals. The BBWR took advantage of their absence and voted the proposals through with the help of Świtalski, the Marshal of the Sejm, who decided that they should be accepted because there was a *quorum* and because over two-thirds of those present voted in their favour. The constitution which was signed by the President on 23 April 1935, the so-called 'April Constitution', really altered the basis of government. The President now became the country's supreme authority. He was given the power to create a government as well as to nominate the Prime Minister. He was entitled to dissolve the Sejm and the Senate, dismiss the Prime Minister and members of the government, the Commander-in-Chief and General Inspector of the Army and the Chairman of the Supreme Board of Control. The President was elected for a period of seven years and had a right to suggest his successor and to nominate his successor in the event of war.

The authority of parliament was considerably limited. The number of Sejm members was reduced from 444 to 208 and Senators were reduced in number from 111 to 96 of whom the President could nominate 32, the remainder elected by indirect voting. Parliament became almost completely dependent on the President.

These measures were tailor-made for Piłsudski. But the 'April Constitution' was one of the last state papers to which Piłsudski put his signature. He was by then a very sick person although he would not allow doctors to examine him. Not until 25 April did he agree to be examined by Professor Wenckenbach from Vienna, who diagnosed cancer of the liver which was inoperable. Piłsudski died on 12 May 1935, the ninth anniversary of the May *coup*.

He was given a royal funeral. On 15 May his body was taken from the Belvedere Palace to Warsaw Cathedral, where hundreds of thousands of people paid homage to him as he lay in state. The army paraded before his coffin on 17 May and it was then transported by special train to Kraków and laid to rest in the royal tombs at Wawel Castle. In compliance with his will, his heart was buried with the ashes of his mother in Wilno and his brain donated to the city's university for the purpose of scientific research.

He had come a very long way from a small estate in Zułów to the royal tombs. Its stages were Siberia, the socialist movement, the Legions, Magdeburg, Head of State and Commander-in-Chief, Sulejówek and full power from May 1926 to his death in May 1935. Piłsudski lived and worked in a number of epochs. He was one of those whose decisions influenced the course of history. Throughout his life what mattered most was the independence of Poland. When it seemed to be just a romantic dream Poland returned to the map of Europe. Throughout his life he determinedly headed for power.

Piłsudski was a politician of great intuition and ability. But on many occasions he lost and on many occasions his plans were completely destroyed by the course of events. He was resilient and could unhesitatingly set aside such plans. He always knew how long to wait. When he was losing, an inner confidence allowed him to be carried along on the wave of events. And every time he found success in defeat.

He was indifferent to the external trappings of power. As a dictator, apart from short periods of time when he was Head of State, he was only a General Inspector of the Army and Minister of Military Affairs and, in contrast to many of his circle, he sought few personal benefits from the positions he held. He was satisfied with very little. But he headed for real power, independent of outward appearances. Piłsudski's influence amalgamated with his legend to become a national legend in his own lifetime. And still is today.

Bibliographical Essay

Andrzej Garlicki's *Józef Piłsudski, 1867–1935* (Warsaw, 1988) is the complete edition of a biography which had been published in four volumes, each covering successive years of its subject's life: *U źródel obozu belwederskiego (At the sources of the Belvedere camp.* Warsaw, 1978) features the years to 1922; *Pzewrót majowy (The May Coup.* Warsaw, 1978) covers the period 1922 to 1926; *Od Maja do Brześcia (From May to Brześć* Warsaw, 1985), the period 1926 to 1930 and *Od Brześcia do Maja (From Brzesc to May.* Warsaw, 1986) from 1930 to Piłsudski's death in May 1935.

Though each volume is fully annotated all lack a bibliography. This omission is, to a great extent, remedied in the richly illustrated edition (see also the wealth of illustration in Aleksandra i Andrzej Garliccy, *Józef Piłsudski. Zycie i Legenda,* Warsaw, 1993) of *Józef Piłsudski, 1867–1935,* Warsaw, 1990, which contains a massive bibliography, compiled by Ryszard Świętek. This lists over 2000 published works on Piłsudski and his milieu, of which more than 85 per cent are in Polish. (See, *ibid,* pp. 721–780).

The English texts in Richard Świętek's list include: Abernon, d'E.V., *The Eighteenth Decisive Battle of the World,* London, 1931; 'An Appeal to Franklin Delano Roosevelt President of the USA on Behalf of Poland Prepared in Commemoration of the Seventh Anniversary of the Death of Joseph Piłsudski'. Presented by a Delegation of American Citizens of Polish Origin, USA, 1942; Bradley, J. *Allied Intervention in Russia 1917–1920,* London, 1968. Budorowycz, B. *Polish-Soviet Relations 1932–1939,* New York, 1963; Carton de Wiart, A. *Happy Odyssey. The Memoirs of Lieutenant-General Sir . . . ,* London, 1985; Ciencala, A., Komarnicki. T., *From Versailles to Locarno. Keys to Polish Foreign Policy, 1919–1925,* Lawrence, 1984; Graig, G.A., Gilbert, F., *The Diplomats 1919–1939,* New York, 1953; Czernow, W., 'Joseph Piłsudski', *Foreign Affairs,* No.1, 1935; Davies, N., *White Eagle, Red Star. The Polish-Soviet War 1919–1920,* New York, 1972; Dębicki, R., *Foreign Policy of Poland, 1919–1939. From the Rebirth of the Polish Republic to World War II,* New York, 1972; Dziewanowski, M. K., *Joseph Piłsudski, a European Federalist, 1918–1922,* Stanford, 1969; 'Joseph Piłsudski, 1867–1967', *East European Quarterly,* Colorado, Vol. II, 1968–1969; 'Joseph Piłsudski, the Bolshevik Revolution and Eastern Europe', *The Polish Review,* New York, No. 4, 1969;

'Piłsudski's Federal Policy, 1919–1921', *Journal of Central European Affairs*, Boulder, Colorado, Nos 2–3, 1950; Eden, A. (Earl of Avon), The Eden Memoirs, Vol. I, *Facing the Dictators*, London, 1962; Fisher, H.H., Brooks, S., *America and the New Poland*, New York, 1928; Fuller, J.F.C., 'The Battle of Warsaw 1920. On the Occasion of the 60th Anniversary of the Polish Victory over the Bolshevik Army', London, 1980; Gasiorowski, J., 'Joseph Piłsudski in the Light of American Reports', 1919–1922, *The Slavonic and East European Review*, London, Vol. XLIX, No. 116, 1971; 'Joseph Piłsudski in the Light of British Reports', *The Slavonic and East European Review*, London, Vol. L, No. 121, 1971; 'The German-Polish Non-aggression Pact of 1934', *Journal of Central European Affairs*, Vol. XV, No.1, 1955; 'Stresemann and Poland before Locarno', *Journal of Central European Affairs*, Vol. XVIII, No. 1, 1958; 'Stresemann and Poland after Locarno', *Journal of Central European Affairs*, Vol. XVIII, No.3, 1958; *Gen. Józef Piłsudski. Founder of Legions and Polish Military Organizations and at Present Provisional President of the Polish Republic and Commander-in-Chief of the Polish Armies*, Chicago, 1918; Goodenough, S., *Tactical Genius in Battle*, London, 1979; Gromada, T., 'Piłsudski and the Slovak Autonomists', *The Slavic Review*, New York, No.3, 1969; *Essays on Poland's Foreign Policy 1918–1939*, New York, 1970; Grove, W.R., *War's Aftermath. Polish Relief in 1919*, New York, 1940; (Hoover, H.), *Herbert Hoover and Poland. A Documentary History of a Friendship*, Stanford, 1977; Hovi, K., *Cordon Sanitaire or Barriere de l'Est? The Emergence of the New French Eastern European Alliance Policy 1917–1919*, Turku, 1975; Humphrey, G., *Piłsudski, Builder of Poland*, New York, 1936; Jędrzejewicz, W., *Piłsudski. A Life for Poland*, New York, 1982; Kessler, H., *Germany and Europe*, New Haven, 1923; Komarnicki, T., *Rebirth of the Polish Republic. A Study in the Diplomatic History of Europe 1914–1920*, London, 1957; Korbel, J., *Poland between East and West. Soviet and German Diplomacy toward Poland 1919–1933*, Princeton-New Jersey, 1963; Landau, R., *Piłsudski and Poland*, New York, 1929; Lee, I.L., *Poland Under Piłsudski. Some Observations on the Economic Progress of (the) Polish Nation*, 1927; (Lipski, J.), *Diplomat in Berlin. Papers and Memoirs of Józef Lipski, Ambassador of Poland*, New York, London, 1968; Lundgreen-Nielsen K., *The Polish Problem at the Paris Peace Conference. A Study of the Policies of the Great Powers and the Poles, 1918–1919*, Odense, 1979; (Łukasiewicz, J.), *Diplomat in Paris 1936–1939. Papers and Memoirs of Julius Łukasiewicz, Ambassador of Poland*, New York, London, 1970; Machray, R., *The Poland of Piłsudski*, London, 1936; Mackiewicz, Stanisław, *Colonel Beck and his Policy*, London, 1944; Musialik, Z., *General Weygand and the Battle of the Vistula 1920*, London, 1987;

Patterson, E.J., *Piłsudski Marshal of Poland*, London, 1934; *Piłsudski and the Polish Tradition*, London, 1935; (Piłsudska, A.), *Memoirs of Madame Piłsudski*, London, 1940; *Piłsudski. A Biography by his Wife Alexandra*, New York, 1941; Piłsudski, J., *Year 1920 and its Climax. The Battle at Warsaw during the Polish-Soviet War 1919–1920*, London, 1972; Polonsky, A., *Politics in Independent Poland 1921–1939. The Crisis of Constitutional Government*, Oxford, 1972; Riekhoff H., von, *German-Polish Relations 1918–1933*, Baltimore, 1971; Rothschild, J., *East Central Europe between the Two World Wars*, Seattle, 1974; *Piłsudski's Coup d'Etat*, New York, London, 1966; Seton-Watson, H., Seton-Watson, C., *The Making of a New Europe. R.W. Seton-Watson and the Last Years of Austria-Hungary*, Washington, 1981; Sukiennicki, W., *East Central Europe during World War I.* 2 Vols, New York, 1984; *Ukraine and Poland in Documents 1918–1922.* (Edited by Hunczak, T.), Part 1–2, New York, Toronto, 1983; Vansittart, R., *The Mist Procession*, London, 1958; Wandycz, D.S., 'A Forgotten Letter of Piłsudski to Masaryk', *The Polish Review*, Vol. IX, No. 4, New York, 1964; Wandycz, P., *France and her Eastern Allies, 1919–1925. French-Czechoslovak-Polish Relations from the Paris Peace Conference to Locarno*, Minneapolis, 1962.

Mindful of the English speaking reader I would add to this list Professor Norman Davies' *God's Playground. A History of Poland. Vol. II, 1795 to the Present*, Oxford, 1981 (widely recognized as the standard work on Poland for the period) and replace Hans Roos' *Geschihte der polonischen Nation 1916–1960. Von der Staatsgrundung in ersten Weltkrieg bis zur Gegenwart*, Stuttgart, 1961 (which appears in the bibliography) with its English translation, *A History of Modern Poland*, London, 1966. I would also recommend Titus Komarnicki's classic (mentioned in the list given above) *Rebirth of the Polish Republic. A Study in the Diplomatic History of Europe 1914–1920.*

Roos and Komarnicki are particularly useful on the history of the Legions during the final year of the First World War when the shifting tide of events on the Eastern Front raised difficult questions for Piłsudski's legionnaires and none more difficult than the question of allegiance to the central powers. The future of the Polish state and army depended on the outcome of the war. Uncertainties over this led to a confused state of affairs inside the Legions, about which, as observed in the Preface (see above), Garlicki writes sparsely in his biography of Piłsudski.

Writing of the situation in mid 1918, Komarnicki (*op. cit.*) states on p. 117: 'The Brest-Litovsk Treaty, which aroused general indignation in Poland, induced the last unit fighting side by side with the central powers, the Second Brigade of the Legion, to cross the frontline at

Rarancza in Bukovina on the 15th February, 1918. From that moment the whole Polish nation was at the side of the Allies, in spite of all the efforts of the central powers, to maintain the appearance of the existence of an Allied State'. Further, (*Ibid.* p. 209) he adds: 'The conclusion of the Brest-Litovsk Treaty led to undeclared war between the central powers and the Polish nation carried out in the homeland by a secret Polish military organization (POW)'.

However, in describing the events of June, 1918, Roos, (*op. cit.,* p. 37), states: 'Governor-General Beseler and the Regency Council even raised two regiments of a so-called "Polish Defence Force" under a German inspector, the Saxon General Barth. This Defence Force included former officers of the Legion such as Marian Zegota-Januszajtis and Marian Kukiel; even the commander of the illegal POW, Colonel Edward Rydz-Śmigly, applied for commissioned rank in it.'

I asked the late General Marian Kukiel to comment on these two differing interpretations of the events in mid 1918, and to comment on conflicts inside the Polish Legion, of which he had first-hand experience. He generously gave me his reply in a hitherto unpublished letter dated 25 October, 1972:

> I am in possession of your writing of October 15th 1972. The matter is really more complicated than presented by my late friend Titus Komarnicki who was a 'Peowiak' (member of the POW) in consciousness and feelings even forty years after.
>
> There was a crisis of the Polish Legion late in 1916. Their battles on the Russian front had greatly enhanced their importance for the Polish cause. After their greatest and most costly one – that of Kosciuchnowka (July, 1916) – Ludendorff himself imposed upon the *Auswartiges Amt* the necessity of the making a '*Gross-Furstentum Warschau*' and 'a Polish army under German command'. Austria announced the transformation of the Legions into one 'Polish Auxiliary Army Corps' of two or three divisions under Polish command. There was an opportunity of increasing the Polish forces fighting against Russia and ensuring a Polish part in political issues. Piłsudski considered the situation of the central powers as critical and the situation as ripe for changing sides. He was unaware of their forthcoming *fait accompli* and hurriedly announced his own resignation. He instructed the officers of his brigade to support him; the Russian subjects simply to resign, the Austrian subjects to demand their transfer to Austrian forces. The order was cruel and contrary to the feelings of the legionaries. Instances of suicide occurred. The First Brigade followed Piłsudski's will with few exceptions; the second formerly under command of Colonel (then General) Zielinski, afterwards of Col. Haller, refused to take part in such a suicidal move.
>
> According to the decisions of both emperors the legions were renamed 'Polish Auxiliary Corps' and transferred on the German Eastern front to Baranowicze under the command of Brigadier (then

General) Count Szeptycki. Efforts were made by Austrians to induce Piłsudski to withdraw his resignation. Both generals governing over two parts of former 'Polish Kingdom', General v. Beseler in Warsaw, General v. Kuk in Lublin issued Nov. 5, 1916 the manifesto announcing the decision of their rulers to restore a Polish State and to create a Polish army. The enthusiastic welcome of the manifesto was decisive for Piłsudski's policy, also he accepted the membership of the delegation from Austrian occupation and invited the legionaries to withdraw their resignations and to continue to serve in the Polish army, whose creation he expected – and he hoped that v. [von] Beseler, invested with full authority in military affairs will invite him as the Polish C. in C. In a few weeks' time he was fully disappointed. Beseler did not consent to Piłsudski's participation in planning and command nor the use of the 'POW' as nucleus of military units. The outbreak of the Russian revolution and the Manifesto of the Prince Lvov's government on future independence of a united Poland (but in frontiers established by the Russian Constituent Assembly) complicated the situation in Warsaw; there were many hundred thousand Poles in Russian ranks and in German and Russian captivity as well – chances of building up a great Polish Army increased on both sides of the Eastern Front. The Polish military in Russia already discussed the idea of putting Piłsudski at their head. And the delegates of the central powers in Warsaw were alarmed about his real aims. They invented a measure of security; imposing upon the new Polish army in building a formula of oath to be taken; the loyalty to the motherland – the Kingdom of Poland and its future ruler – and the preservation of brotherhood in arms with the forces of both emperors – Austrian and German. The first part meant a tremendous progress towards independence – even Piłsudski himself had to accept in September 1914 for his troops the Austrian imperial formula unchanged with no mention of Poland. But the new formula could be exploited for a revolt against binding the Polish soldiers with the central powers in the critical phase of the war. The Polish National Assembly in Warsaw was divided, the unity shaken by an outburst of anti-German feelings, the Polish troops in garrisons and exercise centres penetrated by violent propaganda and ready for revolt. Once more former Russian subjects had to demand dismissal from military service and the Austrian ones the transfer to the Austrian army.

The part of Piłsudski and of the POW as well in that second crisis was evident. Beseler decided for incarceration and deportation. It did not prevent the revolt. It was general in the former troops of Piłsudski's First Brigade and prevailing in the third. The Second Brigade suffered by the secession of most Russian subjects but remained ready for further service. The Austrians ordered the 'Polish Auxiliary Corps' to Galicia for selection and re-organization. The Russian citizens who demanded dismissal were interned by the Germans in war prisoner camps Szczypiorno (near Kalisz), Benjaminów (near Zegrze) and Łomza.

Some hundred officers and other ranks from the Polish Auxiliary Corps were left in Warsaw to help the reconstruction of military training courses and founding military schools. There remained in Beseler's General Staff the section 'Polnische Wehrmacht' – Polish Military Force. Three distinguished legionaries – Berbecki, Januszajtis and Minkiewicz served as inspectors of schools and courses and of training generally. The Officer-Cadet school and the school for non-commissioned officers started almost immediately. The Cadet-Officers had before long to act as honorary Guard in the Royal Palace in Warsaw on the ceremonial instalment of the Council of three Regents (Archbishop Kakowski, Prince Lubomirski and Ostrowski) – being a living symbol of the forthcoming Polish sovereignty. Early next year several hundreds internees from Szczypiorno asked secretly to be admitted back to the ranks and they did with some violation of the regulations and instructions. But we got immediately an amnesty for them and ourselves too.

Before long the same occurred in the officer camp of Łomza and the process continued until the last weeks of German occupation. Starting from scarcely more than 1000 in 1917 the Polish Forces in Royal Poland reached in October 1918 about 10,000 in two schools and two infantry regiments (a third in formation).

Since October 1918 the Polish Regency Council took over the government of the Polish Kingdom and the High Command of our forces. The first government (Swiezynski) included Joseph Piłsudski (still prisoner in Magdeburg) as war minister. It was not until November that Warsaw and large parts of the country were free and the prisoner of Magdeburg brought in hurry to Warsaw under the guard of a German officer and diplomatist. A gesture of goodwill from the side of the crumbling German government (Max v. Baden). In Warsaw Piłsudski was greeted not only by his former soldiers, the POW, the men in the street, but also by the German *Soldatenrat*. They expected of him protection against vengeance by revolting population. This was also the policy of our regular 'Polish Military Force' in the area of Warsaw as well as of Ostrów, Łomza and elsewhere.

Hans Roos is right in what he says about the Polish Military Force under Beseler. About Smigly-Rydz [sic] and his application (in October I think) when the Polish Force in former Kingdom of Poland already was taken over by the Regency Council and Gen. Rozwadowski was Chief of General Staff.

Further details if necessary are to be found in my book *Dzieje Polski Porczbiorowe*, (Polish History since the Partitions), (2nd edn, London, 1962). I found there bits to change, more to add, nothing to erase.

Kukiel's scholarly history of Poland, unavailable in English, is included in the bibliography appended to the 1990 edition of Andrzej Garlicki's *Józef Piłsudski, 1867–1935*.

Ryszard Świętek's list does not however include the author's archival sources. This is an important omission since so much of the book is based on material held at the following Archives: 1. Archiwum Akt Nowych. *VI Oddział. Zespół Polskiej Partii Socjalistycznej* (Warsaw). 2.

Archiwum Akt Nowych. *Zespół Polskiej Organizacji Narodowej* (Warsaw). 3. Archiwum Akt Nowych. *Zespół Komisji Tymczasowej Skonfederowanych Stronnictw Niepodległosciowych* (Warsaw). 4. Archiwum Akt Nowych. *Zespół Rady Ministrów* (Warsaw). 5. Archiwum Polskiej Akademii Nauk (Warsaw). 6. Centralne Archiwum Wojskowe. *Zespół Wojskowe. Biuro Historyczne* (Warsaw). 7. Centralne Archiwum Ministerstwa Spraw Wewnetrznych (Warsaw). 8. Archive of the Józef Piłsudski Institute (New York). 9. Archive of the Józef Piłsudski Institute (London). 10. Archive of the Polish Institute and General Władysław Sikorski Museum (London). 11. Biblioteka Ossolineum. *Dział rękopisów* (Wrocław). 12. Biblioteka Uniwersytetu Jagiełłonskiego. *Dział rękopisów* (Kraków). 13. Biblioteka Uniwersytetu Warsawskiego. *Dział rękopisów* (Warsaw). 14. Biblioteka Katolickiego Uniwersytetu Lubelskiego. *Dział rękopisów*(Lublin).

Of the archives in Poland, the first yielded perhaps the most original of Professor Garlicki's finds: 30 letters from Piłsudski to Leonarda Lewandowska, written between 25 March, 1890 and 11 December, 1891.

The *Archiwum Akt Nowych*, which contains documents for the period since 1918, has, as Professor Garlicki explained to me, an interesting history. Its Section VI (*Oddzial VI*) groups documents relating to the PPS (*Polska Partia Socjalistyczna*), the Polish socialist party. The PPS merged with the PPR, the communist Polish Workers' Party (*Polska Partia Robotnicza*) in 1948 to form the PZPR: *Polska Zjednoczona Partia Robotnicza* (See Coutouvidis, J. and Reynolds, J. *Poland, 1939–1947*, London, 1986, p. 302). As in the case of Piłsudski's letters to Lewandowska, material relating to the PPS since the First World War thus appears in the Central Archive of the Central Committee of the PZPR. The files in Section VI had been split into two distinct and separately administered collections, one of which was a secret party archive accessible only to party members. Symptomatic of much else happening in Poland at the time, this became available to a wider public when the two collections were merged over 1988–1989.

Index